Organizational Identity in Practice

Edited by

**Lin Lerpold, Davide Ravasi, Johan van Rekom
and Guillaume Soenen**

Routledge
Taylor & Francis Group

LONDON AND NEW YORK

First published 2007
by Routledge
2 Park Square, Milton Park, Abingdon, Oxon OX14 4RN

Simultaneously published in the USA and Canada
by Routledge
270 Madison Avenue, New York, NY 10016

Routledge is an imprint of the Taylor & Francis Group, an informa business

© 2007 Lin Lerpold, Davide Ravasi, Johan van Rekom and Guillaume Soenen for editorial selection
and material; individual contributors for their own contributions.

Typeset in Perpetua and Bell Gothic by RefineCatch Limited, Bungay, Suffolk
Printed and bound in Great Britain by The Cromwell Press, Trowbridge, Wiltshire

British Library Cataloguing in Publication Data
A catalogue record for this book is available from the British Library

Library of Congress Cataloging in Publication Data
Organizational identity in practice / edited by Lin Lerpold . . . [et al.].
  p. cm
"Simultaneously published in the USA and Canada."
  Includes bibliographical references and index.
ISBN 0–415–39839–8 (hard cover) — ISBN 0–415–39840–1 (soft cover)
1. Corporate image. 2. Corporate image—Case studies. 3. Corporate culture. 4. Trademarks.
I. Lerpold, Lin.
HD59.2.O74 2007
659.2—dc22

                            2006100810

ISBN10: 0–415–39839–8 (hbk)
ISBN10: 0–415–39840–1 (pbk)

ISBN13: 978–0–415–39839–8 (hbk)
ISBN13: 978–0–415–39840–4 (pbk)

Contents

CONTENTS

Illustrations

FIGURES

TABLES

Contributors

Barbulescu, Roxana, INSEAD, Boulevard de Constance, 77305 Fontainebleau Cedex, France. roxana.barbulescu@insead.edu

Brunninge, Olof, Internationella Handelshögskolan i Jönköping, Box 1026, 551 11 Jönköping, Sweden. Olof.Brunninge@jibs.hj.se

Harquail, Celia Virginia, Stockholm School of Economics, 2 Edgemont Road, Montclair, New Jersey, USA. cvharquail@comcast.net

Irrmann, Olivier, HEC Montréal Department of Management, 3000 chemin de la Cote-Sainte-Catherine, Montreal, PQ H3T 2A7, Canada. olivier.irrmann@hec.ca

Lerpold, Lin, Stockholm School of Economics, Department of Marketing and Strategy, Institute of International Business, Holländargatan 32, Box 6501, 11383 Stockholm, Sweden. lin.lerpold@hhs.se

Monin, Philippe, EM LYON, 23 Avenue Guy de Collongue, 69134 Ecully cedex, France. monin@em-lyon.com

Ravasi, Davide, Universitá Bocconi, Istituto di Strategia ed Economia Aziendale Università Commerciale, Luigi Bocconi Viale Isonzo 23, 20136 Milano, Italy. davide.ravasi@unibocconi.it

van Johan Rekom, RSM Erasmus University, Department of Marketing Management, P.O. Box 1738, 3000 DR Rotterdam, the Netherlands. jrekom@rsm.nl

Rindova, Violina, McCombs School of Business, University of Texas, Austin, Texas, USA, violina.rindova@mccombs.utexas.edu

Rouzies, Audrey, EM LYON, 23 Avenue Guy de Collongue, 69134 Ecully cedex, France. rouzies@em-lyon.com

Sarason, Yolanda, Colorado State University, College of Business, Strategic Management, Rockwell · 225, Fort Collins, Colorado 80523, USA. Yolanda.Sarason@business.colostate.edu

Schultz, Majken, Department of Intercultural Communication and Leadership, Copenhagen Business School, Dalgas Have 15 DK-2000 Frederiksberg, Denmark. ms.ikl@cbs.dk

Soenen, Guillaume, EM LYON, 23 Avenue Guy de Collongue, 69134 Ecully cedex, France. soenen@em-lyon.com

Stigliani, Ileana, Bocconi University, Viale Isonzo 23, 20126 Milano, Italy. ileana.stigliani@unibocconi.it

Sutton, Ciara, Stockholm School of Economics, Department of Marketing and Strategy, Institute of International Business, Box 6501, SE-11383 Stockholm, Sweden. ciara.sutton@hhs.se

Tienari, Janne, Lappeenranta University of Technology, Department of Business Administration, P.O. Box 20, Lappeenranta, FIN-53851, Finland. janne.tienari@lut.fi

Vaara, Eero, Swedish School of Economics, Management and Organization, PB 479 FIN-00101, Helsinki, Finland. eero.vaara@hanken.fi

Weeks, John R., INSEAD, Boulevard de Constance, 77305 Fontainebleau cedex, France. john.weeks@insead.edu

Acknowledgements

The editors and authors of this book would like to express their sincere thanks to Dennis Gioia, Mary Jo Hatch, Cees van Riel and a special thanks to Mirdita Elstak, David Whetten and C.V. Harquail for their comments on preliminary drafts of this book.

We are also indebted to our university environments and colleagues at Bocconi, EM LYON, Rotterdam School of Management and Stockholm School of Economics for both intellectual encouragement and diverse financial support. The Swedish Science Council (Vetenskapsrådet) is also gratefully acknowledged for financial support of our endeavour.

Acknowledgements

Introduction

*Lin Lerpold, Davide Ravasi, Johan van Rekom,
and Guillaume Soenen*

In the early 1990s, Oticon, a leading producer of hearing aids, was losing ground
to its competitors. For decades, the company had dominated the market for
behind-the-ear models. Over the course of the 1980s, the success of smaller in-
the-ear hearing aids – technologically inferior but cosmetically more appealing –
had eroded sales volumes and market share. In spite of this, product developers
at Oticon refused to acknowledge the changes taking place in the market,
and persisted in the design and development of technologically advanced but
cumbersome devices.

To rectify the situation, the newly appointed CEO, Lars Kolind, saw the need
for a radical redefinition of how organizational members understood the company
and its *raison d'être:* "Instead of thinking of ourselves as a manufacturer that has to
serve its customers, we need to see ourselves as a service company offering a
concrete product." Kolind declared: "Oticon has to stop regarding itself as a
'producer of acoustic equipment': our real mission is to help people with hearing
problems live the life they want." This subtle shift of emphasis from the mechan-
ical device to the people that used it carried with it substantial practical
implications.

Psychoacoustic research became paramount. This was carried out directly with
patients and aimed to identify the various ways that hearing problems are perceived, depending on age, work, and lifestyle. The company's product developers
and marketers were encouraged to rethink their approach, expanding their focus
from purely technical performance – such as the clarity of sound reproduction
and the intensity of amplification – to the users' quality of life, in the broadest
sense. New products based on digital sound processing were designed to adapt
flexibly to changes in users' needs and lifestyles. Shapes were redesigned to be
more appealing; the color was changed from the traditional flesh pink to opaque
titanium; and new packaging was created for easy use and safe transportation. A
notebook called "The Oticon Diary" was included in the package, so that new

users could record observations and listening experiences. The logic behind the Oticon Diary was later developed in what was called the "Human Link Philosophy," supporting the transfer of information from patients to audiologists to improve the fitting and fine-tuning of the products.

The new strategic course resulted in a sharp increase in sales and profit margins, as Oticon subsequently regained a leading position in the global hearing aid market. Widespread changes in corporate policies and collective practices had been set in motion by an apparently minor modification in what people viewed as central to what their organization was and was about – in other words, to their identity as an organization.

WHAT IS ORGANIZATIONAL IDENTITY?

"Who are we?" "What kind of organization is this?" "What does it stand for?" "What makes us different from, or similar to, other organizations?" "Who do we compare with?" "Who is our benchmark or role model?" As the case of Oticon suggests, how managers and employees answer these frequently heard questions may often make the difference between success and failure, growth and stagnation, survival and decline. When members of an organization implicitly or explicitly ask themselves these questions – and it happens more frequently than one might think – they turn their attention to an essential aspect of their collective undertaking – namely, the very *identity* of their organization.

In this book, by organizational identities we refer to *engaging and influential conceptualizations of the organization*, which are *relatively shared* by members and/or *upheld by its leaders*, and often *emphasized* in formal corporate statements (mission, vision, etc.) and expressions (logos, buildings, symbols, etc.). In most cases, the overall identity of the organization results from the juxtaposition of different attributes that, taken together, are believed and claimed by members to describe what the organization is and is about (an example is shown in Figure 1).

However, not all internal descriptions and conceptualizations of the organization can be considered to be truly part of its identity. According to organizational

Figure 1 *The organizational identity of a large oil company*

sociologists Stuart Albert and David Whetten (1985), organizational identity refers only to what members believe in good faith to be the most central, enduring, and distinctive features of their organization. In other words, of all the possible definitions that members can provide of their organization in reply to questions such as "Who are we as an organization?" or "What do we stand for?", legitimate identity claims refer to attributes that satisfy three fundamental criteria (Albert and Whetten, 1985; Whetten, 2006):

1 *Centrality*: identity features are believed and claimed as the essence of the organization and central to its success (or survival) in the past. Without them, in the eyes of its members, the organization would not be the same: it would become something else or soon cease to exist.
2 *Distinctiveness*: in the eyes of its members, identity features positively distinguish the organization from others with which it may be compared, and satisfy members' needs for self-distinction and self-esteem. Distinctive features also position the organization within its competitive field, and are believed by members to be crucial to securing support from stakeholders.
3 *Temporal continuity*: in the eyes of its members, identity features are perceived as providing some degree of sameness or continuity over time. Identity features have withstood the test of time and tend to survive organizational restructuring, overriding concerns for efficiency or profitability. The continuity of identity features helps to reinforce individual members' sense of self and stability, when the members identify themselves with the organization. Even relatively new and emerging conceptualizations may come to be perceived as prospectively "enduring," if they are made central to an organization's policies and practices and are backed up by strong commitment (Whetten, 2006).

Broad internal consensus around these claims, the explicit support of powerful actors, and embeddedness in committing institutional statements are what make organizational conceptualizations drawing on these features more influential and engaging for organizational processes than the specific beliefs or aspirations of individual members or fleeting instrumental claims made by individuals or interest groups.

WHY CARE ABOUT ORGANIZATIONAL IDENTITY?

In recent years, a growing body of research in organizational behavior (e.g., Dutton and Dukerich, 1991; Dukerich, Golden, and Shortell, 2002), organizational theory (e.g., Glynn, 2000; Ravasi and Schultz, 2006), strategy (e.g., Gioia and Thomas, 1996; Corley, 2004; Peteraf and Shanley, 1997), marketing and corporate communication (e.g., van Riel, 1995; Balmer and Soenen, 1999) has shown how identity-related issues influence the behavior of organizations and their members in a broad range of situations.

Newly founded firms must put forward explicit claims about who they are and what they want to be in order to secure the resources they need. In doing so, they address two fundamental concerns of critical stakeholders such as venture capitalists or business partners: (i) what business are you in (in other words, what *similar* organizations can we compare you to, to make sense of what you are)? and (ii) why should people buy your products or services, work for or with you, or invest in your shares and not in others (in other words, how will you be *different* from other comparable organizations)? In fact, formulating and articulating a sustainable and appealing identity for the new firm is one of the central tasks of founders and a way for them to leave a legacy and an enduring imprint on the company (Lounsbury and Glynn, 2001).

Later in the life of the organization, identity-related issues are likely to influence strategic decisions. Decision-makers' perceptions of the identity of their organization – in other words, what they believe their organization is and what it stands for – tend to affect the way corporate issues are interpreted, attended to, and addressed (Dutton and Dukerich, 1991). In times of change, aspirations of top managers may even override their beliefs, as the desired future identity and image – how they wish their organization to be perceived externally – may influence the way they interpret key issues and events, and elaborate new strategies and courses of action (Gioia and Thomas, 1996; Corley, 2004).

Identity-related issues also affect everyday behavior, with their influence also reaching far beyond the boundaries of strategic decisions. Organizational identity provides institutional justification for organizational practices, routines, and policies, and provides the context within which members assign meaning to behavior ("This is what we are, therefore this is how we should behave"). In doing so, organizational identities help members make sense of their everyday behavior in the light of their understanding of what their organization is (Fiol, 1991).

For the same reasons, organizational identity can be a powerful force blocking change. When changes are proposed that might clash with beliefs about an organization's identity, they are likely to encounter heated resistance from organizational members (Reger *et al.*, 1994). It is not uncommon for organizational members to come to define themselves in terms of core and distinctive traits and values of their organization (Ashforth and Mael, 1989). Appealing and desirable identities positively influence the way members feel about their organization, stimulating identification, commitment, and cooperative behavior (Dutton, Dukerich, and Harquail, 1994; Dukerich, Golden, and Shortell, 2002). Therefore, changes that violate employees' identity beliefs and expectations may threaten their collective sense of self ("This is not who we are!"), and negatively affect their psychological well-being and commitment to the organization, engendering individual and collective resistance to organizational change.

Finally, there are important connections between the identity of the organization and the various actions and decisions that influence how the organization will be perceived externally. Internal beliefs about central and distinguishing features of the organization shape the set of visual attributes and expressions that form what marketers and graphic designers call a "corporate identity" (Rindova and Schultz, 1998), the policies that promote a corporate brand (Hatch and Schultz, 2001), and the practices that induce the formation of corporate images (Dowling, 2001) and reputation (Fombrun, 1996).

Collectively, this body of research points to the important role of organizational self-perceptions and self-definitions in shaping strategic decisions, driving or resisting organizational changes, influencing commitment and loyalty, and giving shape to organizational images. However, despite the increasing awareness in the corporate world of the relevance of organizational identity in both understanding and handling organizational issues, systematic attempts to organize the growing body of research findings and to illustrate their implications for the practice of management remain largely absent (for notable exceptions see van Riel (1995) and Schultz, Hatch, and Larsen (2000); however, their emphasis is mainly on the management of external expressions and projections such as corporate identity, image, reputation, and brand).

We believe that this collection of cases illustrating the practical implications of organizational identity may be valuable for graduate students, managers, and scholars alike. By combining concise reviews of current theories with complex real-world cases of "organizational identity in practice," this book aims to offer both practical and theoretical insights. On the one hand, our book may help readers recognize and understand identity processes when they occur in their organizations, and stimulate their capacity to address identity-related issues and to apply leverage on identity-related processes and resources. In this respect, our book may be useful to scholars in need of rich empirical cases to illustrate their research and to support their teaching to participants in graduate and executive management courses, and to managers otherwise interested in how organizational identity affects corporate life. On the other hand, we believe that the cases reported in this book may provide scholars with much-needed empirical insights to support and inspire theory-building efforts on the dynamics of organizational identity.

ORGANIZATIONAL IDENTITY AS CLAIMS, BELIEFS, AND ASPIRATIONS

The identity of an organization is the result of the interplay of three closely connected and sometimes overlapping elements: *formal claims* (i.e., "what we say we are as an organization"); members' *beliefs and understandings* about what is central, enduring, and distinctive about their organization (i.e., "what we think we are as an organization"); and managers' *aspirations* about it (i.e., "what we would like our organization to be"), sometimes referred to as *desired identity* (van Riel, 1995).

In this book we will refer to these three elements as *identity claims, identity beliefs*, and *identity aspirations*.

Identity claims

Identity claims are the most tangible element of organizational identity because they can be found in formal statements about what the organization is and is about, as well as being embedded in internal documents, corporate websites, public interviews and speeches made by a firm's representatives. They are often found under the labels "Our mission" or "Our values." Regardless of the medium, any "official" definition of what the organization is, as well as any explicit statement about the essential and distinctive features of the organization, can be considered an identity claim.

Through formal identity claims, corporate leaders and spokespersons attempt to influence how internal and/or external audiences define and interpret the organization (Whetten and Mackey, 2002). Internally, formal claims are likely to influence members' collective self-definitions, because they provide them with legitimate and consistent narratives to construct a collective sense of self (Czarniawska, 1997). As we have seen in the case of Oticon, identity claims may be used to provide a coherent guide for how members should act, how issues should be prioritized, and what behavior should be considered appropriate and desirable. In times of change, these formal identity claims may be closely related to the identity aspirations held by top managers.

Externally, identity claims are expected to influence how the organization is perceived by its audiences in ways that facilitate the organization's goals. On the one hand, identity claims may be used to justify and support managerial strategies and tactics aimed at securing critical resources for the organization. In Chapter 5, for instance, we describe the case of Industrifonden, a Swedish state agency funding technology development projects, whose managing director began to describe publicly the organization as a "venture capitalist" in a deliberate attempt to reposition it within the community, emphasizing its market orientation and distancing it from other state agencies. On the other hand, identity claims may also be used to project appealing representations of the organization that legitimize it in the eyes of internal and external stakeholders – and to back these up with subtle symbolism. We will see this in the cases of Air France and Starbucks in Part III of the book.

Identity beliefs

Identity beliefs are organizational members' collective beliefs about the distinguishing features of the organization that are presumed to be central and relatively enduring. It is not uncommon for each member to develop a personal conceptualization of the organization – organizational behaviorists use the concept of *perceived organizational identity* to refer to individual members' perceptions and beliefs about core, enduring, and distinctive features of their organization (Dutton, Dukerich, and Harquail, 1994). By identity beliefs, however, we refer to *relatively shared* views and understandings about central, enduring, and distinctive features of the organization.

Organizational theorist Dennis Gioia (1998) defines identity beliefs as "mental schemes that members collectively construct about their organization in order to provide meaning to their experience." These relatively shared beliefs can be straightforward associations with little further meaning, such as "we are the bank with the orange logo," or more complex mental schemes carrying deeper implications for corporate policies and practices. In the latter case, members' beliefs may influence not only individual attitudes and behavior, but also organizational behavior. For instance, members of a pension fund may connect their perception of the organization as a "non-profit institution" to the need to behave in a "cost-conscious" and "socially responsible" way, with practical implications ranging from the careful use of organizational funds to programs aimed at supporting the local community.

The greater the number of members who share such beliefs, the higher the likelihood that these beliefs will form a common bedrock upon which members rest their understanding about what their organization is, and that these beliefs will be enacted in collective practices and decision-making.

Identity aspirations

Although the continuity and endurance of an organization's features are important when defining its identity, organizational members may feel the need to "be (or become) something else." At these times, members may collectively re-evaluate, and possibly revise, their identity claims and beliefs. In times of change, during heated discussions about possible future directions, "what do we want to become as an organization?" is a profound identity question. Desires to achieve a certain position for the organization can fuel members' collective aspirations to redefine internal and external perceptions of it.

New conceptualizations of the organization are often promoted by corporate leaders in response to external pressures. As the case of Oticon illustrates, managers' efforts to change members' perceptions of "what we really are about" helped them re-focus attention, change priorities, revise corporate policies and practices, and justify changes in the internal allocation of resources. In such cases, management's changing identity claims not only reflect new organizational aspirations but may also drive strategic repositioning (Corley, 2004). Part I of this book illustrates and discusses the links between organizational identities, strategy making, and responses to environmental threats.

Changing aspirations may also be influenced by an intent to change the way an organization is perceived by and represented to its external audiences (customers, investors, regulatory bodies, the media, etc.). Changes in identity aspirations may reflect a new *desired image* (Gioia and Thomas, 1996) for the organization. In these cases, the desire – or the need – to redefine external perceptions may lead corporate leaders to project new organizational images – through a new catchy slogan, by revising visual identity markers, or similar changes – in the hope that the rest of the organization will align with the new identity claims.

Members' reactions to these projected aspirational images, however, are not always favorable. Depending on the extent to which new identity aspirations are seen as clashing with established beliefs about the organization or seem disconnected from the organization's history and culture, the newly projected images may fail to garner the required support or may even trigger overt resistance to the new course (Reger *et al.*, 1994; Humphreys and Brown, 2002).

THE IDENTITY ARENA: THE INTERPLAY BETWEEN MULTIPLE CLAIMS, BELIEFS, AND ASPIRATIONS

Ideally, in an organization, identity claims, beliefs, and aspirations should cohere around a more or less commonly shared set of conceptualizations of what the organization is and of ambitions for its future. Corporate statements should reflect relatively shared understandings among members, in particular the aspirations and beliefs of organizational leaders. In practice, gaps or inconsistencies frequently arise between the three elements. Official identity claims, for instance, may reflect the desires of senior managers, but might not necessarily correspond to widespread beliefs about what really defines the organization (Corley, 2004). In fact, it is not unlikely that senior managers' ambitions for change will collide with entrenched beliefs and desires of the rest of organization, triggering resistance to any attempt to alter "the organization as we know it and want it to be" (Humphreys and Brown, 2002).

In addition, in large or complex organizations different subgroups may lay different claims to what the organization is, reflecting different social identities (Pratt and Rafaeli, 1997), professional skills (Glynn, 2000), or hierarchical positions (Corley, 2004). Although these multiple claims may rarely surface in official corporate communications, they are occasionally manifested as one or more groups invoke identity-related arguments to justify or object to corporate decisions. While it is not uncommon for these claims to be used instrumentally and rhetorically to further or defend specific interests, multiple identity claims often reflect different views of the organization – in other words, multiple identity beliefs. In Chapter 2, for instance, the case of a large division of the French railroad company SNCF provides a vivid illustration of how, in the face of organizational changes following a new strategic course, tensions may arise between different professional subgroups holding radically different views of what the organization is and how it should function.

In fact, some organizational identities are characterized by a fundamental duality, built on opposing or competing metaphors such as a "church" or a "business" for a university, or a "business" and a "family" for a family firm (Albert and Whetten, 1985). In these types of organizations, alternative interpretations of the organization, its history, and its nature tend to coexist, their internal contradictions surfacing only at critical times. Documented cases include, for example, cultural institutions (Glynn, 2000), rural cooperatives (Foreman and Whetten, 2002), universities (Albert and Whetten, 1985), and nonprofit organizations (Golden-Biddle and Rao, 1997).

It is precisely when diverging interpretations collide that different conceptualizations become visible and can thus be addressed, discussed, revised, or reaffirmed. At these moments we expect the most fruitful debate and collective sense-making to occur. It is significant that very few cases in this book depict situations where the use of organizational identity is simple or straightforward.

THE CONTENT OF THE BOOK

In order to highlight the practical relevance of organizational identity and identity management, the book is divided into three main parts, each addressing specific organizational identity issues. These are (i) how identity beliefs and aspirations influence strategy formulation and strategic responses to competitive threats; (ii) how identities are socially constructed, drawing on multiple cues; and (iii) how identity claims and beliefs support a range of corporate expressions aimed at projecting favorable and attractive images to external audiences.

The purpose of Part I is to illustrate from the outset the influence of organizational identities on organizational processes. In the first two cases, Scania and SNCF, Brunninge and Barbulescu and Weeks show how organizational identities affect strategic decisions – acting as a "court of last resort" in addressing ambiguous strategic issues – as well as daily behavior in organizations. Sarason and van Rekom's analysis of how different organizations resulting from the de-merger of AT&T (the so-called "Baby Bells") followed different strategic routes and shows the influence of identity beliefs and aspirations on various steps of the strategy process, such as environmental scanning, issue interpretation, and the selection of strategic options. Finally, using the Handelsbanken case, Brunninge shows how organizational identities may influence organizational responses to environmental changes, and exemplifies the concept of "identity threat" – an external trend or event that is perceived as a challenge to the identity of the organization.

After illustrating the pervasive influence of identity claims, beliefs, and aspirations on organizational processes, Part II focuses on how members of an organization, in response to internal and external stimuli, socially construct or reconstruct a common understanding of what their organization is. Drawing on the case of the Danish company Bang & Olufsen, Ravasi and Schultz illustrate how cultural values, practices, and artefacts may circumscribe organizational responses, preserving stability in the face of environmental challenges. In Chapter 5, Sutton traces the evolution of the identity of Industrifonden, initially founded as an agency of the Swedish government to fund innovative industrial projects, to show how organizational identities can be constructed by drawing upon, or distancing themselves from, existing social categories such as "bank" or "venture capitalist." In Chapter 7, Lerpold illustrates the influence of cognitive strategic reference groups – groups of competitors that are taken as prototypical role models – on purposeful attempts to reframe the identity of the organization to support organizational and strategic changes. Finally, Chapter 8 discusses the unusual case of Carrie King – a fictitious character developed by marketers at Heartland Co. in order to orient and inspire brand policies – and reveals how symbols initially intended to influence external impressions of the organization may eventually come to be incorporated in internal self-perceptions.

Part III gathers cases that examine the links between organizational identity, corporate communication and expressions, and organizational images. Building on the case of Starbucks and other specialty coffee producers, Rindova investigates how identity-based corporate communication may help build a distinctive and attractive position in the environment and ensure the flow of resources needed for the survival of the organization. Through a historical analysis of the evolution of corporate dress at Air France, Soenen, Monin, and Rouzies show how various artefacts – such as uniforms, products and visuals – may be used to express and project a distinctive set of values. Similarly, based on a study of three corporate museums, at Alfa-Romeo, Piaggio, and Kartell, Stigliani and Ravasi discuss how various artefacts help to foster identification in and around the organization. In Chapter 12, Vaara, Tienari, and Irrmann use the case of the bank multi-merger Nordea to show how organizations can draw upon various discursive resources to build a distinctive organizational image, also discussing the fundamental requirements of a successful image-building campaign.

After having discussed and exemplified throughout the book the multiple ways in which identity claims, beliefs, and aspirations affect organizational processes, in Chapter 13 we introduce a number of concrete tools to help managers address identity issues in practice. We briefly summarize some of the most popular and insightful heuristic devices intended to help managers reflect on the identity of their organization, analyze potential discrepancies between multiple views and interpretations in and around the organization, and make sense of core, enduring, and distinctive features that can be legitimately used to support a common conceptualization.

Part I

Identity, strategy, and the environment

Lin Lerpold, Davide Ravasi, Johan van Rekom, and Guillaume Soenen

How do organizational identities affect individual and collective behavior in organizations? How do members' beliefs and aspirations about what their organization is (or should be) shape the way decisions are made, strategies are formulated, and policies set up and enforced? Past research shows that members' identity beliefs and aspirations frame how they interpret changes in society, technology, and the industry – especially to the extent that these changes are perceived as posing a threat to the preservation of a collective sense of self – as well as how they respond to these changes by formulating new strategies or adapting existing ones.

Organizational identity is often invoked by members to support or justify decisions that are perceived – or presented – as crucial to the maintenance of features, without which "our organization would not be the same." At times, however, changes in the external environment may challenge members' confidence in the viability of current conceptualizations of their organization, requiring them to re-evaluate their beliefs and aspirations as they formulate new strategies for the organization. Often, as organizational strategies need to adapt to a changing industrial landscape, so too do the identity beliefs and aspirations that underpin and support strategies. Strategy formulation, then, becomes a process where members' beliefs and aspirations must be made explicit, re-evaluated, and reconciled with changing environmental conditions.

However, as organizations engage in substantial organizational and strategic changes, it is not unlikely that conflicts arise regarding the appropriate course of action. At times, as the case of SNCF (see Chapter 2) shows, conflicting views and positions may rest on different beliefs and aspirations about what the organization is and should be. For instance, people in different units or with different professional backgrounds may develop partially diverging views and aspirations. These diverging views – or, as they are sometimes called, multiple identities – are often unarticulated, but they may underlie internal tensions or, occasionally, give rise to heated conflicts.

The relationship between identity, strategy, and the environment, then, appears to be a dynamic one where all three elements are interrelated and have important iterative influence on one another. In the remainder of this part of the book, we will briefly introduce how organizational identity dynamics influence strategy making in organizations. The issues we raise will be illustrated and discussed more fully in the cases that follow.

ORGANIZATIONAL IDENTITY AND STRATEGY FORMULATION

The formulation of organizational strategies can be understood as an iterative process involving the collection of information about the environment (scanning), the selective focus of attention on some of this information (attention), the attempt to make sense of this information (interpretation), and the development of potential responses.[1] All these steps are influenced by interpretive schemes that help people assign priority to the various events they are facing, frame their sense-making activity, and guide their selection of appropriate courses of action. These sense-making/interpretive schemes are related to organizational members' current identity beliefs and, to some extent, their identity aspirations (see Figure 2).

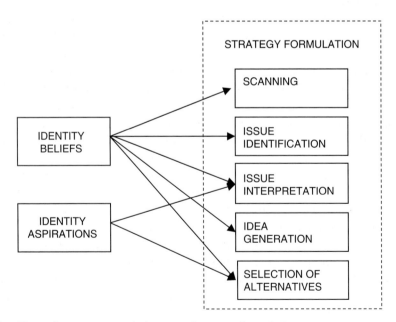

Figure 2 *Organizational identity and strategy formulation*

[1] For the sake of simplicity, we will describe and represent as a linear process what is in fact iterative and unstructured, with frequently interrelated steps (Mintzberg, Raisinghani, and Théorêt, 1976).

Strategy formulation usually starts with the acquisition of information from and about the external environment – a process that has been termed "environmental scanning" (Aguilar, 1967). However, with overabundant information – and a limited capacity to collect, store, and process that information – managers engaged in formulating strategy have to make choices about what kind of information is salient to them and what information sources are appropriate. Their choices are also guided by their beliefs about "what their organization is" (Nardon and Aten, 2004). The case of the three spin-offs of AT&T described in Part I illustrates how managers' different conceptualizations of the organization lead them to gather information about different reference groups – in this case, competitors – with repercussions for the following stages of the process.

However, managers do not attend equally to all the information they gather. While some pieces of information are noticed, others are more or less consciously ignored. In this respect, identity beliefs provide a reference for assessing the importance of an event and the extent to which it is worthy of attention (Dutton and Dukerich, 1991). In particular, an event that seems to challenge or contradict collective identity beliefs is likely to become an "issue" – i.e., an event that members collectively acknowledge as threatening their collective sense of self, and as deserving a response. Later in this section, we will call these events "identity threats."

Identity beliefs, however, do not merely affect the collection of information, they also influence how members process information. They provide a cognitive framework for members' interpretations of events and their subsequent action (Gioia and Thomas, 1996). More generally, organizational identity helps members of an organization relate to the broader organizational context within which they act, and to make sense of events in relation to their understanding of what defines the organization (Fiol, 1991). Jane Dutton and Janet Dukerich's (1991) study of the New York Port Authority shows how identity beliefs tend to constrain the meanings that members give to an issue; they help distinguish aspects of the issue that pose a threat to the organization from those that do not, and they eventually guide the search for solutions that can resolve the issue. At the Swedish bank, Handelsbanken, for instance, the diffusion of internet technology and "e-banking" was initially viewed as a threat to the independence of local branches and to the preservation of close direct relationships with customers – two features that were collectively perceived as central and enduring to the organization. Members' determination to preserve these features eventually led to the development of innovative solutions that reconciled established identity beliefs with adaptation to a changing competitive environment. The case is described in more detail in Chapter 4.

Current beliefs, however, are not the only identity-related frames affecting strategy formulation. Based on their investigation of how top managers in higher education institutions make sense of changes in modern academia, Dennis Gioia and James Thomas (1996: 371) argue that "under conditions of strategic change

15

. . . it is not existing identity or image but, rather, envisioned identity and image – those to be achieved – that imply the standards for interpreting important issues." Whenever environmental conditions are interpreted as requiring substantial changes in the organization, identity aspirations – "what we would like to be as an organization in the future" – may in fact override identity beliefs – "what we believe we are now" – in driving the formulation of new plans. The identification of an "identity gap" between current beliefs and future aspirations (Reger *et al.*, 1994) may thus be crucial to the development of new strategies that effectively reconcile beliefs, aspirations, and external conditions.

ORGANIZATIONAL IDENTITY AND STRATEGIC DECISIONS

The idea that identity claims and beliefs are invoked by organizational members to help them select among alternative courses of action is as old as the concept of organizational identity itself. In fact, Albert and Whetten's conceptualization of organizational identity was initially formulated to explain an organization's surprisingly heated reaction to a proposed 2 percent budget cut, a change that should have been experienced as relatively insignificant (Whetten, 1998). The proposed change raised fierce emotions and heated debates, as it was perceived as leading to the "uncontrollable erosion of the organizational, and by inference personal, identity" (Whetten, 1998: viii). As one of the participants in the discussion observed:

> Would important constituents still think of us as the University of Illinois if we cut out the aviation program, or cut back on agricultural extension services?
>
> (Whetten, 1998: viii)

According to Whetten, organizational self-definitions became a "court of last resort," invoked to support or justify decisions that cannot be settled on purely technical or economic grounds. A similar phenomenon can be observed in the case of the Swedish truck manufacturer, Scania (see Chapter 1). At Scania, organizational members refused to discontinue the production of bonneted cab trucks for years, regardless of commercial considerations, because this particular design was believed to be central to how both employees and customers perceived and defined the organization.

More generally, identity issues are likely to be raised or invoked whenever alternative courses of action seem relevant to or incompatible with existing identity claims and identity beliefs (Whetten, 2006). During major transitions in the organizational lifecycle, for instance, organizational identity may serve as an anchor point to guide major decisions in the absence of more "objective" criteria, such as technical superiority or economic efficiency. Organizational identity issues are also likely to be raised when there are events and actions that imply an alteration of important identity referents, such as the diminishing relevance of local branches as a result of the spread of e-banking described in the Handelsbanken case. In Part II we will refer to these potentially disrupting events as "identity threats."

ENVIRONMENTAL CHANGES, IDENTITY THREATS, AND ORGANIZATIONAL RESPONSES

Organizations and their members respond actively to external or internal events that they perceive as threats to their identity beliefs, identity aspirations, and/or the image of the organization. A discrepancy between how members believe the organization is perceived externally (what scholars refer to as *construed external images*) and how members perceive the organization (their identity beliefs) or wish it were perceived externally (their *desired image*) is likely to trigger a reaction aimed at countering threatening events and representations, and at preserving collective internal and external perceptions of the organization (Ginzel, Kramer, and Sutton, 1993). Unfavorable images of their organization may threaten members' sense of self and negatively affect their psychological well-being as well as their identification with and commitment to the organization (Dutton, Dukerich, and Harquail, 1994). Furthermore, a deteriorating image may eventually undermine the organization's very survival by decreasing the willingness of critical resource holders to support the organization (Scott and Lane, 2000).

Usually, organization members respond to these "image threats" by engaging in impression management tactics to reaffirm the identity of the organization (Ginzel, Kramer, and Sutton, 1993; Sutton and Callahan, 1987) or by adopting "face-saving" strategies (Golden-Biddle and Rao, 1997) aimed at preserving or restoring collective perceptions and self-esteem when confronted with disrupting events. However, insofar as organizational images provide members with feedback from external stakeholders about the credibility of the organization's claims, a serious discrepancy between internal beliefs and external perceptions may undermine members' confidence and induce them to re-evaluate their beliefs. They may do so by asking themselves "Is this who we really are? Is this who we really want to be?" (Whetten and Mackey, 2002).

In fact, external pressures increase the likelihood that organizational members will reflect explicitly on identity issues (Albert and Whetten, 1985). Of particular relevance are events that are associated with shifting external claims and expectations about the organization, and/or which seem to challenge the prospective viability of current conceptualizations of the organization and of the strategies that rest on them (Ravasi and Schultz, 2006). Under such circumstances, these events become real "identity threats," as they are perceived as demanding substantial alterations to core and distinctive organizational features and as challenging the sustainability of organizational identities (Barney *et al.*, 1998). The cases of Handelsbanken in this section (Chapter 4), Bang & Olufsen (Chapter 6), Statoil (Chapter 7), and Industrifonden in the next (Chapter 5) illustrate how relevant identity threats can be to strategy formulation and organizational survival.

Chapter 1

Scania's bonneted trucks

Olof Brunninge

What actually shapes a company's strategy? The normative literature in the field (e.g., Porter, 1980) emphasizes the importance of rational managers, calculating the economic consequences of different options and choosing the one that offers the highest possible return. Critics of this view have remarked, however, that strategy making is not that simple in practice. A variety of aspects that go beyond purely economic calculations need to be taken into account in order to understand strategy processes in their full complexity (Mintzberg *et al.*, 1998). Organizational identity is one such aspect. It has been said to serve as a "beacon for strategy" (Ashforth and Mael, 1996: 32), providing strategic direction to the company. Albert and Whetten (1985), in their classic paper, characterize identity as a court of last resort in the strategy process. In cases where companies struggle with a strategic decision, the question about the company's identity can be decisive for which strategy is eventually chosen. How clear is the guidance identity offered and how strong is this guidance in a situation where identity clashes with more economically oriented rationales in the strategy process? Such questions become critical when tensions arise around controversial strategic issues.

At the start of the new millennium, the Swedish truck manufacturer Scania was one of the few remaining independent companies in the industry. The firm had a tradition of more than a hundred years of truck manufacture and strived to position itself as the premium brand in the industry. A particular characteristic of the company was its so-called modular system, meaning that trucks were assembled from a relatively limited number of components. Thanks to standardized interfaces, the components could be combined in numerous ways like the building blocks from a child's toy.

The present case tells the story of a specific cab design, the bonneted T-cab, which has come to symbolize the distinctiveness and legendary status of Scania trucks. Around the turn of the millennium, there was an internal debate at Scania between proponents of the T-truck and those opposing it for commercial reasons.

At the same time the company began to pay increased attention to identity issues as a result of a hostile takeover attempt by its domestic rival, Volvo. Scania had only recently regained its independence after a period of merger with the auto manufacturer Saab. The Scania case illustrates conflicts that can arise around different identity conceptions in a company. It is also an example of how organizational identity and product identity are intertwined in a single product company.

ORGANIZATIONAL IDENTITY AND PRODUCT IDENTITY IN A SINGLE-PRODUCT COMPANY

At the beginning of the millennium, Scania was an organization with a very clear emphasis on a single category of products, namely trucks. Trucks, buses, and engines, together with the truck-related finance and service businesses, represented almost the company's entire turnover. The dominance of trucks had been a characteristic of Scania for a long period, and managers often emphasized that Scania was a single-product company and, moreover, that the product and the company used the same name. Considering the closeness of the company and its product, it was not surprising that the understanding Scania members had of their organization was difficult to distinguish from their understanding of the product. Organizational identity and members' conceptions of product identity had become blurred.

What was it, then, that the Scania truck stood for? The answer was not self-evident and partially differing views existed in the organization. A crucial issue in the debate surrounding product identity was the question of what customers valued when they purchased a truck. But even this was not easy to answer: Scania's customers were a heterogeneous group comprising both single-truck and fleet owners, with different demands and preferences. For an economically rational customer, the technical characteristics of the truck that affected the haulier's profitability were decisive. However, beyond these "hard" facts there were also non-quantifiable aspects. Particularly at times when it was difficult to maintain a technological advantage over competitors, the emotional appeal a truck evoked gained increasing importance. Scania thus paid increasing attention to non-quantifiable aspects. In a company with a tradition of rational engineering ideals, however, this was not always free of tension. One subject where the issue of non-quantifiable aspects became particularly salient was bonneted cabs. This cab design appealed to many customers on an emotional level, while being questionable from a strictly economic perspective.

Calculative and emotional aspects of purchasing a truck

Even though emotional reasons might be part of the decision in buying a truck, practically all trucks were purchased for some kind of commercial application. In this sense they were investments, and their profitability for the owner could be calculated according to economic criteria. In such a view, a purchasing decision can be seen as based on objective facts, while emotional aspects that cannot be measured play a very marginal role. The calculative aspects of a truck sale might create legitimacy problems for those in the organization dealing with "softer" issues such as industrial design. The journal *Mekanisten* once carried an article focusing on Scania's design: not everyone at the company was pleased with the perspective on their product:

> *Mekanisten* had two articles. One was on Volvo and they had interviewed engine people . . . Then they had another article on the pages following. It was about Scania and dealt with design. After [the journalist] published it, some people [at Scania] were angry. *Mekanisten* is a journal for engineers and that's where they read about it: "That gives a completely false picture! It's about engines! Scania makes engines!"
>
> (Kristofer Hansén, Head of Styling, interview 2003)

However, there were things other than calculative aspects that mattered in the truck business. Truck buyers might actually consider things like the external appearance of the truck or the image of the brand. They might be willing to buy an engine that is larger than necessary because it would give them additional prestige. In some respects economic calculations and soft values could overlap. Good truck drivers who drove in a fuel-efficient way were scarce and difficult to recruit. Hence, there was an incentive for hauliers to purchase trucks that appealed to drivers. Additionally, the non-quantifiable aspects could be decisive if different trucks were similar technically:

> We intend to continue surpassing the technical achievements of our competitors, but it won't get any easier . . . As is the case with many products, both in the trade and consumer markets, it is becoming increasingly difficult to compete on technical excellence alone. Most manufacturers today can produce very good, high-quality products. Therefore, the battle for the customer's favor has now shifted to a platform other than the purely technical.
>
> (Scania, 2000: 7)

Scania's product identity platform

As a consequence of this view, Scania decided to emphasize soft values more explicitly. A 66-page internal company manual entitled *Scania Product Identity: Guiding Principles* (Scania, 2000) outlined the aspects that should be associated with a Scania truck. The company referred to them as quantifiable and non-quantifiable "values." While the former could be measured or assessed numerically, the latter could not. Nevertheless, they were perceived by people and evoked reactions. In the manual, Scania's product identity platform was depicted as a combination of quantifiable and non-quantifiable aspects. *Performance* summarized the quantifiable aspects. These were taken for granted and not elaborated on greatly. The major part of the manual was devoted to non-quantifiable aspects, which were summarized under the label *prestige*. The manual illustrated the various values with examples from both Scania and completely different contexts. Interestingly, when examples from Scania were used, some of the pictures and stories did not show the company's latest trucks; rather, they showed Scanias from the 1960s and 1970s. This emphasized the continuity in Scania's product identity: despite continual development it should be easy to recognize a Scania.

An increasing emphasis on non-quantifiable aspects

Scania's product identity platform was intended to combine the quantifiable and non-quantifiable aspects associated with a truck. The concept of non-quantifiable characteristics as such was not new for Scania. For example, the company had a long history of developing high-performance engines. Beyond the technical properties they represented, they also stood for respect, confidence, and privilege. The two generations of the famous V8 engine in particular had embodied these attributes and contributed to Scania's commercial success:

> V8 was where Scania's name was made in the UK. Scania had the reputation of being the only manufacturer that produces a V8 engine that worked well and it was the owner-driver's dream machine. If you go back ten years people bought V8 and they didn't need them because they had low weights. They were buying with the heart and they liked this noise of this V8 engine and they used to happen to be very efficient on fuel. That seemed to be a side effect, although not today. We have had weight increases up to 44 tons and you still don't actually need a V8 engine of 580 horsepower for 44 tons, but they have a very good fuel consumption.
>
> (Tony Ballinger, Marketing Manager Scania Great Britain,
> interview 2003)

While non-quantifiable characteristics had been ascribed to Scania's trucks for a long time, top management had only recently begun to assign these strategic importance in a more explicit way. Changing market conditions had not been the only driver of this development: the changing ownership constellations had also played an important role. The disintegration of the Saab-Scania group in 1996 and the takeover attempt by Volvo in 1999, although ultimately defeated, had triggered an interest in emphasizing the Scania brand and in reflecting upon what was unique about the company and its products:

> If you look back it was "in the walls" as we used to say. It was a robust product. It was fuel consumption. Scania had the best engine. A good second-hand value because of a good engine, long lifespan, and good quality. That has been the mantra throughout the years Now it has become more sophisticated, and it was perhaps through Volvo we were forced to re-think more intellectually and a little more deeply than just quality and engine about what makes our brand . . . It still builds a lot on the history of the engine and quality and then there is also the macho bit and the perceived values.
>
> (Per Hallberg, Head of Production and Procurement,
> interview 2003)

Among other things, the work resulted in Scania's product identity platform and a separate section on Scania's identity that was included in the 1999 annual report. In this report, Scania placed particular emphasis on the pride truck owners should feel for their Scania. Alongside the traditional technical performance aspects, the non-quantifiable aspects of identity were thus clearly stressed.

Scania's bonneted T-trucks

An area where tensions between hard and soft values arose was design. Design could have a measurable impact on the technical properties of a truck, but it was particularly connected with how a truck was perceived (i.e., a soft aspect). In truck design it is the outer appearance of the cab that most clearly distinguishes different trucks. There were two main ways of designing a cab, depending on where the engine was placed. For a long period the dominant design had been to place the engine under a bonnet in front of the driver's cab, resembling a nose at the front of the truck. With few exceptions, almost all trucks had been designed like this. The bonneted trucks (Figure 3) had been appreciated both for being more comfortable and for their impressive appearance.

The rise of cab-over-engine trucks

The bonneted cab design first began to be questioned in the 1960s. By this time many countries in Europe had introduced length restrictions for trucks, and the increasing performance of truck engines meant that regulations rather than engine performance limited transport capacity. Against this background, using part of the disposable length for a bonnet was waste of money. The solution was to

■ **Figure 3** *Scania's bonneted T-truck has been an important embodiment of the prestige associated with Scania and its products. It is an example of the classic cab design that was prevalent in Europe before length restrictions were introduced. Thanks to their impressive appearance, bonneted trucks are still cherished today as flagships of the fleets of many truck owners.*

manufacture so-called cab-over-engine trucks (Figure 4), with the engine situated under the driver's cab. Cab-over-engine trucks quickly gained market share across Europe. The situation differed to some extent in overseas markets with different traditions and regulations.

In Europe, bonneted cabs became increasingly marginal. Many manufacturers stopped offering them as the low volume did not warrant the additional development costs. Despite such arguments, Scania continued to include bonneted cabs in all its new programs. When cabs were modularized in the 2-series in 1980, the first version to be launched was the bonneted cab, the so-called T-cab, with a torpedo-like design. Thanks to the concept of modularization, the additional investments in development and tools could be kept low. For applications where the length of the truck was not relevant, such as construction vehicles or transports of goods with high density, the T-cab was not a disadvantage.

Figure 4 *Cab-over-engine trucks replaced most bonneted trucks in Europe when length restrictions were introduced. The model is equipped with a V8 engine, which has been an important symbol of Scania's identity alongside the T-cab.*

The bonneted cabs increasingly questioned

Although the bonneted cabs had a number of practical advantages, much of their attraction lay in their impressive appearance. They were also closest to the traditional image of what a truck was supposed to look like. A story often told at Scania was that children who drew a truck intuitively drew one with a bonnet. Finally, American trucks, which symbolized trucker romanticism, typically had a bonneted cab. The reason why Scania's T-cab still attracted customers was to a large extent emotional. Even for applications where the cab length was in fact somewhat of a disadvantage, some hauliers were willing to sacrifice economic gain for the status associated with having a T-truck in their fleet:

> As far as the T-cab is concerned, the problem in the UK is the overall length of course. I mean you are restricted to a 40-foot trailer. You might see it as a flagship vehicle. We have one customer who specializes in plant movements and they have a T-bonneted cab hooked up to a trailer and it's a very impressive rig and it's a flagship thing.
>
> (James Armstrong, CEO of an independent British truck retailer, interview 2003)

As the sole supplier of T-cabs in the European market since 2003, Scania used this to demonstrate its position as the premium brand among truck manufacturers:

> Scania's bonneted T-truck, despite relatively limited sales volumes in Europe, is an important identity platform for Scania. It signals both strength and prestige, showing that the driver is pulling such a heavy payload that he does not need full cargo length. It says that the owner has enough money and experience to offer the driver a flat floor and the superior comfort provided by a driver's seat behind the front axle.
>
> (Scania, 2002: 25)

Despite the possibility of using the T-truck as an identity platform, the cab model was not without controversy at Scania. Was it really worth the money and effort to develop a cab model with low sales volumes? In 2005, less than 2 percent of Scania's trucks sold worldwide had a bonneted cab. Although the modular system made it possible to develop a bonneted cab with relatively little additional effort, there were costs associated with development and production. The question was whether the image associated with the bonneted cab outweighed the additional costs:

> From a purely economic point of view, the profitability of the [bonneted cab] is not good at all. Then of course the soft values can be debated. Is it really the image carrier it is claimed to be? . . . Soon after I started I said we should discontinue the T-truck. We should not do things like that. The result was an uproar. There was a complete revolt. It was unacceptable to even mention discontinuing the T-truck.
>
> [OB:] Despite Scania being so profit-oriented?
>
> Yes. That you can say is really a paradox. There are limits to profit-orientation, obviously.
>
> (Hasse Johansson, Head of Research and Development, interview 2003)

In the discussions surrounding the T-truck, tensions arose between Scania's traditional focus on rationalization and the increasing attention to non-quantifiable aspects. Like the Scania customer who bought a T-truck as a flagship vehicle despite its economic drawbacks, Scania also thought beyond quantifiable calculations when it came to the T-truck. It was of course difficult to put a figure on the value of the T-cab as an image platform. The assumption was that the value outweighed the additional cost. Moreover, the internal discussion on the bonneted cabs was not a simple issue of the marketing side supporting it and the technical side opposing it. There were dealers who would not regret the disappearance of bonneted cabs since they were a marginal product in terms of sales volume. At the same time, there were people on the technical side who identified with the bonneted cab as it represented the essence of Scania.

The STAX project

Given the low market share in Europe and the declining market share in Latin America, the question was how long would T-trucks be included in new cab generations. One decisive issue besides the demand for the cab was the company's ability to design a bonneted cab that was profitable for the company as well as for its customers. At the IAA truck fair in Hanover in 2002, Scania presented a concept study of a future bonneted cab, the STAX. The project began as an internal study by Ola Pihlgren, one of Scania's industrial designers, and three design students on internships at Scania. As there were no plans to present the design study in public, Pihlgren and the students had a considerable degree of freedom in their work. Nevertheless, they did not wish to stray too far from Scania's business reality. The study should comply with Scania's product identity platform and it should take into account that a bonnet that was too long would not be accepted by the market. One of the major challenges was to combine the desire to design an impressive truck with the need to limit the length of the cab to make the dimensions commercially viable. Ideally, the STAX cab should not be longer than the T-cab of the then-current 4-series:

> [In the US you can have] a nine-meter tractor unit. It doesn't matter. But it did not really feel like a Scania. We would have been allowed to do that, but we felt it would be too far removed and would not have anything to do with Scania . . . without any connection to reality. It would never be Scania-like optimizing on such a long cab just for the sake of external appearance.
>
> (Ola Pihlgren, industrial designer, interview 2003)

It was more Scania-like to use the disposable length to increase the driver's comfort. Scania had been trying to increase the status of the truck-driver profession, for instance by organizing pan-European contests for young drivers. The company believes that drivers, whether employees or self-employed, are important in truck purchase decisions. The idea therefore was to make the driver's cabin of the STAX longer than that of the 4-series T-truck at the expense of bonnet length. However, the designers managed to make it look longer than it actually was by extending the edge of the bonnet along the length of the whole cab, giving the STAX a powerful appearance (see Figure 5).

Essentially, the STAX truck was a design study that aimed at testing options for future generations of bonneted cabs. Although the aim was to make the design study Scania-like, the main emphasis was on visual appearance rather than

Figure 5 *The STAX concept truck was presented at the IAA Nutzfahrzeuge trade fair in Hanover in 2002. The design of the bonnet makes it appear longer than it actually is. While the STAX was originally conceived as a concept design for future bonneted cabs, it was reinterpreted as a study for a crash zone.*

commercial reality: some technical aspects of the STAX would be problematic if applied to a real truck. The STAX concept study was therefore not without controversy within Scania's organization, with some arguing that the company should concentrate on selling its current products rather than expending energy on fanciful studies that would not result in any product in the foreseeable future:

> The head of sales from [one country] just scratched his head and almost lost his temper and wondered what kind of crap this was. "I can't sell this tomorrow. What shall we do with it? What kind of nonsense is this?" He did not at all understand that we are boosting the brand a lot by showing this sort of thing.
>
> (Ola Pihlgren, industrial designer, interview 2003)

Despite some resistance among middle managers, Scania's top management liked the STAX and gave approval to present it to the public. The model had a point of reference in Scania's history while at the same time expressing progressive thinking. The STAX was exhibited at the IAA truck fair in Hanover and was one of the eye-catchers on Scania's exhibition stand. The uncovering of the model was the highlight of Scania's press conference. Scania also made a considerable effort to draw customers' attention to the STAX. An article in the *Scania*

World magazine was devoted to it, emphasizing the history of bonneted cabs at Scania. The T-truck was supposed to convey the company's identity, signaling strength and prestige. Moreover, it stood for continuity in the long history of Scania trucks:

> At least as important as identifying new design concepts was the task of conveying the historical identity of Scania bonneted trucks. Put simply, it was all about finding Scania's soul and seeing how it could be expressed in the future. "We looked at T-trucks as part of the history of Scania," says Ola Pihlgren. "Which design features have survived? Which ones are important? Which are not so good?"
>
> *(Scania World*, 3/2002: 26)

Shortly before the STAX project, Scania had been working on another cab design that had at least visual similarities to the STAX. There were ongoing discussions in the European Union about how trucks could be made less dangerous in accidents with passenger vehicles. Frontal collisions between cars and trucks were particularly dangerous for car passengers as truck cabs did not absorb the crash energy. Moreover, the car might end up partially under the truck cab in a crash, potentially increasing the risk of fatalities. There were two competing concepts to make trucks safer. One was so-called front underrun protection, where a metal beam was placed at the front of the cab to prevent cars from being pushed under it in a crash. Scania proposed an alternative solution incorporating a crash zone, visually resembling a very short bonnet, at the front of the cab. In a collision the crash zone would crumple, thereby absorbing part of the energy. The crash zone was not an ordinary bonnet, more a nose in front of the cab – it was not supposed to contain the engine. Therefore, it partially offered the visual flair of the T-truck, though it was not a T-cab in the original sense. Scania presented a study on the crash zone at its road safety seminar in Brussels, but the EU's decision was finally in favor of the front underrun protection solution.

The similarities between the STAX and the crash zone were initially rather superficial. The STAX bonnet was much longer and was not at all optimized to absorb collision energy. Ola Pihlgren and his colleagues had not intended to conceptualize the STAX's bonnet as a crash zone. Nor was there any reasoning about the crash zone in Scania's publicity in connection with the STAX presentation. However, managers had already had the idea of combining the concepts of a bonnet and crash zone:

> The study actually has a hidden agenda – to see if we could make a crash zone. It was last September. We said that we don't have any news for these fairs and the fairs are after all about image building . . . We could show it and show our competence in carrying out studies. That's

something new for Scania. It was a struggle to get it accepted [internally], but some people did not understand that it was open in strategic terms.

(Kaj Lindgren, Chief of Staff, interview October 3, 2002, less than three weeks after the trade fair)

Exhibiting the STAX at the trade fair did not mean that Scania's management had finally decided what the model implied strategically. There was some information on Scania's crash zone in another section of the company's exhibition stand. The two concepts were not yet connected, but the option for this was left open. In the 2002 annual report, published in March 2003, the STAX was given a double meaning: it was a future T-truck as well as a future crash zone:

> The bonneted truck concept combines tradition and new thinking. Scania's own long tradition of bonneted trucks and more futuristic impulses. The sweeping and eye-catching lines of the STAX might serve as an image creator for transport companies in 10–15 years. At the same time, Scania wants to study whether the hauliers of the future are prepared to sacrifice some of their cargo volume and payload capacity for a truck with superior driver comfort and with various safety features such as deformation zones and underrun protection.
>
> (*Annual Report*, 2002: 24)

One month later, the relabeling of the STAX model was taken further, when the issue of the future T-truck was de-emphasized in favor of the crash zone. At Scania's annual general meeting, Leif Östling presented the STAX in his review of product development over the past year:

> Strong product development is our investment for the future. At our exhibition outside this AGM venue, we show examples of this. Among other things, you can view a large cab – the Scania eXc – and a quarter-scale model, the Scania STAX . . . The Scania STAX shows how the truck of tomorrow featuring a crash zone might look. This may save many lives.
>
> (Leif Östling, AGM, April 25, 2003)

Over a period of months, the way STAX was presented had changed from being a future T-truck to a future crash zone. To Ola Pihlgren, this reinterpretation of the concept was not intentional, but was nevertheless an argument that strengthened the project:

> [I wasn't thinking about a crash zone] when I was working on the [STAX]. That job was going on in parallel, but there were no connections . . . Maybe management thought of the crash zone, let the STAX pass and

thought, "If it works we can use it as a crash zone too." I don't think they were reasoning like that, but you never know.

(Ola Pihlgren, industrial designer, interview 2003)

At its current stage, however, the STAX was not a realistic option for a crash zone, not from a safety point of view or considering the economic consequences of the additional length:

[The crash zone] is one of the engineering arguments and a logical argument. As an engineer you always want to be logical and the best logical argument to retain the T-truck is the crash zone. Then if you take a look at the STAX and know something about the industry you can easily say that it's not a real crash zone. The front axle is too far to the front . . . The [collision issue] is something we have to work on from a technical and an image point of view. In that respect a crash zone in the form of a bonneted cab could be an interesting combination.

(Hasse Johansson, Head of Research and Development, interview 2003)

Scania continued to work on a combination of the STAX and crash zone. In fall 2003, at the company's road safety conference in Brussels, Scania presented a new quarter-scale model showing a truck with a crash zone. It was the third conference of this type that Scania had arranged, and a number of high-ranking EU representatives were among the guests. The crash zone concept was presented by Hasse Johansson and Ola Pihlgren, who had also been involved in the project. The model was less futuristic than the STAX and much closer to a solution that could be launched commercially. The crash zone was a "bonnet" of 600 millimeters, much shorter than that of the STAX. However, the influence of the STAX model was clearly apparent. The future of the bonneted cab, whether in its original form or as a crash zone, remained undecided for the time being, with different strategic options left open.

Postscript

After the empirical study for the present case was finalized, Scania eventually decided to discontinue the T-truck in 2005. The decision was not easy and, as the case shows, it had been preceded by a long period of internal discussion. What finally made the company take this step was the fact that the cab model represented less than 2 percent of Scania's total volume and the design no longer seemed commercially viable. In many markets, so few T-trucks were sold that it was in fact debatable how important it was as a symbol of Scania's identity from the customer's perspective. Other truck features, such as the renowned V8 engine, now had to assume fully the T-cab's role as symbols of the company. It remains to be seen what future the STAX will have. As a concept, it was never intended to be launched commercially. Thanks to the possibility of interpreting the STAX in different ways, it may be referred to as a prototype of a future crash zone.

DISCUSSION AND CONCLUSION

The Scania case is characterized by the absence of a clear demarcation line between organizational identity and product identity. As the company offered essentially a single product, which moreover shared its name with the company, the characteristics that were attributed to the product also became attributed to the firm and vice versa. The "Who are we?" question was partly answered by looking at Scania's trucks. This situation became particularly interesting as there were different opinions on what identity the organization and its products should have. Some members of the organization saw Scania as a company that acted according to a calculative logic, and thus the trucks too should be designed primarily to maximize the economic benefit to their owners. Other Scania employees believed, however, that the company and its trucks should also connote non-quantifiable values: the trucks should not only contribute to the owner's bottom line, they should also appeal to his or her emotions.

Interestingly, in the case of the bonneted trucks, Scania's management initially did not take any measures to resolve the conflict regarding the different interpretations of the organization's identity. The two opinions were allowed to coexist side by side, reflected in the two different interpretations of the T-truck within the company. A reason behind the management's tolerance might have been that neither of the two identity conceptions was clearly opposed to what was usually thought of as Scania's identity: both calculative and emotional elements could be part of it. The question was rather on which side to place the emphasis. As a result of the ambiguity permitted by managers, different strategic options remained open. The possibility of launching new generations of T-trucks still remained initially, while it was also possible to interpret the STAX concept truck as a crash zone development, mainly embodying the calculative aspects of Scania's identity.

For the decision finally to discontinue the T-truck, it was important that the bonneted cab was not the only truck feature that could symbolize the non-quantifiable values ascribed to a Scania. The V8 engine had similar connotations to the T-truck, making the bonneted cab somewhat more dispensable as an embodiment of Scania's identity. Over time, different features of a product can come to express the same identity. Hence, discontinuing the T-truck did not mean that the duality of quantifiable and non-quantifiable identity aspects at Scania had ceased. There was still ambiguity in Scania's identity, leaving various options open for future strategies.

Linking the Scania case to theory, the role of organizational identity as a "beacon for strategy" (Ashforth and Mael, 1996: 32) comes into focus. The strategy process at Scania was by no means limited to a series of calculative analyses. Such analyses are important, but when it comes to decision-making, the question of an organization's identity becomes a crucial criterion. Even though rational financial calculations provided strong arguments for discontinuing the T-cab, the decision finally to cease production met much resistance and was delayed for years. The non-calculative values associated with it were regarded as so important to the identity of the company that the cab model was continued until 2005. Here, identity was a court of last resort for decision-making (see Albert and Whetten, 1985), which for a long time meant that rationalities other than the purely calculative ruled at Scania. What made the issue particularly knotty was the fact that Scania's identity contains some inherent ambiguity. This provided proponents of a calculative approach to strategy and advocates of a more emotional view with arguments in strategic discussions. These two sides of Scania's organizational identity were closely linked to that of the company's products.

The interplay between organizational identity and product identity is an issue that was particularly interesting about Scania. We know from previous research that different identity-related phenomena interrelate. However, so far, the identity–image interplay has been particularly in focus (e.g., Dutton and Dukerich, 1991; Gioia, Schultz, and Corley 2000; Hatch and Schultz, 1997), while connections between the organizational and the product level have been much less discussed. The Scania case suggests that the two affect each other reciprocally. While the products affected how Scania's members saw their own company, organizational identity also created expectations regarding what kind of values the products were supposed to express. Considering the mutual relationship of organizational identity and strategy (Ashforth and Mael, 1996), this indicates that strategy and product identity are also related to one another.

Regarding the cabs, the different conceptions of the product identity reflected different ideas about Scania's strategy. At the same time different product identities legitimized or delegitimized different courses of strategic action. It is remarkable that Scania's management consciously tolerated an ambiguous identity for Scania, both as a company and in specific products. The ambiguity literally built into Scania's identity offered room for different interpretations and increased the variety of strategic options for the future. If we use Ashforth and Mael's (1996) metaphor of identity as a "beacon for strategy," it was not perfectly clear in Scania's case in which direction the beacon guided the company. Where ambiguity of identity is tolerated, identity becomes less of a constraint shaping strategic path dependencies – rather it offers general guidance, allowing room for variation and enabling managers to leave a larger number of strategic options open for a longer time. From a normative point of view, an ambiguous identity might thus be a useful means to maintain a fruitful strategic debate in a company.

KEY QUESTIONS

The following concluding questions are drawn from the Scania case.

- How do organizational identity and product identity affect one another in a single-product company?
- Can we also observe an interplay of organizational identity and product identity in companies with multiple products?
- How do different conceptions of product identity affect the strategic choices made in an organization?
- What degree of diversity of different identity conceptions is acceptable in an organization?
- How do conflicting conceptions of an organization's identity develop over time? Can they be reconciled?
- Can an ambiguous identity be used as a means to increase the strategic flexibility of a company?

NOTE ON METHODS USED

The data for this study were collected through document studies, participant observation, and 39 interviews with strategic actors at Scania. Parts of this chapter refer to a document on Scania's product identity platform: although elements of it are communicated relatively openly, the document as a whole is for internal use only. I have therefore refrained from going into too much detail and have limited my description to a few examples illustrating the ideas behind the platform.

I would like to thank Leif Melin, Per Davidsson, and Hamid Bouchikhi for their helpful support and feedback during my research. In addition, I would like to thank Jönköping International Business School (JIBS) and the Marknadstekniskt Centrum (MTC) for financing the study.

Chapter 2

Why do managers talk about identity?

Roxana Barbulescu and John Weeks

INTRODUCTION

Seldom in organizations do people debate questions of their identity for purely philosophical reasons. Organizational identity has the ability to shape the sense people make of events and the decisions they make about how to respond to those events. This makes identity a powerful tool, sometimes even a weapon. Pressing claims about the organization's identity can be a way of influencing the thoughts and actions of others and persuading them to agree with you. Organizational identity provides an account of how the disparate parts of the organization fit together into a coherent whole. This implies the shape that the organization should have in the future. It also provides an account of how the various decisions that the organization has made in the past are consistent. This, in turn, implies the direction that the organization should take in the future. Talking about the organization's identity, therefore, can be a useful way of justifying particular decisions or attacking them as inappropriate.

We are used to thinking that the prototypical invocation of organizational identity occurs when there is deep and enduring disagreement about a decision of major importance, such as an acquisition, disposal, or product launch (Albert and Whetten, 1985: 264–265). The issue of identity is profound and consequential, and high-profile debates about it can be so difficult and distracting that organizations prefer to avoid them under ordinary circumstances. The absence of such debate, however, allows conflicting views of the organization's identity to persist at the individual and group level, and it creates scope for people to use these different claims about the organization's identity as they confront day-to-day issues of relatively modest significance. It may be in these small ways – rather than through explicit deliberation and dialogue – that the organization's identity actually gets worked out.

In an engineering business unit within Société nationale des chemins de fer

(SNCF), the French state-owned railroad operator, organizational identity was invoked often, and different people talked about identity in different ways and put forward different claims about it at different times for different reasons. The unit was in the midst of a great deal of change, both externally in its market and its relationship with its parent, and internally in its structure and culture. People held varying views about what their identity consisted of and at which level of organization identity ought to matter most – SNCF as a whole, the business unit within it, the divisions within the unit, the broader civil service, or the particular profession of engineering. They avoided, however, a high-level public debate about identity. The conflict remained in the background, and people in the organization, depending on their purposes at the time, found it useful sometimes to talk around it, sometimes to highlight it, and sometimes to try to resolve it. They engaged, in other words, in different types of *identity work* (Alvesson, 1994; Sveningsson and Alvesson, 2003).

Identity work refers to the explicit use of organizational identity for some specific purpose by members of the organization: for example, to influence decision-making, to facilitate day-to-day sense-making, or to manage the impressions of outsiders and newcomers. In this chapter, we examine these patterns of identity work. In order to understand the day-to-day consequences of organizational identity it is important to understand how members of the organization approach the question of identity – namely, "Who are we?" That means, first, how do people draw the boundaries of their shared identity? What level of organization do they identify with? Second, what do people accept as legitimate ways of talking about that shared identity? When we look at how people use the idea of organizational identity to help them think, to help them decide, and to help them persuade others, we find that how people define the "organization" and its "identity" depends a lot on – and reveals much about – what they are trying to achieve.

BACKGROUND INFORMATION

The data presented here are the result of four months of fieldwork at RAIL conducted by the first author in 2003. She spent several weeks each with groups from all of the divisions in RAIL, shadowing people as they went about their work and talking with them informally. In parallel with following the specific activities of the groups under observation, she also attended cross-departmental meetings and social events whenever the opportunity presented itself, and collected archival data. She gained access through the invitation of a senior manager who was interested in having an outsider observe the effects of their office relocation and culture change efforts, as well as "holding a mirror up to the organization" to provide a view from which they might learn.

RAIL, a pseudonym, is one of a number of business units within SNCF engaged in design and maintenance engineering work. In 2003, the unit comprised 1,300 people, most of them engineers. RAIL was organized into three divisions: Technical, Projects, and Management.

The Technical division had approximately 900 people. It was structured by technical specialization into three departments: Civil Engineering, Electrical Engineering, and Telecommunications. These departments were strictly separated, and the division was highly hierarchical in structure. Members of the Technical division executed projects that had been sourced by one of the other two divisions, Projects or Management. Technical members had little client contact except on an operational basis.

The Projects division, with approximately 300 people, coordinated the management of projects, handling client relationships and recruiting people from Technical to do the technical work. The Projects division had a flat structure and was divided into departments according to project size: large projects, small projects, and support functions.

Management, the smallest division with fewer than a hundred people, comprised what the organization called the "transversal" functions (i.e., functions that cut across the specialist departments of the Technical division and across the project-based groups in Projects). These transversal functions consisted of Human Resources, Quality, Communication, IT, Logistics, and Strategy and Development. The Strategy and Development group monitored the environment: developing contacts and sourcing new projects. It was also responsible for organizing the proposals made in response to requests from external clients. These proposals typically required input from several different project and technical departments. Strategy and Development was, at the time of the study, still a new function with responsibilities only recently required by the organization and still controversial.

CONCERNS ABOUT CHANGE AT RAIL

In the late 1990s, the market for RAIL's engineering services was deregulated. Previously, RAIL had one client – SNCF, its parent company – and no competitors. Following deregulation it could bid for work from private clients, but it also had to compete against public and private companies for most of its projects. These environmental changes – and the uncertain prospect of further changes ahead – wrought intense concern and self-questioning within RAIL. In top management, department, and team-level meetings, the organization devoted tremendous time and energy to the notion of change: focus groups, working groups, task forces, employee questionnaires, client surveys, strategic meetings, plans, and initiatives of all kinds had all been employed in an attempt to help the organization make sense of the new reality. Changes had been made to the organizational structure and to work roles. New roles, such as project supervisor, quality supervisor, and commercial liaison, had been created and old roles redefined.

Traditionally, there had been a complete separation of engineering and administrative roles, but now most engineers were expected to devote at least 10 percent of their time to administrative tasks such as time and cost tracking for each project they worked on — tasks that in the past either had not been considered necessary or had been carried out by specialist administrative functions.

At the time of our study, the structural changes in the organization of work at RAIL had already been accomplished, and the focus of change had shifted to physical relocation and culture. Geographically, RAIL employees had previously been located in six different locations across the same city. Over a period of four months, they moved in together to a brand-new building on the outskirts of the city. The relocation generated a large amount of discussion among both management and staff about appropriate partitioning of the new space, design of common areas, choice of furnishing, and logistics.

Culturally, a project named *Virage* ("Turning Point") had been initiated with the aim of highlighting the good and bad ways things were done at RAIL and suggesting improvements. The project was led by a nine-person Relay Group consisting of managers from different parts of RAIL who had been asked to volunteer their time because of the energy and enthusiasm they had shown in the past in leading improvement and change. The Relay Group had responsibility for defining the project, proposing a plan of action, and following through with its implementation. The Turning Point project polarized RAIL management and staff outside the Relay Group: it had supporters and detractors, but few people were indifferent to it.

The case study, then, deals with a very special moment in the life of RAIL: one that encompasses changes in the competitive environment, physical environment, and organizational culture. It is not surprising that the issue of organizational identity would come up repeatedly during this time. The identity work that was carried out at RAIL — even within the Turning Point project — did not, however, consist of the kind of high-level debate about major issues concerning the direction of the organization that is assumed in the literature to be prototypical. Instead, claims about organizational identity were made in the context of day-to-day struggles to influence sense-making and decision-making about relatively minor issues by people at all levels of the organization as they went about their jobs and pursued their various interests. It is here, as the consequence of the words and actions of people trying to make sense of the world around them and influence proximate outcomes in ways they believed best, that organizational identity was contested and negotiated.

PATTERNS OF IDENTITY WORK

At RAIL, organizational identity was invoked in casual conversations, in client meeting preparation discussions, in project team meetings, and in strategy meetings. Rarely, though, were the terms "identity" or "organizational identity" used themselves. More often, the reference was to "we," "us," "who we are," "how we do things," or "what we believe."

We observed three types of identity work – three uses that people made of talking about the identity of their organization. These were:

1 *Impression management identity work*: efforts to shape the initial impressions of the organization in the minds of newcomers and outsiders. "Who are we?" is a question that organizational members have to answer whenever they meet new clients, collaborators, employees, or other third parties. The question is often implicit but never ignored. The specific way in which members intro-duced themselves, their work group, department, business unit, or larger organization is very important for how the relationship with the newcomers and outsiders will subsequently develop. Identity work here meant glossing over the conflicts about RAIL's identity to present a favourable, consistent façade that focused on a superficial sense of identity such as the organization chart.

2 *Sense-making identity work*: justifications or explanations of behaviour within the organization. Just as people often invoke individual identity to explain behaviour – arguing that the reason a person did something is because that is the kind of person he or she is – so too people use organizational identity to make sense of what happens in the organization. At RAIL, when people used identity as a way to justify their own acts or account for the behaviour of others, they highlighted the disagreements among them about the organiza-tion's identity. In the way they talked, they revealed the different camps of opinion within the organization and how each viewed the others. This kind of identity work ultimately reinforced differences.

3 *Persuasion identity work*: attempts to influence the behaviour of others. Invoking shared identity – claiming that this is who we are and we are in this together – is a way of persuading others to act in ways they might resist at first. At RAIL, this kind of identity work was used, for example, by managers to try to convince engineers that the commercial activities they disliked performing were now part of their duties. Another successful tactic was to draw upon the image that outsiders had of RAIL, either positive or negative, to motivate others to want to behave in ways that would prove or disprove those external views of the organization's identity.

Managing impressions

In introducing RAIL, people typically spoke of organizational identity in structural terms: how the different pieces of the organization all fit together into a united, coherent whole. This had the advantage of keeping the focus on the relatively superficial aspects of the unit's identity about which there was broad agreement. For example:

> As you know, now at RAIL we have clients and competition. There are three big parts of RAIL. Technical people specialize in precise fields of expertise. They work on studies, and work with us on projects. Projects people are the project heads. Upstream, they do the studies. Downstream, they do the work for the implementation stage. Then, there is Management. They work with us and Tech on everything transversal.

As part of RAIL's ISO 9001 qualification, each department head had a copy of a quality manual that included the organization chart. It was often used as a prop in introductions. Sometimes people explained who RAIL was by simply reading the chart and describing what its different departments and sections did.

The same pattern was evident when the organization being identified was not RAIL as a whole but a division or department within the unit. Members of the Strategy and Development department (SD), for example, often found themselves in the position of introducing RAIL, and their department in particular, to potential clients or external partners. Sometimes they used the organization chart, other times they painted the structure of roles verbally. Either way, they would introduce their department by showing how what they did fit with the activities in the rest of the organization:

> We are a recent part of RAIL. Our roles are: monitor requests for proposals; manage database for answering requests for proposals; close partnerships; market analysis; studies on particular topics; client contacts; support to contract writing; archive past answers to requests for proposals; and store models, contracts, and up-to-date administrative documents.

Structure was not the only dimension of organizational identity that could be invoked to portray a unified front for RAIL. The organization could also be described in terms of the skills and competences that set it apart. For example, a Telecom engineer introduced his department to a group of new interns as follows:

> OK, welcome. So, here at RAIL Telecom we work on different frequencies from what you normally know about radio. They are not part of the public network. We do WiFi too.

Members of RAIL, then, when asked the question "Who are you?" by outsiders and newcomers, answered by talking about the structure of the organization or the competences that differentiated it from others in the industry. In so doing, they emphasized the aspects of RAIL's identity that were uncontested, answering the question "Who are we?" in a way that avoided advertising to outsiders and newcomers the conflicts within the organization about its identity. If they were to move away from this surface definition of identity and talk about the values that united (or divided) the various parts of the organization and the common mission underlying the organization's behaviour over time (or its absence), conflict would come to the fore because at this level opinion was divided about what the organization was and what it should be. Such talk was not shared with outsiders.

Making sense

It did not take long after the introductions, however, for the differences of opinion within RAIL over these deeper levels of organizational identity to become visible. It is not that there was an organization-wide debate about identity, or that people were discussing "Who are we?" in the hallways of RAIL. Rather, the conflict emerged indirectly in the way that people made sense of behaviour in the organization. When justifying their own behaviour and explaining the behaviour of others, people invoked organizational identity not in structural terms but in terms of values. Different values, though, were espoused in different parts of the organization, and different values were salient depending on the particular circumstances.

At the core was the division between those who argued that RAIL was an organization where everyone should think of him/herself as technical *and* commercial, and those who argued that a clear separation of technical and commercial people was fundamental. There were, in other words, two very different ideas about what RAIL's identity should be. Simplifying somewhat, in the same way that people at RAIL found it convenient to reference the differences of opinion in these stereotyped ways, there were *technical* people and there were *commercial* people, and they held opposing views about the organization's identity.

Technical people saw RAIL as a technical executor that took detailed plans given to them by the client and executed them to the highest technical standards of quality. In such an organization, members are highly qualified technical experts who concern themselves primarily with the quality and performance of the product they are asked to deliver. Technical people were those who, for example, joined RAIL because it was a pure engineering organization untainted by commercial concerns, unlike private-sector alternatives. The following quote from an engineer in the Technical division is representative of this view:

> Our job is very interesting, and varied. We follow all technologies that come out. I chose RAIL because, in the private sector, I wouldn't have the same flexibility; here I do everything, it changes so often. We're in

between technologies, we take them, mix and match, and add complexities!

The respondent invoked the identity of the organization – and its congruence with the professional identity of engineers – to justify not only his career choice but also his right, as a member of RAIL, to exercise his profession fully and freely, without unwelcome interferences such as the routine work or narrow specialization that result from a commercial focus on cost and efficiency. In this view, private firms subordinate technical values to commercial ones and place professionalism second to commercial ends. Thus, a commercial identity for RAIL was something to be feared and cut against the very reason engineers joined RAIL.

Commercial people saw RAIL as a commercial decision-maker that helped clients to understand what they needed, even selling them a particular solution, and delivered that solution in a technically excellent but cost-effective manner. In such an organization, members are active collaborators with the client on every project, and they concern themselves not only with technical aspects but also with commercial and business development aspects of their work. They saw the same reality in RAIL as technical people did, but valued it differently. They too projected their professional identity, as managers, onto the organization as a whole, and they resisted the identification of RAIL purely with engineering. For example, a manager in SD had this to say to his staff about the members of technical departments:

> Our group is reactive, responsive. But to communicate this to the Tech people with whom we work is difficult. They are concerned with doing beautiful things, not doing things that are financially viable. It is difficult to make these departments responsive in this sense. There is a large margin of competences, but one has to push to get to it. By and large, they don't know what commercial responsiveness is . . . They are excellent technicians, but execrable business people.

For commercial people, identifying RAIL with doing beautiful things was financially irresponsible: the company would not be offered the chance to build anything if it was not commercially responsive.

This division between technical and commercial identities could be seen most clearly in the justifications people gave for their refusal to do something or their unhappiness at having to do it. There was controversy about who was responsible for commercial activities such as responding to requests for proposals (who should coordinate the answers?), being proactive in lobbying clients (who should address them, and who should prepare the strategy for addressing them?), keeping track of staff track records and collaborators' contacts (who should be responsible for updating the references and competences lists?), and being up to date with members' work charges and availability (who should do the paperwork?).

These differences allowed a new form of identity work: explaining behaviour in terms of RAIL's identity. For example, a manager in a technical department, frustrated after trying unsuccessfully to find somebody to respond to a new request for proposals so that he would not have to do it, said:

> Look, this is not my job. We waste half a day just to figure it out. We need someone who does commercial work for the department, who has everybody's agenda and can plan this.

Officially, it *was* his job, but he implicitly rejected the idea of RAIL as an organization where commercial and technical functions were intertwined. Similarly, a manager in a technical department complained about having to keep track of the offers his team responded to:

> Here, we're technicians; it drives me mad to spend all this time on Excel, timesheets, monthly overviews, project by project, and now invoicing!

At one level, these are arguments about roles and responsibilities. However, the conflict about whether commercial and technical functions should be separate within RAIL corresponds to a larger question: should commercial and technical functions be separate within SNCF, and RAIL be strictly technical? It is a conflict over fundamental assumptions about what RAIL should be.

There was clear awareness within RAIL of these different organizational identities, but also broad realization that the split of views and values had negative consequences. People agreed that it made it difficult to communicate. Within SD, for example, managers and analysts complained to each other that:

> There is a big distinction between commercial and technical people. We, in Strategy and Development, can see the big picture, because of the department we're in. But the engineers cannot see that, they only see the project they're working on, and their specialty of expertise.

Meanwhile, technical people complained that SD were the naive ones, trying to impose responsibilities for decision-making and for commercial activity:

> You cannot have commercial activities without strategy. And the strategy, this must come from the top management. It can't be up to everyone to make strategy. The people in Strategy and Development, they think that empowerment is everything – that just by putting information

about deals and partnerships on our web portal everything will work. That's not true.

This lack of communication and difficulty in working together was perceived to have consequences. If the commercial and technical elements of the organization were completely divided, then the commercial side might make commitments to government or private clients that the technical side could not meet. This came to the surface in a meeting between SD and a technical group. Hearing the people from SD describe their commercial activity, the head of the technical group replied passionately:

> In a team with two people, what should we do first? We just don't have the means. We've been saying for years watch out, people are retiring, training someone takes time, and we don't have enough people! I just want discourse and action to be consistent! Sure, we will always say yes to clients, because commercial and political considerations come first. It's only later that we realize we don't have enough resources and can't fulfill our obligations to the client honourably!

In this example, the technical group's lack of commercial activity was blamed on the organizational "we" in a way that invoked an identity claim – "This is how we are" – and implied that everyone was in agreement with this. Indeed, the response from the head of SD was conciliatory and constructive, even if trying to tilt the balance a little towards the commercial position:

> Those are huge problems indeed, we all know it, and I hope the man-agement acts on it very soon. In the meantime though, we have to do what we can to move forward. We know it's tough, for all of us. And that's exactly what we're here for, to tell you we can help you.

We see, then, two important aspects of sense-making identity work at RAIL. On the one hand, the two conflicting organizational identities – technical and commercial – encouraged people to stereotype one another and to derive straightforward accounts of the attitudes and behaviours of "us" and "them". It simplified the choices confronting the organization: each side believed that their values were the right ones for the organization and that dire consequences would ensue if the values of the other were adopted as the identity of RAIL. On the other hand, because there was agreement that the current situation of segregated iden-tities was undesirable, when members of the two groups talked together organiza-tional identity was invoked in a way that avoided the conflict. The conflict was usually discussed only among groups of people who already shared views and offered no possibility for debate. On those occasions when the issue arose in mixed groups, the conflict remained tacit and unresolved. In practice, it was the norm at RAIL to avoid public conflict over organizational identity. It was seen as part of the RAIL culture.

The head of Quality Assurance explained why such fundamental differences of opinion were not raised even in meetings ostensibly held to resolve them: "It's in their personality, why would they be at RAIL otherwise?" It is as if an agreed element of the organization's identity was not to argue about the elements of identity over which there was no agreement. Often, however, to get things done day to day, the differences had to be overcome and so, as we examine in the next section, identity work of a different kind was an important part of influencing behaviour.

Influencing behaviour

As we have seen, the competing claims about the organizational identity of RAIL were linked to specific ideas about work roles and behaviours that were appropriate and desirable and those that were not. When trying to influence people to do things that do not fit their identity-based beliefs (getting technical people to perform commercial activities, for example), identity work is required. We observed two such tactics for influencing people to do something that contradicted their beliefs about organizational identity: playing down identity and playing it up.

Playing down identity involved framing the behaviour as necessary but posing no threat to anyone's beliefs about organizational identity. This meant separating the question of the behaviour from the tacit argument about identity. Identity was talked about in terms of ideals, separable from the actual behaviour of the organization. Deregulation, competition, client demands, or other economic realities of the changed environment were invoked as neutral, purely pragmatic reasons for why certain behaviours were necessary. For example:

> Competition is putting pressure on us. We have to change our mentality, naturally. We have to be responsive to calls for proposals, to question our costs, because our performance today depends on RAIL's future revenues. So we have to translate the stress that the competition is putting on us into positive energy, improve our communication, lessen the formality of our exchanges, and improve the training of our engineers.

Evidence that such arguments worked, at least some of the time, comes from the fact that people echoed this same reasoning in their explanations for why they were doing things. For instance, when engineers gathered in their daily morning ritual around the coffee machine to complain, they contrasted the ideal work activity with the tangible, immediate dealings they were engaged in:

> Our mission is not work for private clients, it's for the internal clients.
> But now we do it, because we have to!

The organization's mission was thus separated from its behaviour – the environment had changed and so the behaviour had changed, but the mission had not. In this way, the organizational identity, as understood by this engineering group, was preserved and was not considered to be under threat.

Playing up identity worked by invoking the external image of RAIL held by clients as having a claim on the organization's identity. Sometimes this image was positive and the tactic was one of motivating people in RAIL to live up to this image. This is illustrated in the following example of a section leader in the Telecommunications department who attempted to mobilize his staff to accept a new project in addition to their ongoing work, as follows:

> Guys, emergency! This was a call for proposals for the fire department in [major city]. They called us directly. They are asking us . . . How can we say no?! We were recommended to them by the bus people there [the public bus company in the city being a client of RAIL].

The manager invoked the positive image that clients had of RAIL and their work to appeal to the pride of the engineers. At the core of the argument was the proposal that RAIL members should behave in a way that ensured the fit between the identity of the organization and the positive image outsiders had of it as a great engineering company. This was a way of assigning a positive valence to the commercial identity of RAIL.

More often, though, when this tactic was used, the image invoked was negative. The idea was to embarrass members of the organization into changing their behaviour in a way that would improve that image because conflict over organizational identity would be displaced by concern for organizational image. For example, when addressing 200 people at a Technical department meeting, the head of the department argued for change in the way engineers worked with clients – the engineers should engage the client as a partner instead of expecting the client to deliver a complete and exact definition of what was needed that the engineers could simply implement. He substantiated his argument by reference to the client's negative image of RAIL:

> We are seen as overly respectful of the distinction between those who decide and those who implement. They say we are just "yes men." We have to speak up when this way of doing things doesn't work. For a product that is yet to be defined, it doesn't work to think with two separate heads. The decision-makers now often don't have the technical

competences. We don't have to choose for them, but we have to put ourselves in their shoes, and think like them.

The speaker here appealed to the pride of the engineers – we, not the clients, have the technical competences, we can show them how it's done! – to overcome their identification of RAIL as a executor rather than a decision-maker, and their tendency to blame the client and wait for instruction when the needs definition was wrong or incomplete.

DISCUSSION

Because the organizational identity question – "Who are we?" – is difficult and contentious, public debate about it is often avoided at the level of the organization. It may be taken for granted or assumed that it is answered in the organization's advertising slogans or vision and mission statements. If this is the case, conflict about the organization's identity may nevertheless be played out in the day-to-day routines of people. At RAIL, organizational identity was invoked in the context of three different goals: managing impressions, making sense, and influencing behaviour. The talk about organizational identity, the identity work, was done in order to accomplish these other goals rather than as an end in itself. Depending on the situation, and on the goals being pursued, different ways of talking about the "organization" and its identity were appropriate.

People at RAIL rarely mentioned SNCF itself as the organization. More often it was at the level of RAIL as a unit; however, often the organizational "we" was at a level lower than that, such as a division within RAIL, a professional group, or a group of people sharing a set of values. When describing the organization to outsiders, RAIL's identity was invoked in structural terms – how all the various pieces of the organization fit together in a coherent whole. In this way discussion of the identity conflicts in the organization could be avoided. When justifying their own behaviour, or explaining the behaviour of others, however, people invoked the organization's identity differently. They talked about organizational identity in terms of the values and mission that were shared (or not shared) by all parts of the organization, highlighting the division of opinion and multiple professional identities within RAIL, and perhaps deepening and entrenching them while avoiding overt conflict. The divergent claims about the organization's identity were consequential, in part because they were associated with different ideas about the appropriateness and desirability of certain activities. To influence others to behave in ways incompatible with their view of what the organization was, different types of identity work were called for. Sometimes the organization's identity was talked about as an ideal that could be separated from behaviours that were necessary for pragmatic reasons imposed by the organization's environment. In this way conflict could be side-stepped. At other times, identity was talked about in terms of the image that outsiders were perceived to hold about RAIL. This tactic attempted to change people's views about the organization's identity directly either to meet the positive image of outsiders or to contradict their negative image.

Our case study contributes to empirical research aimed at understanding how organizations live out multiple identities. Building on recent work that looks at the drivers (Glynn, 2000; Corley, 2004) and consequences (Humphreys and Brown, 2002) of organizational identity differentiation and conflict, and on work by authors such as Gioia and Thomas (1996) and Dutton and Dukerich (1991) examining the relationship between organizational identity and individual sense-making, our analysis focuses on the practices of identity work where conflict and sense-making get played out. Agreeing with Ashforth (1998: 279) that "identity, to really stick, has got to be something that you enact in a very local, tribal context," the findings of our study emphasize the importance of locating organization-level ideas about identity and conflict in the occasions, mechanisms, and resources for identity work (Alvesson, 1994; Sveningsson and Alvesson, 2003) in the mundane, day-to-day interactions of members of the organization.

It is in these mundane details that the future identity of the organization is mapped out. Where there are conflicting identity claims, so there are conflicting views of what lies ahead. At RAIL, some technical people feared that a commercial identity would be forced upon them and that resistance was required. Some commercial people feared that only an economic crisis would dislodge the identity of RAIL as technical executor:

> RAIL is losing contracts to competition, who are acquiring more and more competences and diversifying their services . . . The problem is that RAIL thinks of itself as a grand lady who does only what she wants.

Others, however, were more optimistic that a gradual working-out of a new identity for RAIL – combining elements of both its technical and commercial identities – could be achieved. As the head of one of RAIL's technical departments said in a meeting with his peers:

> I've heard this for a while now, "What's going to happen to us? Are we going to disappear?" I say we have to phrase it as opportunity. Now, in today's economy, our jobs in fact make a lot of money! . . . Yes, the world changes, but we change with it.

At RAIL, and in any organization, there is no reason to assume that one version of identity will necessarily dominate, or even that the pattern of identity alternatives will reach an equilibrium. The outcome will depend on the day-to-day identity work of people in the organization as they try to make decisions, make meaning, build things, and, yes, make money.

CONCLUSION

1 At RAIL the top management team avoided official pronouncements and formal debates on organizational identity because they felt these could create
   more problems than they would solve. This might not be the case in other
   organizations. How should leaders attempt to shape ideas about organizational
   identity in their organization? Can identity be imposed from the top down?
   What are the costs and benefits of an organization-wide debate about identity?

2 At RAIL we identified three contexts in which people found it useful or
   necessary to invoke organizational identity: when introducing the organization
   to outsiders and newcomers, when justifying their own actions or explaining
   the actions of others, and when trying to influence behaviour. What other uses
   may organizational identity have for organizational members?

3 In SNCF, the boundaries of organizational identity do not always coincide
   neatly with the legal boundaries of the corporation. More generally, finding out
   what level of "organization" people identify with can be an empirical question.
   From a managerial point of view, is it a good thing when people identify more
   with their part of the organization than with the organization as a whole? What
   are the consequences of multiple identities competing for people's loyalty?

4 RAIL was undergoing a period of major change in its competitive and physical
   environment and in its culture. To what extent are the dynamics of identity
   work that we observe in RAIL dependent upon those changes? What does
   identity work look like in periods of relative stability?

5 At RAIL we saw the identity conflict portrayed as competition between stereotyped "technical" versus "commercial" views of what the organization is, or
   should be. What is the influence of these simplified, shorthand ways of talking
   about identity in organizations? Does it aid debate by providing structure or
   impoverish it by oversimplifying?

Chapter 3

Organizational identity and formulating strategy

The breaking and remaking of AT&T

Yolanda Sarason and Johan van Rekom

INTRODUCTION

Identity questions such as "Who do we want to be?" are directly related to strategy questions such as "Where do we want to be strategically?" (Whetten and Godfrey, 1998). The sense-making and sense-giving processes of answering these identity and strategy questions have begun to be explored by researchers (Gioia and Thomas, 1996; Peteraf and Shanley, 1997; Corley and Gioia, 2004; Ravasi and Schultz, 2006). The identity question "Who are we?" influences strategy formulation in ways not fully understood and articulated by the strategists. Issues of "who we are" form self-evident, unquestioned, and sometimes even unnoticed assumptions that influence a company's strategy formulation.

This chapter will show how useful it may be to focus on those occasions where identity catches the strategists unaware. We will look at the history of AT&T, how it was broken up and put back together, and how organizational identity helps us understand how this was done. First, we will describe the divestiture of AT&T and how seven Regional Bell Operating Companies (RBOCs), often referred to as the "Baby Bells," came into being. Next we will focus on how the two types of strategies of the "Baby Bells" evolved. We will focus on three of these "Baby Bells," highlighting how they saw themselves after divestiture and how they compared themselves to their competitors and their corporate siblings. We will then discuss how more recent strategic moves by these organizations can be better understood through the lens of their organizational identities.

AT&T AND THE BABY BELLS

For almost a hundred years, American Telephone and Telegraph (AT&T, also known as the Bell System) accompanied the United States through the industrial age. In the 1970s, AT&T was the world's largest corporation. However, in 1982, with the anti-trust lawsuit that called for the divestiture of all aspects of the Bell System coming to a conclusion, senior management agreed to spin off the 22 operating companies that had been responsible for local telephone services. These were clustered into seven Regional Bell Operating Companies, or RBOCs, which would become known as the "Baby Bells." Figure 6 shows the geographic boundaries of each of these organizations at divestiture.

For 12 years, up until the 1996 Telecommunications Act, the Baby Bells were able to operate in relatively protected home territories. The new law opened up the telecommunications industry to new competition. A wave of mergers and attempted buyouts followed, which consolidated shortly after the millennium (Cauley, 2005). By 2000, Southwestern Bell (renamed SBC) had acquired Ameritech and Pacific Telesis; US WEST was purchased by Qwest, and Bell Atlantic and NYNEX were consolidated under the name Verizon. In 2005, SBC agreed to purchase AT&T ("Ma Bell"), and announced that it would rename its entire telephone business "AT&T" (SBC, 2005). In 2006, the new AT&T entered into arrangements to purchase Bell South. In many ways, the old "Ma Bell" is being reconfigured by the "babies" (AT&T, 2006). Figure 7 shows the reorganized companies as of 2006.

Each Baby Bell provided local telephone services in its geographic area. The companies were prevented from competing in markets in which they might have an unfair advantage. In return, the RBOCs were granted a monopoly on traditional local telephone services in their respective territories. Each Baby Bell was of approximately equal size (Cauley, 2005). The RBOCs had a shared history and culture, and senior managers had similar backgrounds and training – in essence they were as similar as any seven companies have ever been, while still financially and strategically independent. Even at divestiture, the Baby Bells could see the

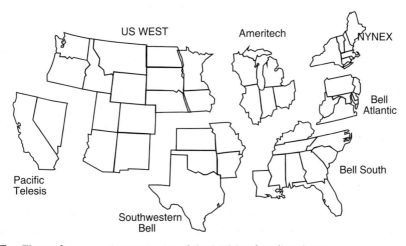

Figure 6 *Geographic territories of the RBOCs after divestiture*

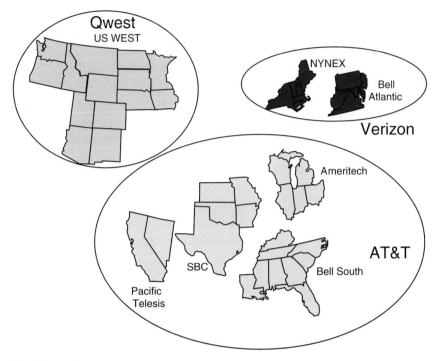

Figure 7 *RBOCs (Baby Bells 2006)*

writing on the wall: though they were cash rich, they were prevented by regula-
tion from entering certain businesses, at the same time as changing technology
would allow competition into their protected business. Since the time of divestiture, the Baby Bells had raced to diversify their businesses in arenas in which they
could compete. The strategies they chose could be categorized either as focused
telecommunication players or as diversified multimedia organizations (Sarason,
1998b).

Focused telecommunicators

The organizations choosing to remain focused on the telecommunications industry are NYNEX, Ameritech, Pacific Telesis, and SBC. Each organization's strategic
trajectory is outlined below:

- *Ameritech.* Ameritech was the least diversified of the RBOCs, with only 13.9
  percent of its revenue generated from diversified activities. The company maintained its geographic organizational structure throughout the 1980s. However,
  shortly before William Weiss retired as CEO he restructured the company
  from being organized by regions to organizing the company around products

and services. Ameritech had been the most vociferous Baby Bell in calling for open competition for local telephone traffic and long-distance calling. In 1999, the company was purchased by Southwestern Bell (SBC).

- *NYNEX.* In an attempt to become a worldwide computer systems company, NYNEX diversified before retrenching to address poor performance in the local exchange business. The company was also part of the alliance with Bell Atlantic, Pacific Telesis, and Michael Ovitz's Creative Artists Agency. It owned 20 percent of Telecom Asia, a company that was about to install two million phone lines in Bangkok. In 1998, Bell Atlantic and NYNEX merged, and in 2000 the company merged with GTE, renaming itself Verizon.

- *Pacific Telesis.* Pacific Telesis set out to become the world leader in wireless networks. In June 1994, the company announced the planned spin-off of a new company, Air Touch, providing wireless services worldwide. The spin-off allowed the company to bid for PCS licenses. Pacific Telesis has adopted the motto "California First," with the goal of making superhighway-type services available to half of all homes in California. In 1997, Southwestern Bell (SBC) purchased the company.

- *SBC (Southwestern Bell).* Starting in the late 1980s the company purchased Metromedia Cellular, doubling its wireless business, and eventually became known as the best cellular operator among the regional Bells. It invested $1 billion to buy 10 percent of Mexico's telephone company, Telefonos de Mexico, which operated next door to SBC territory. This RBOC has emerged as the dominant player in this industry. By 1999, Southwestern Bell (renamed SBC) had acquired Ameritech and Pacific Telesis. In 2005, SBC agreed to purchase their earlier parent company, AT&T, and announced that it would rename its entire telephone business "AT&T" (SBC, 2005). In 2006, the new AT&T entered into arrangements to purchase Bell South. In many ways, the old "Ma Bell" is being reconfigured by one big "Baby Bell" (AT&T, 2006).

Multimedia players

The multimedia players were more likely to enter the cable sector as their diversification strategy. This decision has taken them out of their region, as they were prevented from providing cable services in their own regions in the divestiture agreement. These companies were Bell Atlantic, US WEST, and Bell South. The following description outlines their strategic actions:

- *Bell Atlantic.* Bell Atlantic pursued scattershot diversification until Ray Smith became CEO in 1988. At this time, the company began to focus on offering integrated wireline and wireless services in its region. In 1993, Bell Atlantic proposed to buy TCI for around $33 billion. The much publicized takeover of

TCI would have been the biggest merger in history, but was thwarted in the final stages of negotiations because of cable TV rate cuts ordered by the FCC. In May 1994, Bell Atlantic unveiled plans to build a flexible network architecture in 20 markets by 1990, costing $11 billion. As previously mentioned, in 1998 Bell Atlantic and NYNEX merged, and in 2000 the company merged with GTE, renaming itself Verizon.

- *Bell South.* Bell South is the largest regional telephone company, whether measured by the number of phone lines (19 million) or annual revenue ($16 billion). The growth of Bell South's territory has enabled it to roll out state-of-the-art fiber-optic technology without having to write off existing investments. The company built fiber-optic and coaxial cable networks in its region, and their plans are to develop high-tech networks as demand for broadband services increases. Bell South paid $100 million for a 2.5 percent stake in Prime Cable of Austin, Texas, part of Southwestern Bell's turf. It also joined the bidding for Paramount Communications with an investment in QVC, contingent upon the latter's successful bid. Bell South joined the programming partnership with Disney, Ameritech, and Southwestern Bell.

- *US WEST.* US WEST had been the most active and broadest diversifier, venturing into many activities. Initial efforts after divestiture focused on diversifying into real estate and financial services, but subsequently the company exited these industries. Since 1989, US WEST has diversified into the cable and entertainment industries. In 1993, it paid $2.5 billion for a 25.5 percent stake in Time Warner Entertainment and its cable systems, cable channels, and movie studios. It also purchased two Atlanta-area cable TV companies. In February 1996, the company announced the purchase of Continental Cablevision, which was the largest combination of a Baby Bell and a cable company. In 1997, with its Time Warner properties, US WEST managed 16.2 million domestic cable customers and had access to some 13.9 million homes abroad, making it the third largest cable company in the United States. In 2000, US WEST was acquired by Qwest.

Contrasting visions of identity: telecommunications versus multimedia

The senior managers of the companies focusing on telecommunications saw their organizations very differently than those of the multimedia organizations. In order to investigate these different beliefs, key decision-makers were interviewed at US WEST, Ameritech, and Pacific Telesis – the companies with the most divergent strategies among the seven Baby Bells in the mid-1990s (Sarason, 1997). US WEST was the most out-and-out multimedia organization, and Ameritech and Pacific Telesis were two of the organizations focusing on telecommunications. The following section outlines the findings of this investigation.

Thirty-six senior managers in three organizations were asked (a) to describe their competition, (b) what adjectives described their organization, and (c) what they thought about strategic issues, in a research project described by Sarason (1997). As managers explicated the logic behind their choices, differences surfaced regarding which company types they viewed as their competitors. At Ameritech, most managers cited long-distance providers; at US WEST, about half of the interviewees cited cable companies. The quote below is an illustrative statement by one of US WEST's senior managers:

> I think we have to view our biggest competitor as being the cable company in each market that we are in. So that's going to be TCI primarily. On the other hand, in other markets like Atlanta our biggest competitor is Bell South, so we are just on the opposite side . . . We are going to duke it out with TCI in Denver and we are going to lose some share. But, we'd like to go to Atlanta and duke it out on the other side with Bell South and maybe gain some share. We know we are going to lose something in Denver but we are going to pick up something in Atlanta and Atlanta is a much bigger market.
>
> (US WEST executive)

Executives at US WEST described their own organization in relation to the other RBOCs and to other competitors. The most striking characteristic of US WEST is "aggressive," as expressed by many of their executives:

> Aggressive, tougher, dealt a tougher hand. Takes higher risk. Open to outsiders from outside the industry.
>
> (US WEST executive)

The responses of Ameritech and Pacific Telesis executives showed a distinctly different pattern of responses than those of US WEST. One Ameritech executive stated: "I think probably the single word I would use is realistic." And the following quote from a Pacific Telesis senior manager is typical:

> I think more creative, more flexible, and more focused. And by more focused I mean once it became clear what our core competence was in the wireless and cellular business, then we grabbed that ball and ran with it full speed ahead.

Only one Pacific Telesis manager used the word "aggressive" in relation to his own organization, and then in a way that expressed some incipient aggressiveness rather than a well-established organizational feature: "We are learning, we are becoming aggressive, and it is becoming more and more a way of life for us."

55

When asked to compare their organization to competitors, executives used different adjectives than in comparisons to other RBOCs. Occasionally, admiration for the parent company, AT&T, emerged:

> Region bound, not as deeply endowed with R&D capability as AT&T and less experienced from a competitive point of view and from a marketing point of view.
>
> (Former US WEST executive)

> The only people who are poised and ready to eat our lunch is AT&T. They not only have the technical capability, but they in fact are competent and have resources and have a great name.
>
> (Pacific Telesis executive)

The words "slow" and "bureaucratic" were commonly used by representatives of US WEST, Pacific Telesis, and Ameritech when comparing themselves to competitors. However, in all three organizations the adjectives used when comparing themselves to other RBOCs were more positive.

We explored the link between how managers viewed their organization's identity and how they evaluated each other's strategic actions. In 1993, as stated earlier, US WEST paid $2.5 billion for a 25.5 percent stake in Time Warner. This was the first time an RBOC had engaged in a joint venture with a cable and entertainment company of this magnitude. Executives evaluated this event, as well as Ameritech's strategy of focusing on telephony. Similarly, we asked their view on the decision by Pacific Telesis to spin off Air Touch.

All US WEST executives who responded to this question showed enthusiasm for the alliance with Time Warner:

> The fit was right, it was just sort of a marriage made in heaven as far as the business fit is concerned. There were problems that could be foreseen and have proved themselves in terms of partnership management. I think we are learning a lot in partnership management and how to assert ourselves and not be managed but exercise the control we have the right to exercise.
>
> (US WEST senior manager)

Positive responses were evident even from US WEST respondents who spoke of the difficulties between US WEST and Time Warner. Half of the US WEST respondents qualified their response with the acknowledgement that the relationship had either experienced difficulties or had not met expectations. For example, a senior manager stated:

> I think it was the right deal, it was one of the most visionary steps we

have taken. I think that it will fundamentally reshape the industry. It was the first example of an RBOC that stuck its neck out and will help facilitate the convergence of technologies. On the hand, I think that it is taking more time to realize the potential of the partnership than we had thought. We have had to tone down our original expectations.

(US WEST senior manager)

Ameritech executives' responses were quite in contrast, and showed two general themes. In the first theme, half of the respondents spoke of their belief that the venture was doomed to fail:

A marriage made in hell . . . When you look at it on paper, you say "Boy does this make sense . . . We're going to put this thing together." You also look at a few operating statistics, like, you know, how are these companies measured? And cable companies are basically cash-flow companies, as I'm sure you know, because you work through all that stuff in school. And big old monopolies changing into competitive companies are really not cash-flow based. Their values, both in the market and internally, are based on net income and efficiency and, you know, the production and use of hard assets. So, on paper it looks great, but when you put the cultures together, especially on a merger basis or a partial vs. a total buyout, what happens is, those kind of businesses have attracted entirely different people. And they just don't get in the harness very well together. It's a people issue.

(Ameritech senior manager)

The second theme, voiced by half of the Ameritech respondents, showed uncertainty about the outcome of the venture:

I think the judgment is still out whether US WEST has gotten enough to justify the money Time Warner is getting. I mean I just – the more I look at it, the more I am uncertain how this is going to play out for US WEST.

(Ameritech senior manager)

It is telling that these quotes come from the RBOC that described itself previously as "realistic" or "cautious." The negative reactions to each other's strategies dominate, with the exception of Pacific Telesis' decision to spin off Air Touch, which would allow it to bid for cellphone frequencies in California. This "outsmarting" of the regulators was approved by the "aggressive" US WEST and the "realistic" Ameritech alike.

There is a consistent pattern in how each of these companies viewed themselves. US WEST saw itself as a multimedia company, while both Pacific Telesis

Table 1 Summary of beliefs about identity and strategy

	US WEST	Pacific Telesis	Ameritech
Identity statement	We are a multimedia company	We are a wire and wireless telecommunications company	We are a telecommunications company
Competitors	Long-distance, cable, wireless, RBOC, CAP	Long-distance, cable, wireless	Long-distance
Adjective	Aggressive	Focused	Cautious
Future	Multimedia	California wire and wireless	More diversified, but mostly telephony

and Ameritech regarded themselves as telecommunications companies, though Pacific Telesis included wire and wireless in its identity. Each organization's statements of identity are congruent with its diversification patterns. US WEST's decision to move into what appeared to be more unrelated, less certain diversification is congruent with the company seeing itself as a more aggressive, multimedia organization. Similarly, Ameritech's decision to focus on narrow diversification is in line with their view of themselves as a cautious telecommunications company. Pacific Telesis viewed itself as a California-focused, wireless and wire telecommunications company (see Table 1).

THE RESULTS IN PERSPECTIVE

It is striking to note how the RBOCs developed their strategies in such a way as to reinforce how they already described themselves. US WEST saw itself as bold and aggressive; therefore, it was logical that it moved farthest from its telecommunications roots, viewed itself as a multimedia company, and took the boldest strategic actions in buying cable companies. The company also saw itself as having the broadest range of competitors. It is notable that US WEST is the only Baby Bell to have been purchased by an organization that was not a telecommunications company and not affiliated with the old AT&T.

Similarly, Ameritech saw itself as cautious and conservative and chose to remain close to its traditional, telecommunications roots. Understanding how managers understood their organization and made sense of their environment made their strategic actions not only plausible but also the next logical action. The beliefs about the identity of their organization, in the context of where it has been and where it is going, provide the lens for sense-making surrounding the strategic direction of the organization.

The executives of the three organizations appeared to focus more on the outcomes of comparison with those companies with which they shared an overarching identity than on those organizations whence the danger came. This may help explain, in hindsight, why the "aggressive" US WEST ended up being bought up by Qwest, which could also be described as an aggressive telecommunications company. Did the RBOCs "bask in irrelevant glory"? In part, this may have been the case. Some executives were aware that the comparisons with other RBOCs were more positive than the competitive reality they faced. One US WEST executive commented: "We are clearly best of the litter, but that doesn't matter, we want to be best of show."

The last letter to the shareholders of US WEST is equally revealing. In the year of the merger with Qwest, CEO Sol Trujillo makes one comparison with other organizations, illustrating how US WEST implements its vision:

> We were the only RBOC to reach the milestone we set in early 1999 by delivering our high-speed DSL data product, MegaBit, to more than 110,000 customers.
>
> (US WEST, 2000: 1)

It is interesting that US WEST continued to feel compelled to compare itself to the other RBOCs, even though it had moved furthest from them strategically. Apparently, until the very last moment of a RBOC's life, comparison with other RBOCs mattered.

DISCUSSION: IDENTITY ISSUES IN STRATEGY FORMULATION

The history of the RBOCs shows how, in order to ensure the success of their organizations, managers monitor and interpret organizational performance. This task is facilitated through comparisons of performance (Short and Palmer, 2003), which the RBOCs appeared to make regularly. The need for comparison requires managers to establish competitive benchmarks against which they can measure their own firm (Porac, Thomas, and Baden-Fuller, 1989). This is a critical moment, because notions of organizational identity may influence what comparison partners are chosen, and on what organizational features managers make their comparisons. The outcomes of these choices may diverge widely, depending upon which comparison partners and dimensions are chosen, and can have pervasive consequences for strategic decisions.

Identity can have a powerful impact, because comparisons with other organizations are not neutral, either cognitively or emotionally. Organizations discover and invent who they are and who they are becoming, relative to others who are also changing (Weick, 1995). Being different from others is an important element in how people, as individuals or in groups, view themselves. The features individuals spontaneously mention when asked to describe themselves tend to be those by which they distinguish themselves in their social contexts (McGuire and McGuire, 1981). Distinctiveness appears to be most relevant when comparisons are made with others with whom one shares some overarching identity, and people are more likely to compare themselves with such comparable others

(Miller, Turnbull, and McFarland, 1988). Thus, the analysis of the three Baby Bells shows how organizational identity influenced the choice of benchmarks, both in terms of which organizations were deemed comparable and in terms of the features on which comparisons were made. With hindsight, one might even argue that the Baby Bells were acting out their identities by contrasting themselves further from their sister companies.

This is exactly where the RBOCs were trapped in their strategy formulation. The two main criteria for choosing comparison partners are their relevance and the availability of information about them (Kulik and Ambrose, 1992). Comparisons with others with whom one shares an overarching identity may be particularly relevant, because they are highly informative about how well the organization is doing. The choice of comparison groups can also be deceptive: Miller, Turnbull, and McFarland (1988) found that people preferred comparisons with people with whom they believed they shared a feature that was irrelevant for the task they were trying to perform. The investigated RBOCs seem to be a case in point. Availability may overwhelm relevance in some situations, either by short-circuiting the search for more relevant comparison partners, or by influencing the perceived relevance of those that are available (Kulik and Ambrose, 1992). Because human rationality is limited in scope, the number of benchmark competitors must be small enough to define and regularly monitor (Porac, Thomas, and Baden-Fuller, 1989). Each RBOC had six sister companies, and that number nicely fits this criterion. If certain comparison partners are deemed comparable because the organization shares certain essential features with them, repeated comparisons will enhance the availability of information about them. Notions of what members believe their organization to be steer them towards repeated comparison with a limited set of organizations with which they feel they have a sufficient amount in common to make these comparisons informative, and to compare features in these organizations in which they hope to achieve a competitive edge.

Once this choice has been made, the influence of organizational identity on how progress is assessed and strategy reformulated may be quite invisible, despite sophisticated planning and decision support systems aimed at coercing executives into controlled processing (Palmer and Short, 2001). Monitoring the progress of an organization, vis-à-vis its comparison partners, is prone to automation. It is conducted repeatedly with a small set of benchmark organizations using a relatively small set of features. The necessary and sufficient ingredients for automation are frequency and consistency of the same mental processes under the same circumstances (Bargh and Chartrand, 1999). Without any form of awareness of the potentially biasing effects of old and well-worn interpretations, new diagnoses will be based on old experiences of past issues, leading potentially to inappropriate interpretations and responses (Dutton, 1993).

The perceived relevance of comparison with the peer RBOCs also appeared in the outspokenness with which executives commented on the strategic actions of the other RBOCs. The degree of conviction expressed in the comments on the strategy of the manager's organization was impressive, as well as the firmness of beliefs in the errors in the other RBOCs' strategic behavior. For example, the contrast between the US WEST respondent who called the relationship between US WEST and Time Warner "the most visionary step we have taken" and Ameritech's comment that it was "a marriage made in hell" could not be more striking. The disapproval of the risky alliance between US WEST and Time Warner by Ameritech executives allowed them to contrast US WEST with their own "realism" and "cautiousness." These examples illustrate well how defining who we are, as an organization, is often achieved by defining who we are *not* (Elsbach and Bhattacharya, 2001). Showing how we are different from a negatively perceived organization helps to enhance our self-esteem. Such distancing from others can be highly useful in promoting desirable behavior – it combines the strengthening of one's own identity with the moralizing message contained in much gossip (Wert and Salovey, 2004). In the case of the Baby Bells, we suggest that the depth of their conviction in their own actions and the errors of others may have helped propel each company's trajectory away from each of the other RBOCs.

There is a paradox in this divergence, which merits further investigation. The frequent comparisons among the Baby Bells seem to have been fostered by their common identity. There was a great deal of focus on distinctiveness from other RBOCs, both in the interviews and, even 16 years after the breakup, in US WEST's last letter to shareholders. The RBOCs might have developed less divergent strategies if they had not compared themselves so consistently with each other. Paradoxically, the divergence-promoting comparisons can be taken to have confirmed and maintained their joint identity. This common identity might also help to explain why most "Baby Bells" have cannibalized each other rather than merging with non-"Ma Bell" companies. Bell Atlantic merged with NYNEX and later became Verizon; Southwestern Bell purchased Ameritech, Pacific Telesis, AT&T, and now BellSouth. Only US WEST did not merge with a Bell company.

An important question that might still be answered in the future is whether and how a striving to maintain identity may have inspired Southwestern Bell to buy its two sister companies, Pacific Telesis and Ameritech, and then to rename its own operations "AT&T" after the purchase of AT&T in 2005 (SBC, 2005). The resilience of the old AT&T identity, through the life of its Baby Bells up to its possible resurrection, recalls the resilience that Fox-Wolfgramm, Boal, and Hunt (1998) observed at a bank that had to adapt operations under regulatory pressure. The AT&T case seems more extreme, however: the independent spin-offs clung together in a way that was fairly much inspired by their common identity, and the old organization appears even to have re-emerged. The history of AT&T provides a compelling illustration of the impact of organizational identity on strategy formulation through the continual mutual comparisons made by the

AT&T siblings and the persistence of the awareness of being a member of the AT&T family.

KEY QUESTIONS

1 An organization's identity gives key decision-makers a framework for making strategic decisions. In this case, what was enabling about such a framework and what was constraining?

2 Organizations can decide who they are (identification) and who they are not (disidentification). In this case, what are examples of identification and disidentification? Is one process more useful or important than the other? Are both necessary?

3 How does understanding the identity of a company contribute to an understanding of its strategic trajectory? What does this understanding add to our other models of strategy?

4 Why do you think Southwestern Bell chose to first rename itself SBC, shedding the Bell label, and then adopt AT&T as its name once it had acquired the other telecommunications companies? Can we make any assumptions about their identity based on the choices of names?

5 Three of the organizations that identified themselves as out-and-out telecommunications companies ended up together (Pacific Telesis, Ameritech, SBC), with a Bell name, AT&T. Two of the multimedia players became organizations without Bell names (Quest, formerly US WEST, and Verizon, formerly Bell Atlantic). What does this tell us, if anything, about the competitive advantage of these three corporations? Who do you think will be the dominant player?

6 For the three RBOCs discussed in this chapter, how does "distinguishing yourself" as an organization have different implications than for Scania in the chapter by Olof Brunninge also in this book?

Chapter 4

Handelsbanken and internet banking

Olof Brunninge

Can a company with a well-established identity adapt to a rapidly changing environment and, if so, what change is possible without harming identity? In the literature, organizational identity is often depicted as an inertial force (e.g., Reger *et al.*, 1994), preventing firms from making necessary changes. The rationale behind this view is simple – sooner or later companies will be confronted with environmental changes that they have to adapt to in order to remain successful. If the necessary change is not in line with the firm's identity, the company has the choice of either abandoning its identity or jeopardizing its survival. As identity changes are usually resisted, well-established identities can in the long run threaten success. A crucial question in this context, then, is: How can firms cope with the dilemma of being confronted with changes that appear to render their identity obsolete?

This chapter presents the case of one of Scandinavia's largest banks, Handelsbanken, and its introduction of internet banking. Internet banking was a very sensitive issue for Handelsbanken as it seemed impossible to reconcile the new technology with the bank's identity as a decentralized organization. Handelsbanken built its operations on a large network of local branches that it claimed were the bank's primary organizational units. Now, internet banking seemed to make the branch network obsolete. The Handelsbanken case nicely illustrates how an organization can preserve its identity during times of radical environmental change that threaten organizational identity. In such a situation a company is not necessarily exposed to life-threatening forces, leaving no options other than change or die; rather, organizational identity may offer options in handling environmental change in a way that is novel compared to the approaches taken by industry competitors.

HANDELSBANKEN – A DECENTRALIZED BANK

Immediately after the beginning of the new millennium, Handelsbanken was one of the largest and most successful banks in Scandinavia. Its profits had exceeded the average of its competitors since the early 1970s, and in recent years the bank had expanded its universal banking operations from its home country of Sweden to Norway, Denmark, Finland, and Great Britain. However, the bank had not always been so profitable. The success story began with a turnaround in the early 1970s: after a crisis, triggered by declining profitability and a scandal relating to violation of foreign currency regulations, a new managing director, Jan Wallander, was appointed. The changes implemented by Wallander were based on decentralization, cost-consciousness, and the abolition of budgeting. One of the new managing director's first actions was to reorganize the bank, transferring decision-making authority from the central head office in Stockholm to local branches. Concrete actions included abolishing central units like the corporate marketing department and giving branch managers increased power to make investment and credit decisions. The internal hierarchy was reduced to three levels: the central head office, a number of regional head offices, and local branches. Wallander outlined his business philosophy for the bank in a booklet entitled "Mål och Medel" (literally: "Ends and Means"; official English title: "Our Way") distributed to all employees. Against the background of the crisis at Handelsbanken, and with the support of the board, Wallander succeeded in overcoming initial resistance among managers at the bank's head office. Throughout the branch network his ideas of decentralization were appreciated and the quickly rising profitability of the bank gave additional legitimacy to the changes. Being a decentralized bank and seeing the local branch as the most important organizational unit soon became Handelsbanken's primary identity claims.

After Jan Wallander's retirement his successors continued to develop the bank's strategy according to a philosophy of decentralization. Branch managers carefully guarded their independence against any kind of action that might transfer power to the center at the expense of local autonomy. "The branch is the bank" became a slogan that summed up Handelsbanken's decentralized identity:

> The branch manager is so to speak an absolute ruler. I can't tell him to work with this or that company. It's not me, rather the manager who has full decision-making authority regarding how he wants to do business from the perspective of his local market. I think that some other banks envy branch managers at our bank.
>
> (Thommy Mossinger, Head of the Southern Sweden Regional Bank, interview 2002)

> That the branch is the bank is not just a marketing strategy, it's a concrete expression of how we want the entire bank to be run. The head

office should not decide how we should look after our customers, how we should talk to them, or even which customers we should have. It is not the head office that should decide how we develop our business – these issues are best dealt with as close to the customer as possible – at the branch office.

(Lars O. Grönstedt, Managing Director, in Handelsbanken, 2004: 7)

Decentralization was reinforced by accounting systems that allocated expenses and revenues to branches according to a system of transfer prices that aimed at mirroring actual business activities fairly. In 2003 Handelsbanken branches generated more than 85 percent of the bank's overall profits, with only a minor proportion deriving from central units and subsidiaries. Branches were always responsible for individual customers, even if that customer was a multinational corporation. Central units were only involved in business with a customer if delegated by the responsible branch. Hence, the branches rather than the central development units were considered the places where Handelsbanken's services were produced. In line with its emphasis on branches, Handelsbanken had kept the size of its Swedish branch network almost constant during the 1990s while most of its competitors had closed branches to rationalize operations.

TECHNOLOGICAL INNOVATIONS IN BANKING

The internet has had an impact on the financial services sector greater than most other technological developments. The new technology was a particularly sensitive issue for Handelsbanken since it challenged its identity claim of regarding the local, physical branch as its most important organizational unit. As internet banking emerged in the Swedish market in the mid-1990s, specialized niche banks challenged their established competitors. They did not establish any branch networks, but kept in contact with their customers by telephone or electronic media. In most cases their main product was savings accounts offering high interest rates. The established banks also began to introduce telephone-based services. Customers could get information on their balance or recent transactions over the phone. Subsequently, a couple of banks also introduced separate telephone banks. Customers had to register for these banks and sometimes had to pay an annual fee. In return, they received access to specific products such as savings accounts with high interest rates. S-E-Banken launched its telephone bank *Sesam*, which was clearly separated from the company's traditional banking operations. It was possible to be a customer of both banks at the same time, but accounts were held separately. Handelsbanken was not enthusiastic about establishing a telephone bank in addition to its branch network. Arne Mårtensson, the Managing Director at that time, said that "running a bank on the phone might be all right in other organizations, but not at Handelsbanken" (Einar, 1995). He stressed that in his view the best way of running a bank was still through a branch network. Handelsbanken therefore limited its telephone services to offering better access to its branches. Customers could perform certain transactions outside office hours and without visiting the branch, but they remained customers of their branch and the branch was allocated the costs and revenues for each customer.

BANKING ON THE WEB

Telephone banking did not pose a serious threat to traditional branch networks, as the range of services that could be offered was very limited. However, this changed as both the niche banks and the established conventional banks began to introduce internet banking in 1996. The internet constituted a potential threat to Handelsbanken's identity as the *raison d'être* of an office branch network was called into question:

> There were substantial worries. Our whole strength is built on geographical division and local presence. Then someone invents a medium that aims to erase geography and local presence.
>
> (Lars O. Grönstedt, Managing Director, interview 2003)

If electronic channels replaced local offices, this would provide an opportunity to reduce personnel and premises costs. Handelsbanken's competitors quickly adopted the new technology. The predominant formula used was to treat internet and branch transactions separately. The internet had thus become a separate distribution channel in addition to the branch network:

> It was some time in the early or mid-'90s that the idea of establishing internet banks appeared [in the industry]. All the other banks were doing it. They called them internet banks. On the one hand the customer was a customer at the branch and on the other hand on the internet. There were even separate customer registers. This seemed like a deathblow to our idea of decentralization. It would take away a major share of business from the branches.
>
> (Leif Lundberg, former Head of Corporate Communications,
> interview 2003)

The branch managers at Handelsbanken had mixed feelings about the new technology. On the one hand, they saw an opportunity to eliminate some routine transactions, and increasing numbers of customers began to ask when the bank was going to introduce an internet service. On the other hand, it was difficult to see how internet banking could fit into Handelsbanken's branch-centered identity:

We had a lot of discussions about these issues. During a short period there was also a fear that the time for branches might be over. Would everyone do everything on the web and would anyone still do anything at a branch in the future? I wouldn't say that people were seriously worried, but I know that for some time I really wondered myself what direction we were going in . . . there was fearful delight about what was going to happen.

(Björn Börjesson, Head of the Central Credit Department, former Head of Regional Bank Southern Sweden, interview 2003)

Handelsbanken was relatively late in attempting to find an appropriate internet solution. This may have been partly because some at the bank were not comfortable with the idea. Further, of course, Handelsbanken staff followed the other banks' internet solutions, which were launched one after the other – these were all centralized and did not fit Handelsbanken's identity at all:

There was resistance and hesitance towards the internet. Instinctively. A feeling that the internet was our adversary rather than something we could use, and that is part of the explanation why we were late.

(Lars O. Grönstedt, Managing Director, interview 2002)

Grönstedt's view that there was instinctive hesitance towards the internet was not shared by everyone at the bank, however – at least not at branch level where staff were under pressure from customers who complained that Handelsbanken could not yet offer internet banking while all major competitors did so. Customers at local branches asked when they would be able to make transactions over the web. The feeling of lagging behind all the bank's competitors affected the self-confidence of Handelsbanken branch employees negatively. They were afraid that they would gain a reputation of being overly conservative and less technologically advanced:

When the internet came we were initially a little disappointed that we were so late. We were in fact last. Our colleagues or competitors from S-E-Banken and Swedbank had their solutions much earlier.

(Claes Ericson, Branch Manager, Jönköping, interview 2002)

There were obviously mixed feelings about the internet at Handelsbanken. The employees' conception of the issue was very much influenced by the behavior of other players in the industry. While the predominant recipe for dealing with the internet was one of deterrent, the speed at which the bank's competitors introduced the new technology was also a trigger for people in Handelsbanken's organization to put pressure on Central Development to come up with its own solution. As the person responsible for stockbroking, Lars O. Grönstedt was among the first to experience competition when Swedbank introduced the buying and selling of stocks over the web. At that time, the Central Development department was running a project to develop an internet solution, but there was little progress due to hesitancy about which solution would be suitable for the bank. Grönstedt was not willing to wait, so he started to develop his own solution:

> I felt that we did not have time to wait. I thought the bank could choose whatever option it wanted. I was on the stockbroking side. I have to compete with stockbrokers so we have to set up our own solution anyway. . . . I created a solution, as I thought it should look, on my computer on a flight back from the US and then I gave it to our IT people without asking Central Development for permission. . . . It was a kind of guerrilla action.
>
> (Lars O. Grönstedt, Managing Director, former Head of Stockbroking, interview 2002)

The plan to launch a stockbroking website was not realized, but the initiative from the stockbroking side increased the pressure on Central Development to come up with a solution. Establishing a stockbroking site was less sensitive than the overall internet issue in the sense that it only concerned a limited range of services that were already relatively centralized. Meanwhile, under pressure from Grönstedt's initiative, Central Development increased its efforts to find a solution for the entire bank. There were a number of technical options to choose from, but the most challenging issue was to find a way to reconcile internet banking with the central role of branches at the bank. Handelsbanken strove to carry out most IT projects in-house. For major development projects such as the internet, however, the bank also took advice from external consultants. The problem in this case was that these experts were also influenced by centralized solutions applied in other companies. The people responsible for the project at Handelsbanken felt that the consultants had difficulties integrating Handelsbanken's identity into their solutions:

> We worked with [a firm of consultants] and they made a number of brave attempts, but they were not really much fun. You were supposed to manage your savings by clicking on a piggy bank. That was all they were able to capture of our soul.
>
> (Jörgen Nielsen, Branch Manager, Birger Jarlsgatan/Stockholm, and former project manager for internet banking at Central Business Development, interview 2003)

It looked as though we would have to revert to something really centralized. We started working with a number of consultants in this area.
Experts on internet development. In no way could they handle it. I was
very concerned how this would end up.

(Leif Lundberg, former Head of Corporate Communications,
interview 2003)

As stated above, the consultants' view of internet banking had already been
shaped by the centralized approaches taken by other banks. As Handelsbanken
surveyed its competitors' internet projects it became obvious that a centralized
internet bank was the cornerstone of all the solutions:

In all contacts I had [with other banks], I saw that they were building
[their internet bank] in a completely different way from what we wanted.
For [the consultants] who came to assist us it was just another internet
bank. They did not understand what we wanted at all.

(Jörgen Nielsen, Branch Manager, Birger Jarlsgatan/Stockholm, and
former project manager for internet banking at Central Business
Development, interview 2003)

Finally, Handelsbanken established contact with Johan Wall, the founder and
owner-manager of Net Solutions, a young IT firm. Wall's approach was different
from that of his colleagues. Before starting the development work, he went round
the organization, met various people, and talked to them in order to better
understand the organization:

He did what consultants seldom do. He listened and he did not have a
readymade solution as consultants usually do. . . . We were completely
taken aback when he came to us with the solution that we could have all
[internet users] go via the branches. Each transaction on the internet
goes via the branch accounts. It is done with the knowledge of the branch
and everything stays with the branch. It was such a tremendous relief and
this guy deserves all the credit for this.

(Leif Lundberg, former Head of Corporate Communications,
interview 2003)

Wall's solution was based on the idea of creating an individual website for each
of the more than 500 Handelsbanken branches. When a customer entered the
Handelsbanken website for the first time, s/he was asked to select his or her
branch. A cookie was then stored on their computer, directing the customer to
the right branch each time s/he entered the website. The branch websites were
individually managed by each branch. What was standardized was the general

layout and a number of basic services handled by a central transaction engine. Beyond that, branches were free to design the websites themselves. As Handelsbanken was in a hurry to get the internet banking service up and running, the first version was a compromise, with the branch sites produced centrally but the branch name at the top:

> The branch name was individual and there was one other thing – each branch would submit a photo – a photo of the staff, the branch, the market square or whatever, but something with a local connection. . . . That was the only thing that was individual originally, but at least it was a start and an important signal that the branch was central even on the internet.
>
> (Mats Heidenberg, Corporate Communications, interview 2003)

It did not take long before the branches were able to manage their websites themselves. After some time, the opportunities to individualize the sites went far beyond mere information. Like the original websites, many branches still emphasized the local connection by putting pictures of the office, the staff, or local sights on their home page. It was also common to promote local activities, such as seminars for customers. The presentation of products and services was also individualized, with each branch emphasizing the products it found most suitable for its local market. Branches could put centrally produced product descriptions on their site, but they could also create their own information. Some branches, for instance, had established local alliances with real-estate brokers, which they promoted on the internet. Others had agreements with corporate customers offering products at beneficial terms to employees of those companies. The employees could then obtain information on the products by visiting the website, using a special login. Other branches, however, believed that special agreements were an unprofitable way of doing business in the long term. Consequently, their websites did not have such offers.

Internet banking was offered by all the regional banks. The concept of allowing the branches to have their own sites was the same everywhere. Regional as well as national differences were reflected in the content of the websites. In Britain, where Handelsbanken (Figures 8–11) was a newcomer, some branches published lists of successful deals that might give them increased legitimacy in the market. A peculiarity of the British market was the frequent use of intermediaries, such as accountants and solicitors, to establish customer contacts:

> I know at least two of the branches that use it deliberately for their intermediaries. They say to accountants and solicitors look here if you want to keep track of the sort of business we are doing. They include a deal sheet on their site. They take the names out. These are the most

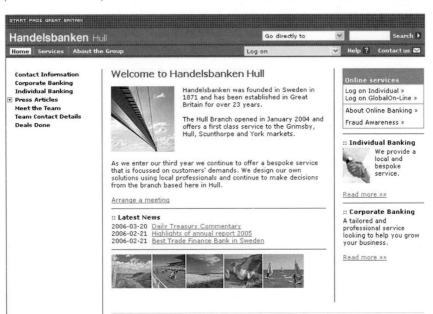

Figures 8 and 9 Handelsbanken's internet solutions allowed branches to give their websites a local touch. The screenshots from the Plymouth and Hull branches from March 2006 illustrate the difference: local photos introduce each branch, and the menus on the left of each page show that the branches chose to emphasize different aspects of their business. On the Plymouth website, branch manager Paul Wilmot appeared on the first page with his direct phone number.

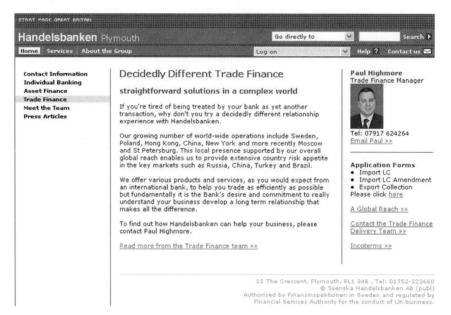

Figure 10 *The Plymouth branch chose to emphasize in particular the bank's trade finance services. According to Handelsbanken's philosophy, each individual branch should decide which services to promote, the local branch manager deciding this based on the local market. The bank had no central marketing campaigns instructing branches to advertise specific products or services.*

recent deals or important deals that we have done. . . . That's one use and I have seen specifically where they use it to establish credibility with people who don't know us.

(Derek Burgess, Area Manager Regional Bank Great Britain, interview 2003)

The opportunity to develop their websites was utilized by branches to varying degrees. As bank staff were rarely proficient web designers, the Corporate Communication department developed a toolbox containing banners, pictures, templates, product descriptions, etc., that could be used by branches. Most branch managers considered development of the website to be important, but at the same time it competed for time with other tasks. Particularly for small branches, time was a restriction:

We have one person who is responsible for updating it [the website] and making sure that there is something happening all the time. Our level of ambition is not extremely high, but it should at least be updated.

(Robert Pettersson, Branch Manager Vaggeryd, interview 2002)

Figure 11 *The Hull branch showed a deal sheet on its website, where potential customers could get an overview of reference deals in which the branch had been involved. Such lists were particularly popular among Handelsbanken branches in Great Britain.*

At the Jönköping branch, which was one of the major branches in the East Sweden Regional Bank, three people shared the task of managing the website:

> It's supposed to be updated and changed continuously so that you really get something out of visiting it. Otherwise it would be better to hand over the task to Handelsbanken in Stockholm. I am the legally responsible editor so once a week we look at it and the rest of the staff can make suggestions. For instance, the end of the year is now approaching and customers might look through their stock portfolios, so we said let's address this on the website.
>
> (Claes Ericson, Branch Manager Jönköping, interview 2002)

The system of an individual website for each branch was launched in 1997. At that time, Handelsbanken lagged behind all its major competitors. For example, SEB had launched its internet bank more than a year earlier. Handelsbanken's solution had been delayed by the difficulties in finding an approach that was congruent with the bank's identity. In the final development phase there were also some problems in implementing the security solution the bank had chosen, resulting in further delays. Further, in order to help customers use the new technology, a support service was needed. Given Handelsbanken's decentralization it was not initially clear whether this should be handled by the branches or centrally:

> The branches had only just introduced PCs themselves. They were a long way from this [technology] and then suddenly the heads of the regional banks proposed that the branches should handle support. That was really interesting. After all, it was the branches that had the customer contact. That was shortly before everything was launched and it was Lars O. [Grönstedt] among others who managed to change their mind. . . . It would have been a catastrophe otherwise.
>
> (Sverker Arvidsson, Central IT Operations, interview 2003)

The regional banks were finally convinced that it was not a wise idea to let ordinary bank clerks handle technical support. Instead, the support unit was located in Malmo, where it shared a building with the Southern Sweden Regional Bank and the Malmo City branch. The support issue was a minor episode in the overall internet question. However, it illustrates how Handelsbanken's branch-centered identity influenced the way the issue was approached. The support unit was likely to have frequent contact with branch customers. Thus people in the branch organization thought it obvious that the branches should handle it.

Unlike some of its competitors, Handelsbanken never considered the internet to be a cornerstone of its strategy. Particularly before the start of the new millennium at the peak of the internet hype, some banks believed that the web would make branches redundant and enable them to expand internationally without having to invest in a branch network. SEB in particular was fond of that idea, proclaiming that it was going to become a European e-bank (SEB, 2000). SEB envisioned that the new technology could give them easy access to various European markets, as essentially no branch network was required to enter a new country. The Danish Codan Bank was acquired with the aim of using it as a basis for e-banking operations in Denmark. SEB saw itself as a forerunner of e-banking in Europe and believed it could gain a considerable competitive advantage by exploiting its technological lead. In contrast to SEB's enthusiasm, Handelsbanken managers never viewed the internet as more than an alternative entrance to the branch. The internet was a useful tool, but not a source of competitive advantage:

> Of course we will provide good internet services. That's an important part of our service and it's a good tool for us to further reduce our costs. So the internet is a matter of course for us, but it will never be a substitute for the branches.
>
> (Arne Mårtensson, Managing Director, interview 2000)

After the IT bubble burst, Handelsbanken felt reinforced in the view that the internet did not have the potential to replace branches. The other Scandinavian banks have also revised their views, placing less emphasis on electronic solutions and more on their branches once again (Tapper, 2001). However, especially during the heyday of e-commerce, Handelsbanken risked gaining a reputation for being a late adopter of technological innovations. Being the last to introduce internet banking did not harm Handelsbanken's business significantly; however, it was not good for the bank's external reputation or the self-esteem of its employees either. Indeed, in the media, Handelsbanken was criticized for being notoriously late in introducing new technologies (Anonymous, 1999; Creutzer, 1998). This prompted the following comment:

> Quality is more important than being early. Other banks being ahead of us is not a problem. Usually they make the initial mistakes.
> (Björn G. Olofsson, Head of Central Development, interview 2003)

Even with Handelsbanken's branch-centered approach, internet banking had a major impact on the way of doing business. The opposite was true of internet banking. Although the new technology did not result in any major reduction in the number of branches, the number of employees per branch has fallen significantly. Self-service has reduced the need to process routine transactions manually:

> Over the course of last year [2002], we have gone from eleven to nine employees. . . . Still we are one of the branches with the highest volume growth in the region. That's possible with current automatization. We feel that it is important to make more money and we do that by doing more business with better margins, but also by adjusting our staff level to the increased efficiency.
> (Jens Claesson, Branch Manager Värnamo, interview 2002)

As branch managers were evaluated according to the economic performance of their branch, there was an incentive to use internet banking for rationalization. Since salaries constituted a major segment of costs, branch managers would tend to keep the number of employees low. More self-service created scope for staff reductions. However, Handelsbanken did not make anyone redundant in this process. The number of employees was instead reduced by not filling vacancies or by offering employees other positions within the bank. As manual routine transactions disappeared, the tasks of bank employees changed considerably. An increasing amount of time was devoted to actively approaching customers and offering them advice. Internet banking had thus dramatically changed the work of the branches without making them redundant.

DISCUSSION AND CONCLUSIONS

Handelsbanken was a highly successful company that viewed its well-established identity as a decentralized, branch-based bank as one of the main reasons for its success. In such a situation, of course, an identity is not easy to relinquish, even if the arguments for an identity change seem obvious and the environmental pressures for change are overwhelming. The present case shows that the possibility of retaining one's identity may often be better than is initially apparent. Handelsbanken did not go through the case without changing. However, rather than following the quickly established industry recipes (Spender, 1989) for inter-net banking, the changes were derived from Handelsbanken's identity. The answer to the question "Who are we?" as an organization (Albert and Whetten, 1985) served as both a source of inspiration and the primary criterion for decision-making. The result of this approach was successful: Handelsbanken's approach to internet banking was accepted by both customers and employees. It allowed the bank to combine the advantages of cost-saving online business and geographical closeness to the customer. Rather than being an obstacle to internet banking, Handelsbanken's identity helped the company to create a novel approach to the technology. Of course, Handelsbanken's success story does not imply that sticking to one's identity in times of change is always the best solution. However, the Handelsbanken case should encourage organizations not to rush to abandon their identity when challenged by change. Identity can be an asset in that it facilitates the tackling of changes in a way that differentiates the company from its competitors.

From a theoretical point of view, the Handelsbanken case highlights questions relating to the dynamics of organizational identity and strategic change, particu-larly regarding an organization's alignment with external changes. The introduc-tion of internet banking is a good example of a radical environmental change, affecting an entire industry. Traditionally, the strategy literature has placed con-siderable emphasis on the question of how organizations align themselves with environmental changes (Andrews, 1971; Porter, 1980). Identity researchers have been interested in understanding what a well-established organizational identity implies for strategic change. A common approach is to view identity as an obstacle to environmental alignment, meaning that it is a source of strategic inertia (Reger et al., 1994). Of course, as identity concerns aspects of an organization that are relatively enduring (Albert and Whetten, 1985), it is difficult to imagine that an organization would easily change things that members consider part of its identity. The range of possible strategic options is thus limited. Change that implies a conflict with identity is resisted, or the need for such change is even not recog-nized (Dutton and Dukerich, 1991), as it functions as a cognitive filter (Reger et al., 1994). Recently, this view has been challenged by researchers claiming that identity is relatively fluid while a sense of stability is created by maintaining certain labels (Chreim, 2005; Gioia, Schultz, and Corley, 2000). However, these labels stand for different things at different points in time, thus concealing the changes in identity that actually occur.

The Handelsbanken case supports the view of a relatively stable identity. Rather than sacrificing the branch-based identity under the pressure of technological change, the company searched for ways to maintain it. This is not limited to the level of labels. Handelsbanken did not merely pay lip service to the centrality of branches: no internet solution was implemented until the bank found a solution that allowed managers to use their website for their local strategy. Strategic options that would jeopardize the central role of the branches in the organization were ruled out in principle from the outset. However, it would be misleading to state that identity was an inertial force: the bank did change, but this was done in a way that was congruent with its identity. Thus, organizational identity does not prevent strategic change *per se*; rather, it channels it in directions that do not threaten identity.

The case indicates that the antagonism between environmental alignment and identity maintenance may be less serious than scholars sometimes assume. One reason for overemphasizing the role of identity as an obstacle to alignment may be an overly objectivist view of the environment. However, as the present case shows, environmental change does not descend upon an organization from above, leaving the company with no choice but to adapt or die. As Smircich and Stubbart (1985) rightly remark, an organization's environment does not have to be seen as objectively given. Rather, strategists enact their environment by making connections between events and situations they experience. There are always multiple ways of making such connections. While Handelsbanken's competitors saw internet banking as a substitute for branches, Handelsbanken ultimately interpreted the technology as a new entrance to the branch. The reconciliation of the new technology with Handelsbanken's identity was first and foremost an act of interpretation and only secondly a technical issue. It was the bank's identity that provided the frame of reference for an interpretation that was novel to the industry. Rather than being a cognitive filter (Reger *et al.*, 1994), identity proved to be a cognitive eye-opener for the bank. In this context, identity turned out to be a counterweight to the institutional pressure emanating from the emerging industry recipe of a centralized approach to internet banking. These ideas of centralization were disseminated by the majority of consultants and implemented by most actors in the field. However, rather than mimicking (see DiMaggio and Powell, 1983) the behavior of its competitors, Handelsbanken chose its own way. The main point of departure for strategic choice was not the industry recipe but the organization's own identity. We should thus be more cautious in emphasizing the inertial potential of identity and instead pay greater attention to its ability to guide companies toward unorthodox strategies.

KEY QUESTIONS

The Handelsbanken case throws up a number of questions:

1 Handelsbanken's identity prevented the bank from launching an internet solution that was similar to that of its competitors. What determines the boundary between what an identity permits and does not permit?
2 The view of identity as an inertial force seems too undifferentiated. How can a well-established identity permit or even support strategic change?
3 If change occurs in organizations with a well-established identity, how does such change happen?
4 Nevertheless, it is not likely that a well-established identity will support any kind of change. What determines which changes are ultimately supported and which are ruled out?
5 Given the indications that Handelsbanken's identity was a counterweight to the prevailing industry recipe, what dynamics arise between institutional forces at field level and organizational identity?

NOTE ON METHODS USED

The data for this study were collected through documentary studies, participant observation, and 43 interviews with strategic actors at Handelsbanken. Interviews were carried out at local branches in Sweden and Great Britain and at the company's headquarters, and included managers as well as specialists involved in the development of Handelsbanken's internet solution. I would like to thank Leif Melin, Per Davidsson, and Hamid Bouchikhi for their helpful support and feedback during my research, as well as Jönköping International Business School (JIBS) and the Marknadstekniskt Centrum (MTC) for financing the study.

Part II

Identity construction

Lin Lerpold, Davide Ravasi, Johan van Rekom, and Guillaume Soenen

How are organizational identities constructed? In other words, how do organizational members develop a relatively shared understanding of what their organization is and stands for? What sources of information do they tap? What cues do they rely on? The answer is not straightforward: research has yet to explain fully how individuals in organizations develop identity beliefs and aspirations, how these individual beliefs about organizational identity are negotiated with or imposed on others, and how they eventually become embedded in institutional claims and collective understandings. However, scholars have already uncovered a number of cues that organizational members seem to rely on – consciously or unconsciously – as they address questions such as what kind of organization is this or what is this organization really about? Here, for the sake of simplicity, we focus on how organizational members try to make sense of who they are as an organization (their identity beliefs) rather than on what they want to become (their identity aspirations). How managers should and do address a related question – i.e., "what do we want to be as an organization?" – has been examined elsewhere relatively extensively (e.g., Balmer and Soenen, 1999).

As individuals collectively try to make sense of who they are as an organization, many different answers are likely to be proposed. In fact some scholars (e.g., Pratt and Foreman, 2000) talk about organizational *identities*, emphasizing how most organizations, at any given point in time, are internally conceived and described through a plurality of labels. In the same way that individual self-conceptions tend to result from the juxtaposition of multiple "identities" – for instance, "Irish," "father," "environmentalist," and "physician" – so organizational identities may be composed of a number of different claims and beliefs. A large institute of higher education, for example, may be internally perceived and described as "international," "research-oriented," "not for profit," and so on.

Building on related work in social psychology (Brewer and Gardner, 1996), David Whetten argues that organizational identities may be classified as *social identities, relational identities*, and *personal identities* (Whetten, 2006). Organizational social identities refer to broad categories such as "bank," "multinational company," or "dot.com," which in a given social setting identify a specific type of company, and are used to *categorize* the organization – i.e., define it as *similar* to other members of that social group. Relational identities by contrast describe the organization in terms of its role towards one or more of its stakeholders. A university, for instance, may describe itself as a "leading contributor to the global scientific community" or a "provider of high-quality education." Similarly, partners in a consulting company may conceive their organization as an "all-round advisor for small businesses" or a "long-term partner for human resource managers." Finally, personal identities refer to specific traits of the organization – such as "cost-conscious," "independent," or "dynamic" – that, combined with relational identities, contribute to define how an organization is *different* from others.

The cases in this section illustrate how members draw on various cues to make sense of – and give sense to – what their organization is, and how different types of identities are likely to arise and be invoked in different situations. Some of these cues – which we may describe as *category based* – are mainly used to classify the organization as "similar to" other types of organizations by drawing on existing social categories. Other cues – which can be labeled *trait-based cues* – are used to make sense of the way that the organization is "different from" others (Figure 12). Among sources of trait-based cues are material features, symbols and objects, collective practices, and values.

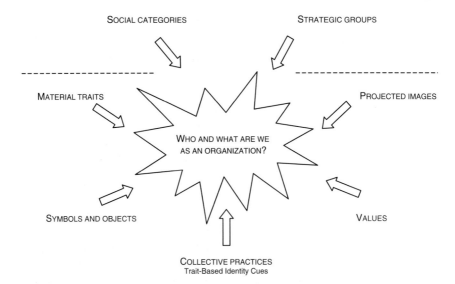

CATEGORY-BASED IDENTITY CUES

SOCIAL CATEGORIES   STRATEGIC GROUPS

MATERIAL TRAITS   PROJECTED IMAGES

WHO AND WHAT ARE WE
AS AN ORGANIZATION?

SYMBOLS AND OBJECTS   VALUES

COLLECTIVE PRACTICES
Trait-Based Identity Cues

Figure 12 *Constructing organizational identity: potential sources of cues*

CATEGORY-BASED IDENTITY CUES

Social categories and strategic groups ("We are one of them")

Making sense of an organization is a process based largely on interorganizational comparison. In other words, developing an understanding of what an organization is and stands for requires members to position their organization within a social space, by defining how and to what extent it is *different from* and/or *similar to* other comparable organizations (Whetten and Mackey, 2002). Organizational members use two types of category-based identity cues: social categories and strategic groups. Members may draw on existing social categories – i.e., broadly accepted labels that are used to encompass a certain type of organization. While some of these categories, such as "bank" or "not for profit," may have precise objective referents, in many cases the boundaries may be purely based on social conventions and not entirely clear. Does merely selling or manufacturing in other countries make you a "multinational company"? How large should your sales or workforce be for you to be considered more than a "small business"? What exactly are you required to do to be allowed to call yourself a "research university"? While scholars or regulators may have established conventions to address definitional issues such as these, it is unlikely that they coincide with those of clients, employees, bankers, and other stakeholders. Locating an organization within one or more of the existing social categories, therefore, seems to be more a deliberate choice rather than a simple acknowledgement of an objective reality. In this respect, the social and cultural context acts as a reservoir of cues that members draw upon – often unconsciously, sometimes explicitly – in order to make sense of their organization.

For organizations engaged in market competition, a particularly relevant subset of categories is represented by clusters of related organizations called "cognitive strategic groups." The concept of strategic groups was initially put forward by industrial economists to explain how in many industries competition takes place within and between subsets of competitors sharing a similar size, strategy, structure, etc. (McGee and Thomas, 1986). Later studies observed how these groups may influence identity construction in organizations, as they provide members with a rough classification of their immediate social space – i.e., their industry (e.g., Porac, Thomas, and Baden-Fuller, 1989; Reger and Huff, 1993; Peteraf and Shanley, 1997). The position of the organization within this social space, defined by its fundamental strategic choices, may provide additional cues to organizational members. In turn, to the extent that members actively categorize their organization as a member of a particular group, they may come to – consciously or unconsciously – assimilate the common wisdom regarding appropriate ways of structuring the organization and competing in the market. The case of Statoil, for instance, described in Chapter 7, illustrates how members may enact changes in their organization – such as becoming a "true" international company – by modeling themselves on prototypical reference group members, and assimilating behavioral models that are considered appropriate for the strategic group. In this way, in-group dynamics become salient at the industry level as organizations' identities are socially constructed in interactions with industry actors.

Both social categories and strategic groups influence the way people understand their organization in that they compare it to other organizations or to general ideas about important differences between groups of organizations. This process of *categorization* helps members to make sense of the extent to which their organization can be grouped with similar others; in other words, of what we have called its social identities. To the extent that they carry practical implications – in that they influence the way people behave in or towards organizations that are labeled as such – social categories act as institutions, providing members with a socially endorsed template for decision and action.

In organizations, however, identity claims and beliefs need to address both issues of similarity and issues of differentiation. When attention shifts to issues of differentiation, members are more likely to reorient their search for identity cues from the outside world to inside the organization.

TRAIT-BASED IDENTITY CUES

Material traits ("We are what we are")

At the individual level, the formation of one's identity is largely influenced by objective identity referents. To some degree, the way we perceive and define ourselves is shaped by objective features such as our sex, somatic traits, age, marital status, and nationality. Refusal to acknowledge or accept one or more of these traits is likely to generate social and psychological tension, if not serious emotional distress (think, for instance, of an elderly person acting like a teenager, or a husband and father persistently behaving like a bachelor). Under extreme circumstances, individuals may even attempt to alter the objective conditions (for instance, by changing their marital status) in order to realign "what they are" and how they view themselves.

Similarly, in organizations, as members collectively construct or negotiate an understanding of their organization's identity, they may turn to objective, material traits. Compared to individuals, in organizations it is far less likely to find features that are truly "objective." Rather than being "given" or unalterable, organizational features are most often the outcome of deliberate decisions and/ or can be altered relatively easily if members choose to do so. To varying degrees, even fundamental material features such as geographical origin and location, business sector, ownership structure, or legal form are the results of implicit or explicit choices. Nevertheless, these features provide important identity cues insofar as they are perceived as central and enduring, and relevant to guiding major decisions as well as ordinary behavior (Rao, Davis, and Ward, 2000).

It is worth noting that despite their level of "objectivity," most of these material features are open to multiple interpretations. What does it mean to be a "Japanese company," a "family business," or even a "university"? While in some cases broadly accepted understandings come to our aid, in others material features may not lend themselves well to easy and univocal interpretation. Is a large multinational, listed on the stock exchange and managed by professional managers, still a "family firm" simply because the largest shareholding is still in the hands of the founding family? Can a company still call itself "Japanese" if it is owned by large global investors, run by an American CEO, and has most of its sales and production outside Japan? In these situations – and they are more frequent than one might think – supposedly objective traits are less likely to provide answers than to raise questions. Their increasing ambiguity may eventually lead members to search for other sources of cues that can help them make new sense of what their organization is.

Values ("We are what we care for")

When asked to reflect on what is unique about their organization, people often mention traits of the organization – customer care, technological excellence, reliability, etc. – that describe what is considered appropriate behavior and that characterize organizational policies and decisions. Culture researchers refer to these traits as *values*, and consider them to be the link between an organization's deeply held assumptions and more visible social norms (Schein, 1992). Often these values rise above the threshold of awareness and are referred to explicitly in conversations, speeches, and corporate documents. When values are referred to explicitly, they may inform collective self-reflections about unique organizational traits (Corley *et al.*, 2006).

Despite the fact that some traits, such as "customer orientation" or "cost consciousness," could be reasonably claimed by many organizations, it is often the combination of these traits that is perceived as unique and distinctive. Southwest Airlines, for instance, used to combine a strong drive for efficiency with an emphasis on how work should be "fun," which distinguished it from most other low-cost carriers. Incidentally, the difficulties that other airlines encountered in attempting to replicate the same unusual combination of values are cited as the reason for their failure to achieve the same outstanding results (O'Reilly III and Pfeffer, 2000).

Collective practices ("We are what we do")

Research on communities of professionals shows that what people do to get work done influences how they define themselves (Brown and Duguid, 1991; Wenger, 1998). Similarly, in organizations, what members do – their tasks and occupation, their daily routines, their practical skills – may influence how they come to perceive and interpret their organization.

Different professional subgroups engaged in different collective practices may even develop multiple and partly diverging understandings of the organization. For example, a study by the organizational behaviorists Michael Pratt and Anat Rafaeli (1997) of a hospital rehabilitation unit revealed that nurses on different shifts and dealing with different practical issues held conflicting views of what defined their organization. Nurses working during the day and performing ordinary care defined their organization by its educational and rehabilitation mission. In contrast, nurses working the evening shift, and mostly facing emergency situations, defined their organization as an acute-care unit. These diverging views surfaced as differences in dominant role behavior (instructing patients on rehabilitation vs. providing acute care) and dress code preferences (wearing street clothes vs. operating room "scrubs").

Similarly, the organizational sociologist Mary Ann Glynn, investigating the causes of a musicians' strike at the Atlanta Symphony Orchestra, observed how conflicting views of the orchestra's identity rested upon the division of employees into two groups: administrators and musicians (Glynn, 2000). While musicians perceived the organization as "a world-class orchestra in a world-class city" and emphasized its artistic quality, administrators facing challenges to the economic viability of the orchestra emphasized economic efficiency. When they used the orchestra's lack of financial resources to justify denying tenure to six musicians, the administrators triggered a highly emotional confrontation with the musician group – a confrontation that exposed a radical division between the two groups' beliefs about the organization's identity.

When multiple, possibly divergent, views are present, invoking common "values" may help bind the organization around a common set of beliefs and facilitate coordinated action. Such was the case, for instance, with a boat excursion company studied by one of the editors (van Rekom, 1997), where a shared conceptualization of the organization as "being a good host" ensured integration of the behaviors of the personnel.

Symbols and objects ("We are all these things")

Research on organizational behavior shows how individuals may develop a powerful emotional connection to certain objects, which are perceived as tangible evidence or expressions of their personal identity (Belk, 1988; Elsbach, 2003) or social identity (Pratt and Rafaeli, 1997). Even when members are asked to describe what is central, enduring, and distinctive about their organization, it is not unusual for them to mention people, products, logos, and other visible and tangible objects that, in the collective imagery, have marked the organization's collective history and have come to symbolize its uniqueness.

In Chapter 1 we saw how the bonneted cab played a prominent role in members' understanding of what Scania is, despite the marginal contribution of these models to the organization's overall sales. Similarly, a Lego brick, the Volkswagen Beetle, or the "prancing horse" of the Ferrari logo are likely to be central to people's perceptions and understanding of their organizations, as these artefacts have long been associated with the organization and because they symbolize important organizational values. To the extent that these objects epitomize past success, they infuse people with pride and may become organizational "myths" around which members sustain a sense of unity and belongingness to a unique collective endeavor.

Often the decision by managers to change or drop an important organizational artefact or symbol – for example, discontinuing the production of a "classic," transferring operations out of a historical building, or changing long-standing visual representations such as logos or color schemes – is felt by employees as a severe loss, after which "things will not be the same." Conversely, managers may readopt old logos and bring revamped versions of milestone products back into production in an effort to recapture the "spirit" that characterized the organization's earlier days, and to send a signal to both internal and external audiences that they intend to refocus on the organizational values that these historical artefacts represent (see the case of Bang & Olufsen in Chapter 6).

Projected images ("We are what we would like to be")

Finally, in some cases individuals' understanding of what their organization is comes to be influenced by specific images and representations of the company that do not necessarily correspond to its reality but rather to a desired or envisioned future identity. In fact, projecting ideal images of the organization – images that may correspond only in part to its reality – is one way that organizational leaders may use to try to fulfill their own identity aspirations, by encouraging a modification in members' beliefs accordingly (Gioia and Thomas, 1996).

At Penn State University in the mid-1980s, for instance, the new board of directors tried to stimulate change in members' behavior by encouraging them to view their institution as a "Top Ten" university – a category that seems concrete and objective but was actually a largely undetermined metaphor. They hoped that members who accepted this idea would raise their ambitions for the organization and support changes in its policies and processes (Gioia and Thomas, 1996). Similarly, more recently senior officers and professors at Bocconi University in

Italy advanced the aspirational identity of a "research university" to promote an intensification of research efforts across departments. This aspirational image was gradually embedded in daily conversations and official debate long before the real transformation of organizational policies, incentive systems, and widespread values was completed.

Whether Penn State was *really* a top ten university or whether Bocconi was *really* a research university was beside the point. What matters is that an increasing number of members began to accept these aspirational images as a matter of fact and acted accordingly. These cases are instructive in that they show how some images expressing the views and aspirations of part of the organization may gradually be assimilated into shared identity beliefs (Gioia and Thomas, 1996).

CONCLUDING REMARKS

In the previous paragraphs we have briefly reviewed a variety of cues that organization members may draw from as they collectively construct an understanding of their organization's identity: selectively highlighting belongingness to existing social categories, letting themselves be inspired by more or less unique traits of the organization, and occasionally engaging in creative acts encouraging a revision of the way members collectively view their organization (such as the Oticon case described in the introduction to this book).

However, as members invoke the identity of their organization or ask questions about it in different circumstances, they are likely to produce different answers. It is not that organization members change their minds or contradict themselves over time: more simply, not all these "identities" are equally relevant to each situation. In organizations, different claims and beliefs may be more or less *salient* (Ashforth and Johnson, 2001) to the issue that members are called to address. For instance, as senior managers of the previously mentioned fictitious university allocate the yearly budget, their actions may be guided by the idea that their organization is and must be "a research university" rather than a "teaching university." In this specific circumstance, its "not for profit" nature may be less relevant, but this trait may be later invoked by the team or some of its members, for example, as they discuss the option of increasing student fees.

Thus, whether members draw on existing categories or search for inspiration in specific traits of their organization will depend on context and circumstance. The cases in this section will cast a revealing light on this issue.

Chapter 5

The Swedish Industrial Development Fund

State trust, bank, or venture capitalist?

Ciara Sutton

INTRODUCTION

Identity issues influence the behavior of organizations in a variety of situations. This chapter focuses on an organization's identity orientation towards existing social categories in the face of imposed strategic developments and external survival pressures.

In 2005 the Swedish Industrial Development Fund, *Industrifonden*, formally claimed that it was a "leading Swedish venture capital player," an espoused identity orientation that was far removed from its organizational origins in 1979 of a state-founded trust providing funds to large stagnating companies. While the mandate of the organization to facilitate industrial renewal had remained unchanged for 25 years, threats to its survival and specific statute changes in the 1990s marked turning points in the organization's identity claims. Threats to its survival came from the basic questionable activity of a government entity channeling public funds to private enterprises under favorable conditions. The legitimacy of the organization's activity and institutionalization of the organization itself was created by invoking different existing social categories of actors over time and clearly distinguishing the organization from these other actor categories. In this way the continuation of the organization could be justified and a distinct identity used to convince the salient stakeholders and constituents of Industrifonden's legitimate existence.

Through this case,[1] this chapter explores and illustrates how category-based identity claims are drawn upon in order to construct and reconstruct organizational

[1] The following sections report the finding from a content study of Industrifonden external representation in Swedish Business and daily press for the period 1990–2005. In addition, archival material of press releases (1996–2005), the organization newsletter "Industrifonden Nytt," and organization representation brochures were reviewed. Data collection also included personal interviews with organization employees. The data analysis focused on quoted identity expressions and industry comparisons to develop the identified themes.

identities in the face of threats to survival and abrupt strategy changes enforced by external stakeholders. The claims are connected to an effort to preserve the consistency of the core organizational identity while maintaining a position of relevance and uniqueness.

By observing the public identity expressions of the organization we find a development pattern of post-adaptation to imposed conditions as the organization matures and adapts to become an institution in its own right.

CHANNELING PUBLIC MONEY TO INDUSTRIAL RENEWAL

History in brief

Celebrating 25 years of "Industrifonden" in 2004, the Swedish Industrial Development Fund released an anniversary edition of its newsletter, "Industrifonden Nytt":

> Is there anyone who remembers Sweden in 1979? Only two TV channels, no commercial radio, no personal computers, and no internet. Swedish companies were in crisis and everyone was talking about "Industriakuten" (the Industrial Emergency). The realization grew that the state and industry needed to be more forward thinking instead of putting all their energy into saving companies facing the threat of closure. This is the background to the establishment of the Swedish Industrial Development Fund, with the task of providing loans for high-risk projects in large companies.[2]

When Industrifonden was established in 1979 it was intended to support the technical modernization of Swedish industry and create new employment opportunities. Funds were primarily directed to large established companies who borrowed to finance new technology projects. These companies included ABB, Allgon, Atlas Copco, Celsius, Investor, Saab, and Kabi Vitrum. Operating with a small core of individuals with high technical competence, Industrifonden cooperated with consultants and researchers both in Sweden and overseas to judge the quality and promise of the various projects. Apart from the financing arrangements, the approval of Industrifonden for a new idea often functioned as a catalyst in these large firms, leading the industry players to gain confidence in the value of their specific internal projects. An initial public contribution to create the fund was followed by annual subsidies in the form of cash and the state equity claims on Volvo and Saab. With established success, Industrifonden became a permanent organization in 1984.

---

[2] This quotation, and all subsequent quotations in this chapter, has been translated from Swedish by the author.

In 1992, a new ordinance permitted the fund to support commercialization and marketing projects in addition to technology-based development projects. Further, it was now possible for the fund to support individuals in business start-ups through entrepreneur loans, including a special loan for women. The fund changed its name to *Industri- och Nyföretagarfonden* (the Industry and Entrepreneur Fund). The fund administered start-up loans for three years and during this time the state transferred its ownership in another financing venture, the Small Business Fund, to Industrifonden. Among the assets received was a portfolio of smaller companies.

Up until 1996, Industrifonden offered three types of finance: conditional loans, guarantees, and capital in exchange for royalties. Conditional loans were interest-bearing loans that could be written off if the project failed. Capital for royalties was a project-specific subsidy with a requirement to pay a royalty to Industrifonden if the project was successful. A guarantee was a commitment to pay a proportion of the incurred costs if a project was unsuccessful.

In 1996, Industrifonden underwent another statute change allowing for the provision of equity capital, primarily aimed at firms in early development stages. This year also marked the beginning of the regional concentration of Industrifonden, resulting in the part-ownership of 11 regional venture capital firms throughout Sweden.

The success of Industrifonden reached a peak in 1999/2000 with its best annual results, but this was short-lived due to the crisis in 2000 affecting both industry and the capital markets. The investment projects encountered difficulties and Industrifonden struggled to find co-investors willing to take risks. The financial results were negative for the subsequent three years, and in 2005 a new director, Claes De Neergaard, took office. A year earlier, De Neergaard had presented his state-commissioned report on proposals for an improved system for complementing the market for early stage venture capital.

THE EARLY YEARS

As stated earlier, Industrifonden was established with a government contribution, receiving annual subsidies for the first four years. In 2006, after 27 years, it was still under state control. Formal regulations are set by the government, who also select the board. Structured as a foundation, there is technically no formal owner of the fund. As previously outlined, the foundation's original focus was to assist large established corporations by assessing new high technology projects and providing financial support. As a consequence of the well-established integrated networks between the government and upper echelons of the dominant industry players (a specific characteristic of the Swedish economy), the state nature of the fund created the belief among the early recipients that the repayment terms and obligations were negotiable. Focused actions were required and pursued by the

fund to counter attempts by these large firms to minimize repayment requirements, and counter the idea that the fund was providing subsidies to Swedish
industry. This included rigorous negotiations to collect the contracted returns. In
doing so, the fund maintained that it did not support providing grants or subsidies,
publicly backing up its stance by pointing out the overall benefits to the recipients
when market-based criteria for support were applied.

The first identity threat: 1989

In 1989 the government initiated a process reviewing "state financial support."
It was proposed that Industrifonden should be dissolved and become a government department, retaining the function of providing risk guarantees but losing
the ability to provide funds for industrial development projects. While this
indicated an imminent crisis for Industrifonden, the Minister for Industry, Rune
Molin, eventually decided against this move. It was concluded that Industrifonden fulfilled a necessary role, and that a cautious approach would be to
maintain a functioning system, given the difficulty of recreating it. It was
determined there was no need to change the activities or support forms of the
fund.

The assessment process highlighted the underlying general and widespread
belief that the market should take care of financing, and that Industrifonden was,
in fact, a vehicle of "state financial support." The government had a long-term aim
of complete privatization of the capital market, including the removal of forms of
selective support to be replaced by general incentives to small companies, for
example, tax rebates. Facing a strong and widespread external belief from constituents such as the state itself, the media, and the interested business community
that Industrifonden should be a private entity, or alternatively that a public organization should not fund industrial development projects, the fund had come to a
crisis of existence and received a reprieve from the government.

Within a month of the media debate this review attracted, the director of
Industrifonden, Bo Lundqvist, responded with the message "We are now needed
more than ever." The banks were becoming increasingly cautious, and against this
backdrop Industrifonden pushed its message that "You can't just ignore good,
high-risk projects" – stressing its role as a partner to banks, and emphasizing that
there were many projects that it was willing to invest in that had fallen through
because the banks or other financiers had pulled out. Directly confronting the
general criticism, Lundqvist stated:

> A state organization is conducting the risk assessment and determines, in
> practice, whether a new technology will be developed further or not.
> Often you hear that a state bureaucracy shouldn't have this role, that this
> should be determined by the private sector at company level . . . we

don't buy that argument . . . those of us that work here have 20–25 years' experience in industry, and we also make use of consultants.

(Dagens Industri, 911116)

Second identity threat: 1992

However, the uncertainty over the existence of Industrifonden continued. Once again, in March 1992, with growing doubts in the government that the fund was necessary, the government decided to review its future. Motivated by developments in the capital market, it was thought that the banks and other financial institutions could to an increasing degree contribute to the financing of various projects, and in more diverse and more flexible forms than previously. If the review determined that in fact there was a need for Industrifonden, then proposals of how the organization should be structured were to be put forward, including options for full or partial privatization. By September 1992, the outcome of the review was delivered by Lars Vinell: "Don't break up an organization that works, it only increases uncertainty in the market without contributing any solutions" (TT Nyhetsbanken, 920914).

The review weighed up the evidence regarding the many improvements in general conditions for financing of small business development projects, but concluded that there still remained a number of reasons for the state to continue to contribute to this form of funding. This time it was suggested, therefore, that Industrifonden should remain under state ownership for the time being, but should concentrate on smaller companies and individuals. Suggestions also included a reduction of the total amount of financing allocated to new projects, and a cancellation of a planned repayment to the state of initial fund capital.

Concurrently with the review of the fund's continued existence, a new initiative for state financing began through a new form, an entrepreneurial fund. Financing for the new loan-based organization was partly drawn from capital that had been under the control of Industrifonden.

The debate in the media pointed out that the proposal that Industrifonden should continue, with a new name (Industri- och Nyföretagarfonden) and altered direction, was strongly indicative that the fund had proved itself in terms of its ability to work specifically with development projects. Criticism was directed at the regulations that restricted Industrifonden to investing in "young" companies – the suggestion was that this should be redefined as "youthful" companies – meaning they could be active with "innovative" companies irrespective of actual firm age. In November 1992, the Minister for Finance, Per Westerberg, presented the structure of the future state involvement in company financing. Industrifonden was to focus on new and young firms, and exclusively through loans and guarantees.

The separate state-financed entrepreneurial fund to which Industrifonden had previously contributed was subsequently listed, becoming Atle and Bure, during a short-lived undertaking, as the directives pushed the return requirements so high that rather than being venture capital funds, as intended, operations were more similar to an investment or private equity company. The government elected to place their shares with Industrifonden with the intention that the funds would be used for their original purpose – to benefit innovative, growth companies.

During the discussion stages of this plan, Lotta Löfgren of Industrifonden commented:

> [We are] convinced that the money will be used for small companies and that Industrifonden will in the future be able to go in at a much earlier stage of development than before. For this to happen, though, requires new state directives on how the money can and should be managed. We need to be able to take bigger risks than we do today. But it would seem that it is precisely along these lines that the government is thinking and a decision on new directives should be made in May.
>
> (SAF tidningen, 950217)

Shortly after, in a debate article, Aapo Sääsk expressed the view that Industri-fonden remained relevant in the prevailing economic climate, where there were so many short-term and relatively safe investments that only enthusiasts would be willing to put money into uncertain and long-term projects:

> It is therefore necessary that the state step in . . . to do this . . . [We] need to increase Industrifonden's funds and remove the 50% limit from their instructions.
>
> (Dagens Industri, 950606)

Industrifonden had clearly moved away from its strategy of supporting high-risk projects in large firms to focusing on lending money and providing guarantees to small and medium-sized firms. Industrifonden had survived its second crisis.

A NEW DIRECTOR IN 1995

In September 1995, Lars Öjefors was appointed director of Industrifonden, and simultaneously the fund released news of its intentions to broaden its activities to become a player in the "growth capital" market (*Riskkapital* in Swedish). Reference was made to the lack of growth capital and the problems this entailed for many of Sweden's small and medium-sized companies.

Lars Öjefors came to his position to head Industrifonden in the new direction of investing in small and medium-sized firms with an expressed desire to direct more funds to the commercialization of innovation. His own background included a period as a researcher, with a Ph D. in chemistry and a teaching position at the Royal Institute of Technology, as well as experience as an industry executive. He believed that this gave him insight from two relevant perspectives – as a provider and recipient of capital funding. He reiterated that Industrifonden was market driven, and that a decision had been made by the state that they were now to enter the growth capital market.

Within a few months of assuming his position, Öjefors expressed a desire to concentrate more on high technology. Very few of the previous investments in smaller firms, through loans, had been in high technology – the majority were in light industry, for instance small workshops and trades of various sorts (e.g., glass-making, car workshops). In hindsight, Industrifonden admitted, these were areas where the fund did not have sufficient industry competence for involvement. Technology projects had been their strength historically, coupled with an internal technology culture that had been further embedded under the directorship of Öjefors. Now, for the first time since its inception in 1979, Industrifonden was planning to become a part-owner in developing companies:

> We are going to engage in the companies we believe in with more than just finance. We need to support and follow up. And for that, we have qualified people. But I want to emphasize that the fund doesn't give pure grants or subsidies, rather it works on commercial grounds – even if the demand for returns is low.
>
> (Dagens Industri, 951211)

With the new direction, Öjefors commented on his desire to combine his knowledge from his professional experience. Öjefors saw Industrifonden as a vehicle through which he could contribute to change attitudes in Sweden to be more like the Americans – believing in an idea and really backing it.

A survey commissioned by the fund at this time examined bank activity. The results showed that the banks' loans were insufficient and that the lack of financing options was hindering companies' growth. Drawing on the results of the survey, Öjefors concluded:

> the most interesting message of all was that companies are more interested in borrowing money than receiving subsidies, and that the risk-willingness of banks is limited . . .
>
> We need to have a complement to the banks – the best complements put forward by the survey were active board membership, conditional loans, and credit guarantees . . .

[We] don't want to compete with the banks, rather create new options for co-operation.

(Dagens Industri, 951230)

Concern was expressed that the financial crisis led to the unsatisfactory functioning of the growth capital market compared to the US market where there was considerably more risk-willing capital. From this perspective, Industrifonden was put forward as having an important role to fill – by taking more risks than the banks, and by daring to stick out its neck and make credit evaluations based on industrial and technical factors rather than economic ones.

By mid-1996, the fund was receiving more in-depth press coverage. The director, Öjefors, was portrayed as having many plans regarding the new option of taking a minority share in companies. Comments by Öjefors stressed the potential for Industrifonden to increase its returns by becoming part-owners:

There are so many projects that are interesting. Reviewing the fund's previous unsuccessful projects through the years shows that it is almost never a problem with the technology. It is often weak leadership in combination with poor liquidity that causes a project to fail.

Of what I have seen, it appears that in the USA there is a completely different follow-up of growth capital projects. In Sweden the follow-up of conditional loans has sometimes been a matter of ticking a box according to whether the project is going well or not.

In the USA the payments of growth capital are staged and are only made after project developments have been presented. But this requires a careful going through of the companies, which is resource intensive.

(Sydsvenska Dagbladet, 960614)

Öjefors emphasized his satisfaction with the market-based activities of Industrifonden.

Subsidies and grants are like drugs, and the dependence can be very strong.

(Sydsvenska Dagbladet, 960614)

In the mid-1990s, Industrifonden was doing well financially, and it was portrayed as a successful example of state involvement in the growth capital market.

In November 1996, the fund announced that it was able to make a larger number of investments, but, given that small companies demand high involvement from those who provide growth capital, it would lend only as much as it had the resources to follow up. This would appear to be in response to criticism that

Industrifonden (along with other state funds) held on too tightly to its funds and invested only in high technology projects. Öjefors reasoned:

> If you only engage financially, the effectiveness is low. Investments in small companies require active governing and are more demanding than investment in large companies.
>
> (Svenska Dagbladet, 961203)

In discussing the development from working only with large firms to a focus on small to medium-sized firms, Öjefors made it clear that this was not a case of a natural or emergent adaptation; rather, he claimed, it had been a difficult change-over.

Again in response to the low investment level, he stated:

> The reason is that we go through every project with a fine-toothed comb. Investing wrongly in a project only creates problems. Growth capital is not for creating short-term employment.
>
> (Svenska Dagbladet, 961203)

Given the loan and investment parameters, it was stressed that the fund was not intended for the very smallest companies. There was an increasing focus on firms that had just passed the prototype phase – the period after the patent and product were in place. This phase is often capital intensive due to product development, marketing, and sales. According to Öjefors, this phase could last up to ten years, requiring on average three new investment rounds before the company showed positive results. To some extent contradicting his own technology stance, Öjefors offered the opinion that in Sweden there was too strong a fixation on the innovation phase, as it was after this phase that the company had the greatest need for capital.

From January 1997, the strategy change was clearly visible in press releases, with a majority of the communication being statements or interviews with Öjefors. While 20 percent of the fund's activities remained with large companies (such as ABB, Atlas Copco, Sandvik, Volvo), this was being phased out. According to Öjefors, the change meant that:

> It will be much more difficult for Industrifonden now with more activities in small and medium-sized firms. We have strengthened and reinforced the organization to be able to effectively deal with regular follow-ups.

> Industrifonden's average customer losses are 10–12%, with the banks averaging 1% of loans. Industrifonden is to take bigger risks than the

banks. A proportion of the projects we enter into are high risk. Our goal is to reduce customer losses to 5–6%.

Previously Industrifonden carried out annual follow-ups. It is very clear indeed that we can provide greater benefit and save projects if we have tighter contact and better follow-up and control. By going in with equity capital, taking a seat on the board and providing competence, we at once increase our insight into the company.

(Dagens Industri, 19970114)

In early 1997, Industrifonden representatives joined a Swedish delegation (led by the Royal Swedish Academy of Engineering Sciences – IVA) to California to study the venture capital market:

We will be now increasing our level of direct investments and with this board membership, to a large part via venture capital companies.

(Dagens Industri, 19970114)

A STATUTE CHANGE

A statute change allowing equity ownership by Industrifonden came into effect in early 1997. The official strategy stipulated a minimum investment of one million Swedish kronor (SEK) and a general guideline that the majority of investments should be between SEK 4 and 6 million. The view was to own on average a third of the shares of the portfolio firms, up to a maximum of 49 percent. Öjefors remarked:

The fund is like a mother – currently she is the guardian of 240 firms. A mother doesn't just hand out an allowance and serve food. She also needs to provide an upbringing. Just think how well brought up you need to be to be listed.

(Finanstidningen, 19970926)

According to Öjefors there was plenty of funding available on the market, but this was coupled with a financial overconfidence. His own view was that money could do as much harm as good, unless it was combined with competence. In a detailed interview published in the Swedish business press, Öjefors expanded on Industrifonden's position. He stated clearly that the organization was market based, and that handing out economic subsidies and allowances to the wrong entrepreneur with the wrong project could do a lot of harm, misleading other financiers to invest and misleading the entrepreneur into wasting his or her best years, in addition to losing money. Öjefors expressed a strategy to combine

Industrifonden's capital with competence and engagement, and emphasized the investment managers' high level of technical education and their experience of company leadership.

Öjefors remarked that one of the main difficulties faced by new firms is that entrepreneurs often do not fully appreciate or calculate the costs of commercialization: the costs of finding the right suppliers, of building up production facilities, and of marketing, and recruitment. In the majority of failures the company's original management was insufficient to meet the new demands of the commercialization and selling phase. This situation made it even more important for the fund to go in as part owners. This would mean that Industrifonden gained board influence over both CEO selection and important strategic issues.

For the same reasons, Öjefors argued, it is often necessary to begin exporting worldwide immediately. The traditional way of gradually taking market share country by country was, according to Öjefors, less applicable to industries that developed short-lived advanced technical equipment. Time shortages and the necessary rapid expansion entailed a high risk for a financier. For such products with a short intensive window of opportunity, it was necessary to exploit it fully.

Industrifonden was in a position to take substantial risks, but, Öjefors emphasized, this was done on a market basis – the greater the credit risk, the higher the royalty. Alternatively, Industrifonden would provide equity capital where the returns were in line with the company's share value. Overall, the results showed that approximately 20 percent of the funding was written off, an equal portion gave a high return, and the rest a normal return.

The fund defended accusations that it might create an uneven competitive field by offering selected companies both competitive financing and competence. While Industrifonden recognized this issue, it countered that it was less relevant given that the companies they invested in usually did not have Swedish competitors, but rather competed internationally.

In addition to promoting industrial technological modernization, Öjefors saw another important role for the fund: Swedish innovations should be developed and sold by Swedish companies, rather than produced under license abroad as was often still the case:

> To a large extent it is a question of attitude. Creativity is admired in Sweden, but not building companies and making money. We also have the problem that newly graduated engineers in Sweden either go into academia or into industry. It's a lifestyle choice. In the USA it is quite common for a university professor to take time out to commercialize a discovery. This results in more growth and more employment opportunities.

> The prognosis is better for a good entrepreneur with a bad product than

a bad entrepreneur with a good product. It is quite simply easier to improve the product than improve the company.

(Finanstidningen, 970926)

Öjefors's emphasis returned to the technical culture at Industrifonden:

It makes us a good complement to venture capitalists who have a financial focus.

(Finanstidningen, 970926)

A(NOTHER) LEADERSHIP CHANGE

Early in 2005, Lars Öjefors stepped down from his position and was replaced by Claes de Neergaard. De Neergaard had been the reviewer of state growth capital to new companies. His suggestions, presented in 2004, included more funds to Industrifonden and a new venture capital fund "Kickstart Sweden" with a focus on young, high-tech companies. De Neergaard commented:

In Sweden there is agreement that we need to focus more on competence-based new firms, and here Industrifonden has an important role as a supplier of growth capital and competence.

(Teknikbrostiftelsen, 050202)

The new choice of director was a move away from technology leadership: de Neergaard's greatest strength was in the finance arena, and he was clearly viewed by staff at Industrifonden as representing a strong connection to venture capital.

In a press release in 2005, Industrifonden described itself as one of Sweden's leading venture capital players. Following this, at the annual public meeting in November 2005, the new director spoke about the promising state of the venture capital sector to the audience, including a large number of Swedish venture capitalists. He took the opportunity to emphasize Industrifonden's important role as an investor partner in early-stage growth companies. Behind the scenes, a debate was ongoing about the future strategy of the fund, which internal sources speculated concerned possible changes in the minority ownership restrictions. The theme for the evening was, however, how young, technology-based growth companies could grow internationally. De Neergaard commented:

Industrifonden now has – more than ever – an important roll to fill as an investment partner in the early stages. We have a high risk profile as a result of consistently making early stage investments. It is however important that every investment is conducted on businesslike terms.

(PIR, 051116)

CASE DISCUSSION

The directional changes that Industrifonden underwent, from large firm to small firm and loan capital to equity capital, are presented by industry experts and internal actors as natural adaptive developments. However, close examination of the public debates, identity claims, and aspirations of Industrifonden over the 25-year period reveals a more disjointed pattern. A subheading of the fund's own anniversary publication refers to the development "From Large Industry to High-Tech – 25 years with Industrifonden 1979–2004." Arguably, this comparison does not fully capture the organization's identity development and, while intended to provide a "then" and "now" contrast, a question could be raised about what exactly the difference is between "large industry" and "high tech." Are they talking apples and oranges?

In two significant periods, 1989 and 1992, the very existence of the foundation was seriously in question and its survival under threat. Following each of these crises, the organization altered its formal identity claims to realign to its new mandated activities and maintain its position in its environment. In addition, statute-based strategy changes (in particular in 1996) resulting from a political and interactive process between the organization and the state were linked to changes in identity claims in relation to other salient actors belonging to legitimate institutionalized social categories.

Industrifonden appears to have striven for continuity by keeping many aspects of its identity consistent over its history. The core role of the organization, mandated in 1979, was to support the technical modernization of Swedish industry and create new employment opportunities. This element of its function remained consistent throughout, as well as some elements of how it was performed – namely, the provision of finance and competence. Although this core function remained stable, Industrifonden altered its declared claims in reaction to rising challenges and changing external expectations. The most remarkable outcome of each external shock was the resultant claim about what and who the organization was "not" in relation to other social actors. Following each of the external shocks and statute changes, the organizational form that Industrifonden held up for comparison or association was changed. As the strategy of Industrifonden changed and the focus of activity and the project management behavior adapted, the organization's espoused claims about what they were not doing and what category of organization they differed from also changed. In doing so, they countered the external threats and emphasized their uniqueness and distinctiveness, and thus the continuing need for their existence. By claiming partnership with these other organizational categories, the opportunity consistently arose to highlight what made them complementary rather than the same.

While formal identity statements were noticeable by their absence, the organization maintained its relevance and uniqueness as an entity by publicly communicating the differences between the fund and the model of "otherness," this being successively of importance to (1) the government, (2) the banks, and (3) the venture capital firms. Obviously, given the nature of being a "provider of finance," Industrifonden could and did use these comparisons throughout its history, but they are significant to differing degrees in different periods:

1 *Not a state entity*. Industrifonden stated specifically that it was a "state entity," but then distinguished what was different about its organization and the institutionalized role of a state entity. The fund emphasized the industry experience of its employees, the use of consultants, and stressed that its function was not to provide subsidies and grants.
2 *Not a bank*. As it moved into loans targeted to small and medium-sized firms, Industrifonden invoked bank actors as its comparison. The statements positioned the fund as not being a bank, although its activities were clearly bank-like once the focus shifted from large organizations. Instead, Industrifonden expressed a desire to complement the banks and highlighted its greater risk willingness.
3 *Not a venture capitalist*. In 1995 Industrifonden discussed a new strategy, clearly influenced by the US model of venture financing and approach to entrepreneurship, and without a doubt moving them in terms of their proposed activities to become actors in the venture capital market. However, the comparisons to US industry were made with quite different actors. Reference was to the venture capital market in the US – characterized by activities including active investor involvement, strong follow-up, a focus on management team competencies and staged investments – and the growth capital market in Sweden, which comprises a spectrum of financing forms including private equity, loan capital, and venture capital, and comprises all levels of active involvement by the finance provider from completely hands-off to micromanagement of daily activities. The fund's technical focus was highlighted and contrasted with the financial prominence in venture capital firms.
4 *A venture capitalist?* The move into the venture capital market marked a significant shift from previous identity stances. It was the first time that the organization actually stated what it believed it was. It is interesting, however, that following a short period the emphasis moved back to being a "complement" to the private venture capital actors, primarily drawing on the statutory restrictions on minority ownership. In addition, when discussing the nature of their organization, Industrifonden staff emphasized the evergreen nature of the fund and its consequent ability to extend investment terms, as well as the fund's reduced return requirements and thus its wider scope for possible investment objects.

Industrifonden made category-based identity claims drawn from the conventions of what were appropriate and meaningful categories (Whetton and Mackey, 2002). Each of the categories (state entity, bank, venture capitalist) were drawn upon, creating an association based on the principal activities of the fund. Distance was then created by stressing elements that distinguished the organization. Much of what Industrifonden did with its identity claims could be viewed as impression management (Elsbach and Sutton, 1992) to maintain legitimacy in the face of continuing crises of survival. The greatest threat to the organization was the view that the funding of innovation should be a matter for the private sector, that the market should be left to operate freely, and that public money should not be channeled to these ends. This belief stems partly from the view that a public organization should not be profit-motivated, partly from the idea that a public organization should be focused on social needs and redistribution rather than on channeling taxpayers' money to selected firms in the for-profit sector, and to a lesser extent private sector crowding-out arguments.

It can be argued that the pure organizational forms of banks and private venture capital firms are better suited to the task of allocating funds to private companies to stimulate growth. Industrifonden, however, has successfully defended its legitimacy and unique position in its role as a support for the technical modernization of Sweden – and the creator of employment opportunities – through the provision of finance and competence.

KEY QUESTIONS

1 The case does not provide a detailed account of the internal dynamics at Industrifonden. To what extent do you believe that changing claims reflected actual changes in beliefs and aspirations, rather than attempts at impression management?

2 The story of Industrifonden highlights a link between organizational identity and changing expectations regarding the role of the organization in society. How is organizational identity likely to affect the capacity of the organization to secure the support of critical stakeholders?

3 Industrifonden is a government entity. Are identity issues likely to differ between organizations working in the private and the public sector? And what about between companies and non-profit organizations? If so, how and why?

4 Industrifonden made considerable use of existing social categories in its public statements on what the organization was and how it functioned. What are the benefits – and drawbacks – of this?

Table 2 Societal changes and organizational responses at Industrifonden, 1978–2005

Period	Foundation and early years (1978–1988)	First identity threat: survival (1989)	Second identity threat: survival (1992–1995)	Rising aspirations: statute change (1996–1997)	Re-positioning (2005)
Environment and society	Industrial emergency State/industry networks	Increasing belief that the market should be responsible for financing	Improving capital market conditions – is the fund really necessary?	Rapid increase in venture capital sector	Shortage of willing co-investors
Role	Supporting technological innovation and employment	Supporting technological innovation and employment	Supporting technological innovation and employment	Supporting technological innovation and employment Change attitudes	Supporting technological innovation and employment
Claimed identity	State organization Competence provider: assessor of new technology projects	Partner to banks, not a state organization	Complement to banks, plus entrepreneurial fund	Growth capital actor, not a bank Complement to venture capitalists Competence and "upbringing"	Venture capitalist With unique characteristics • Lower return requirement • Evergreen fund Lead investor role?
Core policies and structures	Investment in large firms Conditional loans Guarantees Capital for royalties	Investment in large firms Conditional loans Guarantees Capital for royalties	Investment in new and young firms Individuals	Minority equity capital investments High technology	

Chapter 6

Organizational culture and identity at Bang & Olufsen[1]

Davide Ravasi and Majken Schultz

INTRODUCTION

The *culture* of an organization rests on a set of taken-for-granted beliefs and norms that guide the everyday behavior of its members: how they think, feel, and act; how they relate to one another and to external counterparts; and how they handle ordinary work activities as well as unexpected events (Martin, 2002; Schein, 1992). Research on organizational identities has shown tight interrelations between identity and culture, as organizational symbols, traditions, and consolidated practices provide cues that help members make sense of – and give sense to – what their organization is.

Organizational identity and culture are often associated, and it is not uncommon to see official corporate documents describing the "identity" of the organization in terms of a long list of "values." However, as we shall see in this chapter, while there may be a close relationship between cultural values and collective self-perceptions, it would be incorrect to assume that they are essentially the same thing (Hatch and Schultz, 2000, 2002). On the one hand, organizations – or organizational members – may justify cultural norms and practices by invoking the identity of the organization (Fiol, 1991). In other words, organizational members may draw on broad social categories such as "family firm," "university," or "socially responsible" – and on widely accepted beliefs about the way such organizations should be structured and function – to account for established norms or major decisions. This is what happens, for instance, whenever issues are raised or handled according to the principle that "this is – or is not – appropriate behavior for this type of organization."

Culture, on the other hand, also plays an important role in inspiring and shaping the construction and reconstruction of organizational identities. In fact,

[1] The authors are very grateful for the openness, time, and support of all at Bang & Olufsen, and in particular Anders Knutsen, CEO, and Francesco Ciccolella, Director of StoryLab.

many organizations explicitly define themselves in terms of cultural beliefs and values. Furthermore, practices, symbols, rituals, and other cultural expressions provide visible manifestations of patterns of meaning, which are perceived as unique and distinctive. Indeed, understanding and managing the multiple inter-relations of organizational identity and culture may be crucial for leaders engaged in redefining the strategic position and conduct of an organization.

In this chapter, drawing on a longitudinal study of identity management at Bang & Olufsen, the Danish producer of audio and visual systems, we show how explicit reference to cultural expressions (stories, artefacts, etc.) and established collective practices (the way products are designed, customers served, and alli-ances managed, etc.) helps members make sense of what their organization is and what it stands for. Such embedding in culture preserves a sense of continuity and distinctiveness, as identity claims and beliefs are periodically revised to address environmental changes and new challenges.

ORGANIZATIONAL IDENTITY AND CULTURE

Organizational culture can be conceived as a set of assumptions that guide inter-pretation and action in organizations by defining appropriate behavior for various situations (Martin, 1993). These largely tacit assumptions and beliefs are expressed and manifested in a web of formal and informal practices, rituals, stories, artefacts, language, and other forms of collective expression, which represent the most visible, tangible, and audible elements of the culture of an organization (Schein, 1992; Trice and Beyer, 1984).

Early research on organizational cultures emphasized the consensus of mem-bers around a set of tacit assumptions and beliefs. Cultural norms and values were defined as largely shared among members, and strongly influenced by the founders and/or leaders of the organization (Schein, 1992). Later studies challenged this monolithic view of organizational cultures and observed how in many organiza-tions subcultures and countercultures existed, resulting in different – and often opposing – views among members about appropriate ways of behaving (Martin, 1993). Other studies highlighted how the interpretation of cultural manifestations such as stories, slogans, and symbols is not always univocal and that occasional fragmentation and confusion among members may arise. However, consensus, divergence, and confusion tend to coexist in most organizations. While some groups hold different views on appropriate ways of thinking and acting in specific situations, and some issues are left open to multiple interpretations, it is likely that most members agree on a core set of values and beliefs, which underpin formal and informal rules and practices, and are sustained by and expressed in organizational symbols, rituals, mythology, and language.

The idea that organizational history, traditions, symbols, and practices tend to influence identity construction in organizations has been advanced since the very formulation of the concept (Albert and Whetten, 1985). Early studies of organizational identity suggested that understanding identity processes in organizations requires the investigation of the tacit mental frameworks that produce "characteristic ways of doing things" (Dutton and Dukerich, 1991) or "regular practices, familiar habits and operating routines" (Ashforth and Mael, 1996). In fact, established practices and operating routines are often invoked by organizational members as they search for self-defining features, because in the members' view they "embody or come to symbolize the identity itself" (Ashforth and Mael, 1996: 50).

By their own nature, then, cultural forms, such as stories, sagas, corporate architecture, dress or other physical artefacts, reflect the distinctiveness of an organization and are often interpreted by its members as evidence of it. In this respect, organizational culture supplies members with cues for making sense of and giving sense to what their organization is about, as unique values, beliefs, rituals, and artefacts can help organizational members substantiate their identity claims and express their perceived uniqueness.

HISTORICAL BACKGROUND [2]

Bang & Olufsen is a Danish producer of high-quality, stylish, and expensive audio and video systems. The company was founded in 1925 in the village of Struer in northern Denmark. Significant technological innovations and the use of unusual components soon established a solid reputation for the company, as reflected in their first slogan: "B&O – the Danish Hallmark of Quality." Already at that time the company's products were characterized by technological excellence, faithful sound reproduction, and user-friendliness. In the 1960s, the new company motto – "Bang & Olufsen, for those who discuss design and quality before price" – followed a strategic reorientation that associated style and design with technical quality, and a new marketing strategy based on the identification of a global segment of customers interested in their highly differentiated product. The company saw its natural target in the very high-end, style-conscious segment of the global consumer electronics market.

In the late 1960s and early 1970s the company grew significantly, driven by a strategy that focused on the distinctiveness of the product. Attention to design and style intensified, with the company's products receiving several national and international awards. In the following years, however, increasing competition as well as changes in the external environment periodically led top managers to address explicitly the identity of the organization and to ask themselves "What is Bang & Olufsen *really* about?" (see Table 3).

---

[2] The following sections build on a longitudinal study of three identity management programs over the course of 25 years. Data are drawn from multiple sources: semi-structured interviews, archival data, transcriptions from internal workshops, and participant observation at company events. Further information on the study can be found in Ravasi and Schultz (2006).

Table 3 Environmental changes, identity threats, and organizational responses at B&O, 1972–1998

	Environmental changes	Shifting external claims	Identity threats	Identity-related response
Early 1970s	Increasing pressure from large-scale, cost-efficient Japanese competitors	Distributors demand conformity to the hi-fi trend in product design and performance	Perceived need for clearer differentiation (what is distinctive?)	Focus on design principles (7 CICs)
Early 1990s	General recession, decline of the yuppie culture, and loss of market appeal	Drift towards luxury brand. Journalists and retailers question the technology behind the product aesthetics	Need for restructuring (what is really central?) and perceived need for repositioning (what is distinctive?)	Focus on core competences and brand values (New Vision)
Late 1990s	Competitors enhance the design content of their products	Some competitors (Thomson, Sony) portray their strategies as attempts to imitate Bang & Olufsen	Perceived need for further differentiation (what is distinctive?)	Focus on brand values (Fundamental Values) and full identity expression

In 1972, the challenge came from growing external pressures to alter the product design to conform to spreading Japanese standards (modular, square, abundance of controls, hi-fi performance, etc.). Organizational leaders felt that conforming to external expectations would mean the loss of an important aspect of their organization's identity. They therefore felt the need to re-evaluate and formalize what really made them (and thus their products) different from the Japanese – which at that time was the relevant identity issue. In 1993, a tacit drift towards luxury business, abruptly halted by economic recession and changing societal values, caused managers to question themselves about the essence of the company, about those features that distinguished Bang & Olufsen from its competitors. Issues of differentiation and centrality also arose in relation to a need to downsize, forcing managers to decide what should be kept in-house and what should be outsourced. Finally, in 1998, a perceived threat of imitation – and the potential loss of distinctiveness – led managers once again to question themselves about the profound roots of their identity as a basis for countering competitors' moves and fostering international growth.

The Seven Corporate Identity Components

In the early 1970s, as previously stated, with increasing competition from Japan, Bang & Olufsen began to feel growing pressure from dealers to imitate Japanese technology and design. Top managers, however, believed that only by maintaining its position as an alternative to Japanese competitors could the company maintain its credibility and image. In 1972, therefore, Managing Director Ebbe Mansted asked a small group of product developers and marketing managers to reflect on what distinguished Bang & Olufsen from its competitors. As a participant reported later:

> The task was not to lay a new foundation, but to formulate values that were already part of Bang & Olufsen's identity and then select the strongest elements for the company's international future.
>
> (Bang and Palshøy, 2000: 86)

Existing mottoes like "Bang & Olufsen – for those who discuss design and quality before price" were felt to be too generic. The aim of the group was to identify and describe "the company's goals and personality." Codification had the purpose, as one of the participants recalled, of "interpreting existing, but unexpressed attitudes." Eventually the group converged on a set of principles that in their view characterized product design at Bang & Olufsen – expressed as Authenticity, Autovisuality, Credibility, Domesticity, Essentiality, Individuality, Inventiveness – and distinguished the company's products from mainstream audio and video systems. These principles came to be known as the Seven Corporate Identity Components (or Seven CICs).

Although initially intended for communication policy purposes, these claims soon came to be considered the basic components of Bang & Olufsen's identity. The identity was intended to be reflected in the products and also serve as a guide for action for marketers and designers. In differentiating Bang & Olufsen in the marketplace, conscious and consistent efforts to communicate the essence of the product were considered as important as technical quality. The perceived uniqueness of the company was reflected in the new slogan "We think differently." This was expressed in detail in a small manual and a poster, later to become a corporate icon, explaining in detail the practical implications of the Seven CICs.

The New Vision

Throughout the 1970s product development and communication followed the Seven CICs. Between 1979 and 1981 Bang & Olufsen introduced a complete range of new products with innovative technology and features that enhanced the quality of sound reproduction, allowed easy remote control, and had fully integrated system components.

Over time, however, managers, designers, marketers, and retailers seemed to develop diverging interpretations of what Bang & Olufsen represented. Product developers designed increasingly sophisticated and expensive equipment, with little regard for what was really valued by customers. Powerful subsidiaries positioned products and ran advertising campaigns with little awareness or regard for central strategies. And communications concentrated on luxury symbols to justify the high price of the products. Gradually, Bang & Olufsen began to be perceived as an expensive luxury brand, while the communication strategies over-looked the technical and design qualities. In the early 1990s, however, a sudden decline in sales forced managers to conclude that changes were required in both the product range and communication policies.

In 1993, therefore, the new CEO Anders Knutsen initiated a change program, called Break Point '93, aimed at ensuring coherence of action among all members engaged in design, manufacturing, advertising, and retailing. At the heart of this concerted effort was an explicit attempt to refocus the organization on what constituted the "essence" of its identity, the "distinctiveness of its product and its spirit." The process was based on two teams working in parallel and was explicitly designed to explore whether the perceptions of the company by actual and poten-tial customers (i.e., the image of the organization) corresponded with how the organization perceived itself (i.e., its identity beliefs). A field survey with four groups of actual and potential customers reported a consistent perception of the organization across groups: Bang & Olufsen was regarded as a company that created a harmony of aesthetics and technology; all other distinctive features, such as the integration of audio and video, were ranked lower. A second team was assigned the task of reflecting on what made Bang & Olufsen unique: the distinct-ive features of the organization and its products. The Seven CICs were perceived as being related "more to the products than to the company." The purpose of the group was to produce a statement that expressed more clearly what was unique about the company and its people. Reflection on Bang & Olufsen's uniqueness eventually evolved into an attempt to codify the essential values that distinguished the company and its products from its competitors. After several informal meet-ings, the group produced the following statement: "The best of both worlds: B&O, the unique combination of technological excellence and emotional appeal."

A comparison with the results of the work of the first group reinforced con-fidence that the selected features – technological excellence and emotional appeal – were also perceived as distinctive and valuable by customers. What was later termed "The New Vision" became the formula used to convey the essence of the organization's identity.

Bang & Olufsen United

Between 1994 and 1996, sales and profits rose rapidly, spurred by a regained coherence of new products, corporate communication, and sales behavior (see Table 4). At the end of 1996, however, the high growth rates of the previous years began to slow. In the subsequent months, some competitors declared their inten-tions to invade the profitable niche for "design products," threatening the unique

■ *Table 4* *Bang & Olufsen, financial figures, 1993–2001*

	1993	1994	1995	1996	1997	1998	1999	2000	2001
Turnover (DKK million)	2,126	2,409	2,618	2,711	3,008	3,117	3,380	3,722	3,810
Op. profit (DKK million)	8.7	155.3	289	236.6	303.3	299	333	337	271
Cash flow (DKK million)	97	539.6	89.7	89.4	63.6	−148	−356	19	−157
Return on equity (%)	−6.4	12.9	19.7	16.7	18.5	21	24	22	13
Profit ratio (%)	0.4	6.5	11	8.7	10	10	10	9	7
Share price (DKK)	23	91	145	200	395	441	462	283	268
Employees	2,298	2,393	2,492	2,495	2,395	2,615	2,668	2,797	2,776

position of the company. A one-off restyling of one of its products by well-known designer Philippe Starcke led low-cost producer Thomson to enthusiastically declare that it would soon compete in the same league as Bang & Olufsen. Furthermore, multi-brand shops did not always emphasize what managers perceived as distinctive attributes of the company and failed to convey the desired image.

Eventually, to counter imitative attempts and support growth on a global scale, managers felt the need to formulate new plans, creating a new retail concept and introducing new product lines and accessories. An essential part of this strategy for international growth was a much stronger reliance on own-brand stores or shop-in-shops in upscale department stores. Bang & Olufsen products had previously been distributed through a wide range of multi-brand dealers, their products displayed and presented along with many other brands. Managers, however, were unsure about the possibility of fully expressing the uniqueness of the products in such a retail environment, and felt that their dealers had to possess a profound understanding of the philosophy behind the products. Their impressions were supported by market data that indicated stronger growth in markets dominated by stand-alone Bang & Olufsen stores.

As part of the new strategy, the top management set in motion another wave of initiatives aimed at further reviewing and clarifying the identity of the company, internally and externally. In their own words, they focused on "restating and debating the fundamental values" of the company, as these values were meant "to provide the foundation for strategic change." This further change effort was labeled "Bang & Olufsen United."

In late 1997, therefore, CEO Anders Knutsen set up a task force to "identify the fundamental values of Bang & Olufsen." Despite the formal mandate, the team soon redefined its purpose and explicitly positioned the company's heritage in opposition to what was described by the task force as the "drift to an international look-a-like luxury brand," which had occurred in the mid-1980s. The task force argued that the fundamental values needed to be situated "within the culture of the company." They further stated as one of their methodological principles that fundamental values could not be "constructed, claimed or copied" but should be "found, discovered and revealed."

The starting point was an investigation of the earlier and recent history of Bang & Olufsen. The group observed how the company had lost touch with its heritage during the 1980s, when the notion of "exclusivity" became essential in defining Bang & Olufsen as a producer and purveyor of luxury goods. The drift towards "exclusivity" was seen as a move away from the company's heritage embedded, according to the group, in the Bauhaus tradition reflected in the motto "Better products for a better world." The Bauhaus movement in architecture and design developed in the early 1920s around the work of the architects and designers Walter Gropius, Marcel Breuer, and Mies van der Rohe. Examples of the Bauhaus tradition were explicitly traced in early products, like the bakelite Beolit 39 cabinet radio and in the sober elegance of the first Bauhaus-inspired trademark, readopted in 1994 as part of the Break Point program. Eventually, the group identified a fundamental challenge of revitalizing the company heritage, rooted in the Bauhaus-inspired balanced combination of design, aesthetics, and technology.

The task force also interviewed leading international brand experts about their perceptions of the values behind the Bang & Olufsen identity. Interviewees generally associated Bang & Olufsen with "Balmain, Château Margoux, Dior, Mercedes; status symbols, trend setting and smartness." In other words, regardless of recent efforts by the company, they still identified Bang & Olufsen with other international luxury labels. According to the task force, these perceptions reflected a mistaken understanding of the company's past and did not capture its desired future. The task force explicitly rejected the notion of "exclusivity" insofar as it indicated that the company's products were intended only for specially selected target groups contrary to the inclusive and accessible image desired by managers.

Based on these reflections, top managers developed a new set of identity claims – defined as the three Fundamental Values – that would support Bang & Olufsen's future strategy: Excellence, Synthesis, and Poetry.

CULTURAL VALUES AND IDENTITY CLAIMS AT BANG & OLUFSEN

Both in 1993 and 1998, pressurized by competition and poor financial performance, top managers at B&O expressed an urgency to renew their organizational identity. However, while formal identity claims changed over time, their underlying meanings and practical implications seemed to display much less variation. Although changing environmental conditions and strategic goals urged managers to revise institutional claims and shared understandings about Bang & Olufsen's distinctive traits, they ultimately seemed unwilling – or unable – to depart from their organizational culture.

Invariably, the collective reflections that followed resulted in values that were perceived – and presented – as already belonging to the organization. As a member of the top management team remarked in 1998, in the early stages of the B&O

United project: "Values must be found within the company, not defined . . . Our values cannot be discussed: they are there where we have found them."

Revised identity claims were framed as a rediscovery of values that had always been part of a collective heritage. Managers illustrated new claims by referring to current practices and shared history rather than expectations of future behavior or exemplary recent actions or decisions. They supplemented analytical descriptions of identity claims with reference to established practices – routinized patterns of behavior, such as the selection of components or testing of sound reproduction – and to material expressions of distinctiveness embodied in physical artefacts such as products, advertising campaigns, corporate architecture, etc. (see Table 4). Illustrations of identity claims emerged substantially from a web of cultural expressions interpreted as the legacy of a shared past.

Rooting new claims in the organizational culture, however, did not seem to be merely a rhetorical device. Despite the initial mandate, collective reflections invariably concluded that external expectations could be met with elements that were already part of the identity but that over time had drifted aside. In 1994, for instance, the New Vision was presented and promoted partly as a result of the past and partly as an expression of an envisioned future:

> We have to adjust and adapt our identity to the coming period. Not because we want to be different or wish to change the B&O identity. On the contrary, we want to maintain and strengthen it. But over the years we have become a bit careless – so when the surrounding changes we have to adapt ourselves. To maintain our identity we thus have to renew it.
>
> (*What?* Bang & Olufsen house magazine, no. 2)

In fact, comparison of identity statements and their espoused interpretation across the three periods reveals an enduring set of cultural values underlying changes in formal identity claims. Drawing on evidence from our study and on discussions with a number of key informants, we suggest labeling these values as *Imagination, Full aesthetic experience, Uncompromising quality*, and *Simplicity of form and function* (see Table 5).

Imagination

As a company whose total sales were often less than the research budget of its main competitors, Bang & Olufsen survived through the years thanks to the creativity and ingenuity – or the "fantasy," as founders Peter Bang and Sven Olufsen used to refer to it – of its designers and engineers. As CEO Anders Knutsen observed, exploring "unconventional solutions to conventional

Table 5 Core cultural values underlying different identity claims

Excerpts from identity statements*	Core values	Manifested in	
		Collective practices	Physical artefacts
"B&O – we think differently." *(Corporate motto, 1970s)* "New approaches to solving practical tasks should characterize the company and its products." "As a small company, we cannot conduct basic research in electronics, but we can implement the newest technology with creativity and inventiveness." *(CIC – Inventiveness)* "The key to B&O's product strategy is the diversity of ideas and how they solve different tasks in different ways." "[Ours] are products that in an original – often unexpected – and elegant way solve a common problem." "We want to change the rules of the game. We want to set new trends." *(NV – Technological excellence)* "Synthesis does not mean easy solutions. We have a tendency to search one more time, to go the extra mile." "Innovation requires participation by talented people with strongly opposing views." *(FV – Synthesis)*	IMAGINATION	Dialectical interplay between external designers and engineers In-house technicians periodically embark on technological development to meet the challenges set by designers' ideas	Five Lamper (first radio powered by mains electricity) Beogram 4000 (first tangential-arm record player) Beolab 6000 (pencil-shaped loudspeakers)
"The aesthetic senses must be employed to bring together the idea behind the product, its mode of operation, and the materials used in manufacture to a state of mutual balance." *(CIC – Autovisuality)* "We appeal to human needs for pleasure, confirmation, and surprise." "Attractive design, materials, and surface treatment all support the products bearing the Bang & Olufsen name." *(NV – Emotional appeal)* "B&O creates the original, which has a substantially new message – the opening of the doors is like an unfolding flower. It talks to people." *(FV – Poetry)*	FULL AESTHETIC EXPERIENCE	Reproduction of sound and image is tested using panels of trained listeners and viewers Use of superb materials (from the walnut cabinets of earlier products to bakelite and anodized aluminum) Design of micro-mechanical movements Careful design of all the aesthetic aspects of Bang & Olufsen stores	The automatic sliding doors of CD players The multicolored covers of loudspeakers The pivoting AV9000 television, orienting towards the viewer The silent opening of the curtains of the AV5 television

Value	Quotes	Key points	Product examples
UNCOMPROMISING QUALITY	"B&O – The Danish Hallmark of Quality." *(First corporate motto, early 1930s)* "The company develops, manufactures, and markets for the people who place greater demands on quality and individuality than the average user." *(CIC – Individuality)* "It is the company's aim to manufacture products that ensure faithful reproduction of program material." "The best sound or picture reproduction is that which comes closest to reality – as experienced by human beings and not by a measuring instrument." *(CIC – Authenticity)* "No first and second class products or product categories!" "Excellence means the quality of materials and finish, and quality in performance – two of our core competences!" *(NV – Technological excellence)* "Credibility means that the wood is real wood. Honesty is a metaphor for the product and the company." "Excellence is doing things the right way, down to the smallest detail." "B&O products take time to develop. Some things can't be rushed." *(FV – Excellence)*	Only premium components selected Extreme attention to detail in product and retail design: "God is in the details" (P. Mondrian) Designers dedicate as much attention to the rear of products as to the front No compromise acceptable in product innovation	Beolab 5000 ("the world's most perfect hi-fi system") Beogram 4000 (tangential-arm record player, reproducing music the same way as recorded)
SIMPLICITY OF FORM AND FUNCTION	"Products are designed to be used by people in their homes. Technology is for the benefit of people and not the reverse. [Products] must be problem-free and easy to operate – even though they are technically advanced." "We must endeavor to present our products simply and precisely." *(CIC – Domesticity)* "We must act and communicate honestly and accurately. Product specifications must be given as minimum data to which every product must conform." *(CIC – Credibility)* "The company's products must allow immediate understanding of their capabilities and manner of operation." *(CIC – Autovisuality)* "The products must be concept-bearing. Design should be focused on the essentials of the concept. We must simplify and avoid whims and fancies that have nothing to do with the real purpose." *(CIC – Essentiality)* "Poetry is about Bauhaus, minimalism. It's a Japanese garden with a fountain." *(FV – Poetry)*	"Seamless integration" (of surfaces, commands, functions, and units) Careful design of interfaces, tested by a panel of users. Human–machine interaction The architecture and interior design of the new headquarters is inspired by functional simplicity "Better products for a better world" (Bauhaus motto)	The B&O trademark designed in 1932 and readopted in 1994 Beolit 39 (bakelite cabinet radio) Beomaster 1900 (concealed technology and easy access to music reproduction) Beolink 1000 (one-thumb, integrated remote control) The subtle understatement of graphic designer Werner Neertoft's advertisements in the 1970s

Note *CIC = The Seven CICs, 1972; NV = The New Vision, 1993; FV = The Fundamental Values, 1998 problems", unusual applications of existing technologies, and original combinations of standard components was essential in a small company in an industry of giants. As earlier managers had put it in the Seven CICs:

> As a small company, we cannot conduct basic research in electronics, but we can implement the newest technologies with creativity and inventiveness.
>
> (Seven CICs – Inventiveness, 1972)

In 1993, under the label of Technological excellence, the New Vision reaffirmed the value of creativity, pointing to the fundamental role of engineers in realizing the designers' bold ideas. A popular anecdote about the development of the Beolab 6000 loudspeaker was used to illustrate the dialectical interplay between designers and engineers. In 1999 managers elaborated on this relationship further and the anecdote was repeated in a video used to illustrate *Synthesis*, one of the Fundamental Values:

> David Lewis, the chief designer, walks in with a cardboard tube that looks like a pencil and says: this is the new B&O loudspeaker . . . He passes this on to the people in Business Development where they tear it apart and scream: that is no loudspeaker! . . . Much discussion between them and David, and then they produce a synthesis: let's make a prototype of the speaker. They then pass the prototype on to Operations. They in turn shout and scream: we can't and won't make that. After another new round of yelling a new synthesis emerges: the product . . . The following round of discussions involves Sales and Marketing: they in turn claim that nobody will buy it. Endless fights result in a new synthesis: the marketing concept. Now marketing has the problem. The dealers kick up a fuss, claiming it won't sell. The result is a new synthesis: how to present the product in the stores . . . Half a day later it has been sold. That's the way we work.

Eventually, *Synthesis* came to be associated with innovation and the ability to realize ideas that initially seemed unachievable.

Full aesthetic experience

From the outset, Peter Bang and Sven Olufsen displayed a rare attention to the aesthetics of product design: products used superb materials and tried to appeal not only to the ear but also to the eye. During the 1960s, attention to design and user experience intensified under the leadership of the product developer, Jens Bang, and the chief designer, Jacob Jensen. Panels of trained listeners and viewers were set up to test the fidelity of sound and image reproduction as perceived by human senses rather than by an artificial device. Design principles codified in the Seven CICs (see Table 5) underpinned an approach to product design that, as one of our informants put it, unlike most of its competitors started from users and developed products around them rather than the other way around. *Emotional Appeal* and, later, *Poetry* were illustrated by the silent opening and closing of the infra-red-controlled sliding doors of Bang & Olufsen CD players or the multicolored covers of loudspeakers.

In 1992, while other facilities were closed and production outsourced, managers saved a small plant where a complex anodizing process produced a particular surface treatment on aluminum which gave Bang & Olufsen products a unique look and feel. As CEO Anders Knutsen told us, referring to a competitor striving to imitate Bang & Olufsen:

> Just because they have hired Philippe Starck to design a TV set, they think they have become like Bang & Olufsen! But it's not just the look: it's the way a product smells, the way it feels to the touch that makes the difference.

In 1998, the value of *Poetry* emphasized the excitement and emotion that customers (and employees) experienced in Bang & Olufsen's products. In a corporate video illustrating the new identity statement, *Poetry* was defined as the "difference between Bang & Olufsen products, such as the new integrated AV5 system, and products by SONY and Philips." One manager explicitly related *Poetry* to the way products were designed, as he observed: "Poetry is the surprising, silent opening of the doors and the unfolding of the product like a flower."

Uncompromising quality

Bang & Olufsen's first corporate motto, "The Danish Hallmark of Quality," reflected the founders' extreme attention to the quality of design, components, and manufacturing. Even after the loss of the founders, managers at B&O maintained strict quality standards, manifested for instance in the exclusive purchase of premium components and in the careful testing of sound and image reproduction. In the 1950s, the new company motto – "For those who discuss design and quality before price" – reaffirmed the centrality of quality and product integrity.

Quality, however, was also reflected in painstaking attention to detail in design and manufacturing, as testified by the adoption of artist Piet Mondrian's words, "God is in the detail," as a corporate slogan. The Seven CICs, and later the concepts of Technological excellence in 1993 and Excellence in 1998, elaborated on the concept, emphasizing at different times the authenticity of the products and materials, the strict quality standards, and the attention to detail.

Simplicity of form and function

Simplicity and essentiality seem to have characterized the philosophy of the company and the design of its products since the very beginning (Bang and Palshøy, 2000). As previously stated, the influence of the Bauhaus movement in art and design is evident in early material expressions of the company: from the first B&O logo, dated 1932 and readopted in 1994, to products like the bakelite Beolit 39 radio. Later, the Seven CICs elaborated on the concept, observing how simplicity should inspire concept development (*Essentiality*), the design of human–machine interfaces (*Domesticity* and *Autovisuality*), and even customer information (*Credibility*).

Over the years the search for simplicity inspired such milestones as the Beomaster 1900 audio system, where user interfaces were designed to facilitate access to music reproduction, and the one-thumb integrated remote control, the Beolink 1000, connected to all the video and audio sources in a house (Bang and Palshøy, 2000). During the 1990s, managers defined "seamless integration" as a core capability underpinning an elegant visual style and the capacity to simplify connections between commands, functions, and units. Eventually, in 1998, the team in charge of the revision of identity claims saw in the revitalization of the simplicity and sobriety associated with the Bauhaus tradition a way of recovering from the drift towards luxury and status.

Reference to the Bauhaus tradition led managers to associate *Excellence* with "simplicity and modesty" and the company's ability to "make choices on the basis of patience and persistence, honesty and decency." Excellence was illustrated through the spare and functional design of an egg or nail, and contrasted with the image of "exclusivity" that was equated with snobbery, opulence, lavishness, and fashion – or, using the group's own metaphors, with "gold, marble and empty palaces." A manager referred to anodized aluminum, a widely used material in Bang & Olufsen products, as a practical illustration of the concept: "Aluminum is excellence. Gold is exclusive."

DISCUSSION

The case of Bang & Olufsen that we have summarized in this chapter highlights the connections between organizational culture and identity, and illustrates how members may draw on a rich web of stories, myths, symbols, and artefacts reflecting deep underlying cultural values in their conscious efforts to make sense of central, distinctive, and enduring features of their organization. Furthermore, the way that managers at Bang & Olufsen managed different threats to their identity over time suggests a possible strategy for coping with conflicting pressures for continuity and change in organizations, based on the periodic revision of identity claims, offering new interpretations of otherwise untouched underlying cultural values.

Organizational culture and the construction of organizational identities

At Bang & Olufsen, as managers engaged in the revision of identity claims, they found in visible and tangible expressions of organizational culture a rich source of cues to make sense of core and distinctive features of the organization. Significant milestones of technological innovation and distinctive design were highlighted as managers reflected on the company's inherent ability to create products that were perceived as genuinely distinctive and interacting with customers in new ways. These unique products were interpreted as manifestations of established practices in areas such as product development (pursuing simple, self-explanatory excellence; avoiding the lowest common denominator; adapting manufacturing to design rather than the reverse), design management (e.g., use of talented external designers), and attitudes towards the marketplace (never imitate mainstream players such as Sony and Philips). Organizational stories and myths – such as the development of the Penta loudspeakers, the "impossible" task of developing the AV5 TV, or Bang & Olufsen's special exhibition at the Museum of Modern Art in New York – helped managers to situate and make sense of established practices and the underlying values.

What we observed at Bang & Olufsen is illustrative of a more general phenomenon (see Figure 13). The idea that tangible, material differences in product design or the content of advertising reflect deeper, less visible differences in goals, values, and competencies is not new (Olins, 1989). When these cultural expressions – products, practices, myths, etc. – are perceived as a legacy of a shared past they provide members with a sense of continuity. When they are interpreted as material manifestations of distinctiveness, they act as a reservoir of cues helping members understand what makes their organization unique; and when

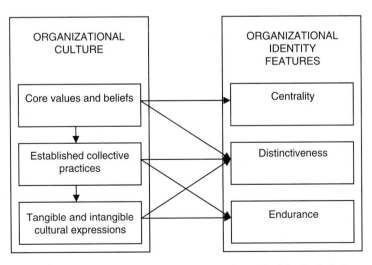

Figure 13 *Organizational culture as a source of cues for identity beliefs*

expressions of differentiation are related to past achievements, they become embedded in the cultural heritage of the organization and can plausibly be interpreted as manifestations of fundamental values that have been central to survival and to the company.

In this respect, cultural practices and organizational artefacts provide members engaged in the re-evaluation of their organization's identity with a less ambiguous starting point than, for instance, formal values, goals, and mission statements, which often reflect managerial aspirations or image-management tactics. As members face a highly ambiguous cognitive task – such as answering the question "What is this organization really about?" – familiar manifestations of a shared culture may provide them with a starting point for making sense of their organizational identity.

Change and continuity in identity claims and beliefs

The concept of "identity threat" refers to environmental changes that challenge the prospective viability of current conceptualizations of the organization and of the strategies that rest on them. Indeed, at Bang & Olufsen, between 1972 and 1998, competitive threats and environmental changes questioned existing identity claims and beliefs on three occasions and induced top managers to reflect on core and distinctive traits of the company.

In organizations, internal and external forces may urge members to revise their core beliefs in order to cope with new expectations and adapt to new requirements (Bouchikhi and Kimberly, 2003). External and internal occurrences that challenge organizational claims and beliefs are, however, likely to trigger individual and collective responses aimed at countering identity-threatening events and preserving personal and external perceptions of what the organization is or stands for (Elsbach and Kramer, 1996; Golden-Biddle and Rao, 1997). New conceptualizations that are perceived as incoherent with the organizational history and tradition and with members' sense of self are likely to be rejected, along with the changes they are expected to promote (Humphreys and Brown, 2002).

Organizational leaders, therefore, often find themselves struggling with conflicting pressures for continuity and change in self-conceptualizations. While inertia may not be a desirable option in the face of external changes, internal resistance makes radical transformation – conceived as a substantial change in identity claims and beliefs – barely feasible. In fact, there are very few organizations that have successfully managed to rapidly and smoothly become "something else," as radical identity changes tend to occur only in exceptional circumstances or when the very survival of the organization is threatened (Albert and Whetten, 1985).

In order to reconcile inherent tensions between change and the endurance of identity traits, organizations may undergo periods of *adaptive instability*, in which

118

the labels that define core values may remain stable, while members of the organization periodically renegotiate the attached meanings, ensuring a smooth adaptation to changing internal and external conditions (Gioia, Schultz, and Corley, 2000). The case we have described suggests a complementary perspective, which we may label as *identity reclaim*, whereby connection with cultural practices and artefacts may contribute to preserve a sense of self in spite of a shifting array of identity claims (see Figure 14).

At Bang & Olufsen, top managers implemented "continuity within change" by periodically selecting subsets of identity claims that on the one hand were firmly rooted in established practices and embodied in cultural forms (and therefore preserved a sense of self and continuity) and on the other addressed changing external conditions by refocusing people's attention onto subsets of values that were salient to the current strategic context (see Table 3).

New identity claims were presented as an expression of values, behaviors, and experiences that were already part of the organization, but that needed to be articulated and given renewed prominence in order to realign collective understandings so that each member could contribute effectively to counter external threats. Objects, images, stories, anecdotes, slogans, and other cultural expressions were used as concrete illustrations of values, attitudes, and behaviors, which, in the managers' view, should support the strategic response to environmental changes.

Embedding new claims within the culture of the organization helped managers to preserve a sense of self and continuity in the face of changing self-definitions. Changes in identity claims are likely to generate distress and encounter resistance. Enriching the illustration of identity claims with specific details from the company's history and culture, however, helps to convincingly present them as a "rediscovery" of shared values. This emphasizes the connection with "who we have been" rather than "who we want to become," and provides credible support to a claim of continuity in the face of a management-driven attempt to refocus collective attention in view of new environmental conditions.

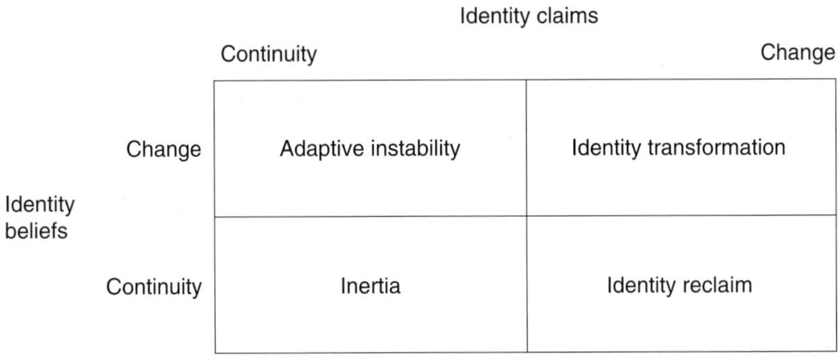

Identity claims

		Continuity	Change
Identity beliefs	Change	Adaptive instability	Identity transformation
	Continuity	Inertia	Identity reclaim

Figure 14 Responding to pressures for continuity and change

KEY QUESTIONS

1 As external pressure induces members to ask themselves "What is this organization *really* about? What do we *really* stand for?", organizational culture gives stability to identity claims and beliefs. What are the benefits and the disadvantages of this phenomenon?

2 What seems to have occurred at Bang & Olufsen is a revision of identity claims, which did not substantially alter members' collective sense of self. Nevertheless, it had positive effects on the future development of the company and on its capacity to face external challenges. How can this happen?

3 At Bang & Olufsen, essential reaffirmation of core and distinctive features was eventually crucial for the survival of the company. Under what conditions is a profound change of identity beliefs required? How can managers cope with conflicting needs for change and stability in collective self-perceptions?

4 At Bang & Olufsen, products and product features were central to members' reflections and debate about the identity of the organization. Is this pattern generalizable? To what types of organization? If not, what could replace products in driving interorganizational comparison and reflections on identity features?

5 The search for further expansion has led Bang & Olufsen to engage in co-branding initiatives with Samsung (phones) and Audi (audio equipment for cars). Do you think this will challenge the organizational culture and collective self-perceptions? How far can organizational strategies "stretch and adapt" the identity of the organization before internal and external tensions offset the expected benefits of the alliances?

6 In 2006, in an interview in a Danish newspaper celebrating the collaboration with Samsung, the current CEO, Torben Ballegaard Sørensen, traced a link between the expanding scope of operations and the preservation of a clear identity when he stated: "When the world becomes global, a very strong identity is the all-encompassing goal – what we call the company DNA." Yet, how can companies balance the need to "be themselves" with the need to adapt to local requirements and specificities?

Chapter 7

An identity-based internationalization process

The BP and Statoil alliance

Lin Lerpold

INTRODUCTION

Before its alliance with BP, Statoil was undergoing a strategic change to internationalize its operations. As Gioia and Thomas (1996) found, strategic change can be a trigger to evaluate organizational identity in terms of identity, image, and desired future identity. Statoil earned a good proportion of its income outside Norway and maintained operations in North America, Asia, and numerous countries in Europe. Yet this was not sufficient for the organization to feel international. Instead, the definition of being "international," and thus by definition "successful," was related to an internalized self-conception along with a publicly recognized and accepted image of Statoil as an international corporation. Statoil wanted to change its identity beliefs and organizational image from that of a relatively little-known domestic firm to that of a successful, international company. Respondents discussed Statoil's "desire to become" something other than it was. The self-conception of Statoil respondents about their organization was to a large extent dominated by a sense of being a domestic, state-owned company with a traditional minor emphasis or focus on international projects. They believed that they were already a "successful" company, but to become and be considered a "major player" they had to become "serious" in the international arena: the alliance with BP was the first step in this proclaimed process of adapting their identity.

In this chapter we illustrate organizational identity dynamics within the context of a strategic alliance between the Norwegian oil company Statoil and the larger, multinational British Petroleum (BP). The identity dynamics are illuminated through understanding Statoil's identity aspirations to be an international player and the company's partnering with the more internationally recognized BP as a vehicle for adapting its organizational identity and image. The case describes how Statoil, stating the publicly articulated motive of learning or transferring international knowledge or internationalization skills from BP, attempted to adapt their organizational identity from "national" to "international." Thus, using the context of an alliance partnership, we explore organizational identity and image, identity aspirations, interorganizational emulation, and cognitive strategic reference group dynamics.

THEORETICAL POINTS OF DEPARTURE

In line with extant theories of organizational identity, the separate concepts of organizational identity and organizational image are especially important. The study of organizational identity at different units of analysis is not a new construct in the organizational literature; rather it has resurfaced in the context of turbulence, diversity, and rapidly changing technology. The remarkable heterogeneity of contemporary society naturally leads to changing and reassessed organizational identities. Identity (as the way insiders make claims about how they see their organization and how they believe their organization is viewed externally), identity beliefs, and organizational images are seen as dynamically intertwined. Acknowledgement of this interrelationship can be traced from individual or personal identity theories (Cooley, 1902) to more recent work at organizational identity level (Albert and Whetten, 1985; Dutton and Dukerich, 1991; Gioia and Thomas, 1996). Organizational image has had numerous conceptualizations in different fields. The most prevailing view, used in recent studies of organizational identity, is based on Dutton and Dukerich's (1991) definition. In their study of the attempts by the New York/New Jersey Port Authority to deal with the problem of homeless people frequenting their facilities, they argued that the perceived deterioration of image was an important impetus for action, leading to changes in identity. Discrepancies between identity and image were thus linked to adaptation processes and organizational strategic action.

Organizational identity or future desired identity is purposely represented in what has been termed a "projected image" (Gioia and Thomas, 1996; Gioia, Schultz, and Corley, 2000). A projected image is focused on an externally projected identity in order to convey a socially desired and managed impression rather than necessarily some ostensible reality (Bernstein, 1984). Berg (1985) went even further by defining image as the public's perception or impression of an organization, usually associated with a given action or event. Corporate identity and image can be understood as a form of manipulated projected image. Theorists in the areas of public relations and marketing have been most concerned with the visual representations of the corporation, most clearly manifested in the design and management of corporate symbols and logos (see e.g., Hatch and Schultz, 1997). In this instance, it is natural to associate identity with reputation. Reputation is how the external world defines an organization; though that reputation impacts on an organization's self-reflection (identity), it is not a component part. They depend on and feed off one another, and whether they are coupled depends on the actions that different actors take to manage their identities and their reputations (Rao, 1994). Though informants regularly use terms such as "corporate" and "reputation," as reported in this case when referring to our understanding of organization and image, and since there are many conceptualizations of organizational identity within the organization and in marketing and strategy research fields, for the sake of simplicity we will use here the understanding of organizational images when referring to the different facets of organizational and corporate image and reputation.

Furthermore, social identity theories posit that groups engage in categorization, identification, and comparison in their construction of a self-image (Tajfel and Turner, 1979) or pursuit of a positive social identity. The view of self is thus socially defined and derived largely from membership of certain social categories (Ashford, 2001). Organizational identity is formed through membership of formal groups or through benchmarking processes (Gioia, 1998), or through more informal networks: the industry to which one belongs, the organizational form used, or through the membership of accrediting bodies (Sarason, 1998a) and cognitive strategic reference groups (Peteraf and Shanley, 1997). By identifying, individuals within organizations perceive their organization as psychologically intertwined with the fate of the social category, sharing its common destiny and experiencing its successes and failures (Deaux, 1996). And, as individuals, groups, or organizations begin to identify, they usually assume the perceived prototypical or exemplary characteristics of the category as their own (Ashford, 2001). A key concept in this area is in-group and out-group dynamics. Thus, group memberships play an important role in defining the self, with people using the salient dimensions of groups to which they belong to define the salient dimensions of themselves (Tyler, 2001). Role prototypes or models are important for identity construction (Ashford, 2001; Ibarra, 1999) and, in the same way that individuals model themselves on other individuals, firms emulate other firms with an admired image and reputation. The choice of role model influences changes in image and identity (Elsbach and Kramer, 1996; Labianca *et al.*, 2001).

THE STATOIL–BP ALLIANCE

The alliance between BP and Statoil was announced in August 1990. The two companies were to cooperate in exploration and production in three regions: Southeast Asia, the former Soviet Union, and West Africa, at that time considered the world's most promising geographical areas. The companies also intended to cooperate in marketing natural gas to continental Europe and jointly to fund technological research and development. This study is located in the strategically most important and largest part of the alliance, international exploration and production. The alliance lasted until February 1999, a period of eight and a half

123

years. The end of the alliance coincided with the BP and AMOCO merger, which was given as the official reason for termination.

While BP started in Iran in 1901 as a privately held international company, wholly state-owned Statoil had a more recent and domestic beginning in 1972 (Yergin, 1991; Ritchie, 1995). Statoil's first international project involved legal, economic, and technical advice on exploration and production for the Chinese government in 1979. Six years later, in 1985, Statoil was awarded a small project in the Netherlands and two small projects in China. In 1986, the company was further awarded small projects in Denmark and the UK. Though the list of international projects began to expand, none of the projects was considered very promising, and expected investments and associated profits were minimal. The global trend and political acceptance of internationalization strategies in Norway during the mid-1980s was a significant change in Norwegian political policy (Ryggvik, 2000). Given the fact that Statoil was at the time a wholly state-owned company, very much considered the property of the Norwegian people, there was surprisingly little national debate on the company's internationalization. In fact, the Norwegian government approved Statoil's "internationalization" plans without debate or committee analysis (Ryggvik, 2000).

In 1989, Statoil consulted with McKinsey & Company to evaluate the company's international efforts. The report (McKinsey & Co., 1989) was written in close cooperation with Statoil management and thus represents the strategic thinking on internationalization at the company in the late 1980s. McKinsey's conclusion was that Statoil's lone efforts had failed miserably; however, they maintained that the company should pursue an international strategy in the exploration and production arena. The McKinsey report did not discuss the requirements for successful international operations, nor did it analyze Statoil's organizational competencies. It did, however, discuss four areas where the consultants believed Statoil had a competitive advantage. All three areas were connected to the political arena, or Norway as a country, represented by Statoil. The company could have an advantage in countries where Norway had contributed substantial development funds, where it was important to be perceived as state-owned rather than "capitalist," and where the interest and influence of the Norwegian government could be traded for interest and influence in frontier countries. In the McKinsey analysis it is significant that no importance is attached to intra-firm organizational competencies or resources. Three strategies for becoming an international exploration and production company were also discussed in the report: "go it alone," "acquisition," and "partnership." Though none of the three strategies was actually recommended in the report, Statoil eventually chose partnership in the alliance with BP.

BP's motives for the alliance with Statoil appeared much simpler. Going from producing in excess of 3 million barrels per day in the 1970s to only 1.5 million barrels per day in the 1980s meant a significant decline in profits (Yergin, 1991).

Compounding this was the fact that BP's production was strongly concentrated in high unit cost production, particularly in the British part of the North Sea and the United States. In addition to its declining production portfolio, BP's profits from downstream activities were also severely hit by the oil price fall from 1986. There is evidence that BP was actively trying to increase its production by exploring for low unit cost production possibilities in frontier areas in the latter half of the 1980s (Ritchie, 1995). Frontier areas were associated with high financial and political risks, which BP had experienced first hand in both Iran and Nigeria when the company's assets were nationalized in both countries in 1979. By the late 1980s, therefore, BP was in urgent need of financial assistance for current operations and future exploration, while Statoil was still earning enormous profits – and would continue do so for some time – from huge oilfields on the Norwegian continental shelf.

STATOIL STRUCTURES BEFORE THE ALLIANCE

In 1989, shortly before the alliance with BP, Statoil had many operations outside Norway. Its Danish wholly owned subsidiary operated 400 retail outlets, a refinery, and a sales office for plastic raw materials. In addition, the company was involved in Denmark in offshore exploration drilling. Similarly, Statoil's Swedish subsidiary ran 450 retail outlets, a petrochemicals business and plant, and a sales office for plastic raw materials. In Germany the company also had a sales office for plastic raw materials; it further operated a plant specializing in petrochemical products and was exploring for oil offshore. In the Netherlands, Statoil was involved in exploration activities in the Dutch North Sea, and in Finland and France the company had sales offices for plastic raw materials. In Great Britain, the company participated in exploration in the British North Sea; it also marketed oil, gas, plastic raw materials, and other products worldwide. In Belgium, Statoil was joint owner of a plant under construction near Antwerp for the production of propylene and polypropylene. In North America, Statoil sold crude oil and products to the American market from its sales office in Manhattan, and in Asia the company was involved in offshore exploration and production in China and was also preparing to participate in the development of a major offshore gas field in Thailand. The following figures, in Norwegian kronor (NOK million), are drawn from Statoil's annual reports and accounts from 1989 to 1991:

	1988	1989	1990	1991
Total net operating income	47,291	59,594	72,356	78,292
Total foreign sales	31,169	44,103	53,007	60,202

Thus, at alliance formation, much of Statoil's revenues were generated internationally. The firm had international subsidiaries and sales offices and was involved in projects in Europe, North America, and Asia. By most measures Statoil was a large company, and international in structure and revenue. Yet, as we will show below, the organizational identity was clearly embedded in that of a domestic company aspiring to be, and be seen as, an international corporation.

ALLIANCE FORMATION AS A TOOL FOR IDENTITY AND IMAGE ADAPTATION

Identity beliefs

The desire of Statoil managers for the company to be perceived as a successful international oil company, both by the international oil industry and internally by itself, was a significant motive for the alliance. It was speculated that Statoil wished to be regarded as a "major player" and could do so by allying with an acknowledged "major player" such as BP. Further, Statoil could use BP as a role model in finding its feet as an international corporation. Managers at both companies discussed the alliance as a vehicle to adapt Statoil's internally held organizational identity and to change the externally construed image or reputation. Though more economically rational motives for this alliance were discussed, changing the company's perceived identity and organizational images was often inferred:

> This is where I saw it coming from. It was through bringing the companies together to share ideas, share cost, share technology, and use the big brain. The other aspect was Statoil's side. Statoil was looking for ways of getting into the international oil and gas business. They wanted to become a really international company and they knew they had to change their *mindset and reputation*. Everyone knows that Statoil is using BP in the alliance to do just that.
>
> (BP manager, 1997)

As the above informant describes, "mindset and reputation" can easily be understood as the internally perceived organizational identity and organizational images. Statoil's identity was often referred to as domestic or national, meaning in this case Norwegian. On identity, both BP and Statoil managers believed that although Statoil had numerous international operations and had been successful on the Norwegian continental shelf, the main reason for its perceived lack of success was a lack of organizational and political self-confidence rather than a genuine lack of resources, knowledge, or skills. Furthermore, respondents felt that the Norwegian government, which wholly controlled Statoil, was very wary about investing large sums of money outside Norway over long periods. Thus, what appeared to be a lack of self-confidence was in part a consequence of what some termed the "mindset" of Statoil employees.

However, being "international" was not only about having substantial investments overseas or being geographically dispersed, but rather about changing the mindset of employees – both those working abroad and those at home. The following quotation illustrates the apparent paradox between being structurally internationally dispersed yet cognitively domestically anchored in identity beliefs and organizational image:

> Well, the alliance with BP was important, but more for legitimacy than anything else. I know that in the beginning we talked about learning all sorts of things, but we're just as good as they are. Probably better in a lot of areas. I go around and hold all these presentations, and I try to get our people to understand that we already are international. They just don't seem to get it. Look [shows us overhead materials of Statoil's operations]: we are all over the world and have been so from the start. You can't be in the industry without being by definition "international." We participate with foreign firms in equity projects both here in Norway and abroad. We transport oil and gas through international pipelines. We sell crude oil in the international commodities market from offices in Asia. And we do it all well! It's not about becoming international. We already are. It's about getting our people to accept and understand it . . . and yes, act like it!
>
> (Statoil corporate manager, 1997 [translated from Norwegian])

Organizational image

The reported alliance motives addressed how Statoil itself believed the international oil industry perceived the company. According to respondents, a major theme was the importance of having the reputation and image of an international "player." A positive organizational image (meaning an international image) was thus discussed as being an important part in gaining access to interesting exploration projects in the frontier areas where major oil discoveries were expected. Apparently, in the words of informants, BP had the international reputation whereas Statoil lacked it. We explored further what this "reputation" actually consisted of: though having a good international reputation presumably consisted of possessing unique competencies, it was argued that "reputation" was more about an organizational image built up over a considerable period than any actual possession of specific competencies. In other words, even though a company such as Statoil may have developed capabilities as strong as any other company, without a prominent international "reputation" it would not be as successful internationally as a more internationally reputed corporation:

To be successful in negotiating with governments in the peculiar places where oil is found, you have to have a good international reputation or at least an image of being a successful oil company. It doesn't really matter whether or not you are actually any good, that will come out at a later stage. It's all about what they [meaning the developing countries] have heard about you that matters.

(Statoil middle manager, 1997 [translated from Norwegian])

The trouble with the thing at the moment is that everybody seems to *want to become* an international, global company. It's the flavor of the year or something. I think those people think it must somehow be good to be considered an international company. And I suppose, you know, for Statoil, and the same with all of the other exploration and production (E&P) companies, E&P upstream skills are transferable around the world, and there isn't a special knowledge of any particular thing that means that you have to stay rooted in Norway. You can take those skills elsewhere, which is probably why all of the E&P companies are *looking to be international*.

(BP engineer, 1997)

If you are going to be seen as *a real player* in the E&P business you have to be *considered* an international company, rather than a domestic one like Statoil. Who better to learn from than BP?

(BP engineer, 1997)

However, BP too was interested in overcoming what it perceived as its negatively laden and unfairly held *externally construed* image – though not internal organizational image – of being an "old, colonial oil company." This was to be achieved by allying with, and fronting, Statoil as a state-owned, traditional "national oil company." It was argued that newly emerging oil- and gas-producing nations, such as Nigeria and Vietnam, were keen to establish their own national oil companies. Fronting a perceived "successful" national oil company like Statoil was expected to improve the potential for good relations, successful negotiations, and a more palatable BP involvement. Added to this were the anticipated "anti-imperialist/capitalist" sentiments, seen in Nigeria, where BP's assets had been nationalized in 1979. It was assumed that any repeat involvement of BP in Nigeria was feasible only with less visibility. Projecting another, more "positive" organizational image to governments in developing countries by fronting the more neutrally perceived, Norwegian Statoil was assumed to be a main reason for entering the alliance for BP. Though BP was concerned with its externally construed image, it was less concerned about its internally perceived identity beliefs or image.

Thus, the motives for alliance formation for Statoil were related to the benefits of allying with an acknowledged international player. This component is related to the first two since it was used more as a tool to facilitate the internal and external adaptation processes. As with playing the national oil company card, allying with another company reinforced what was believed to be a more positive external image: in this way BP could be seen as less colonial, and Statoil more internationally competent, by association. Though BP respondents discussed their external "colonial" image, they felt that they were neither imperialistic nor colonial, and were thus not especially concerned about adapting their organizational identity. Statoil, on the other hand, was interested in changing both its perceived internally held identity and its externally construed image. By allying with an international "player" like BP it could believe that it too was an international "player."

IDENTITY ASPIRATIONS, COGNITIVE STRATEGIC IN-GROUP, EMULATION, AND ROLE MODELING

According to respondents, Statoil wished to join the group of international oil companies considered the most successful. This included Shell, Mobil, Texaco, Elf, Agip, and Conoco, in addition to BP, and thus comprised Statoil's cognitive strategic reference group (Peteraf and Shanley, 1997). Statoil wanted to be seen to be in the same league as these organizations – as one respondent put it, to "join the top table" (Norwegian geologist, translated from the Norwegian adage "invitert i det fine selskapet"). However, not only did Statoil want to be perceived as in the same group, it wanted to become *like* those organizations. In this way, the organizations at the "top table" were perceived as collectively embodying characteristics that could be appropriated. The following illustrate this motive:

> Statoil had grand plans. They wanted to join the gang of major exploration and production players. I know they were contemplating several other companies before the alliance with BP was announced. I've heard Shell was a serious possibility. Anyway, the alliance with BP was, at least from Statoil's side, a means to hook up with the right connections. With BP guiding them, they thought that they overnight could become a major international company.
>
> (BP middle manager, 1997)

> Let's face it, Statoil's riding on our coat tails.
>
> (BP manager, 1995)

Alliance formation motives also included emulation and use of BP as a prototypical in-group role model. There was a belief that Statoil would learn about how to be and act as an international company from the recognized international company BP. Typical examples reported by respondents were imitating practices in business processes and procedures associated with international operations. For

129

instance, changes in dress from less to more formal and in the company's working language from Norwegian to English were also symbolic manifestations reported by respondents:

> I think it was clear from our point of view that it was about international-ization and learning. BP would teach Statoil about what it really means *to be an international player*. They are obviously not best at everything even though they seem to think they are. But the rest of the international industry still looks up to BP even though they keep making mistakes. In that way, they could be a pretty *good role model*. We could learn from their experiences and kind of copy what works well and fits with our organization.
>
> (Statoil manager, 1999)

Thus, BP's motive for the alliance was to utilize Statoil's more palatable national oil company organizational image, particularly in Nigeria, while Statoil's motive was to change its identity beliefs and its organizational image by using BP as a role model and an entrance ticket to the industry strategic in-group.

ORGANIZATIONAL IDENTITY ADAPTATION AS A MOTIVE FOR THE ALLIANCE

Statoil's organizational image, or what it believed was its external image, seemed fairly consistent with its perceived organizational identity or self-conception. The belief was that outsiders viewed it as a successful, albeit domestic, state-owned company. This belief was reinforced by the strategy of fronting Statoil in the alliance, when it was felt politically/strategically advantageous to do so, in negoti-ations with emerging oil nations interested in establishing their own national oil companies. Despite a wish to become strongly established in the international field, along with the economic strength to do so, the fact remains that Statoil had only invested in minor, dispersed international projects before partnering with BP. This supports the argument that Statoil's identity beliefs mirrored its organiza-tional image in being primarily domestic and state-owned in nature.

Adapting Statoil's organizational identity involved the construction of a desired future or new possible identity (Gioia and Thomas, 1996) in the company's aspiration to be international. Who it wanted to be in the future was not specified exactly, but was rather more vaguely described as "internationally suc-cessful" and a "major player." By allying with BP, Statoil could – by "basking in reflected glory" (Ashford, 2001) or by association – become part of the in-group and assume the in-group's attributes and characteristics through a type of "legitimate peripheral participation" (Lave and Wenger, 1991). Allying with BP as a role model, or prototypical member of the in-group, also allowed Statoil to experiment with and adapt to a new "possible self" (Markus and Nurius, 1986) or "possible social identity" (Cinnirella, 1998). What it really meant to be an international company could be experienced through close proximity with BP: this would allow the company to try out "provisional selves" (Ibarra, 1999), as exemplified by respondents' reports of Statoil's proclivity to choose and/or imitate "best practices," such as an international operations manual, attire, or language that were in line with the company's own organizational sense of self.

In the study we found that Statoil's identity was fairly well mirrored in its image. Rather than a disjuncture between the two, it was the changing contextual environment in which Statoil was embedded that was the impetus for strategic change. Since the diminishing oil reserves on the Norwegian continental shelf necessitated a change in Statoil's initial purpose, maintaining a going concern served as an impetus or trigger for a perceived need to adapt the company's organizational identity from domestic to international. As the mirror image of the firm's organizational identity seemed fairly congruent, it was identity aspirations rather than discrepancies between image and identity (Dutton and Dukerich, 1991) that drove the adaptation process. These identity aspirations provided the necessary link to organizational action – "action" in this case being an alliance between BP and Statoil. BP was chosen as a prototypical member of the in-group, or what Elsbach and Kramer (1996) term Statoil's perceived "strategic reference group." This type of self-categorization, as described by social identity theories, resulted in interorganizational emulation (Labianca et al., 2001) involving both cooperation and competition between the alliance partners.

The focus of this chapter has mainly been on Statoil's organizational identity adaptation, since this was the most obviously identified in our case study. However, organizational identity can also be understood in BP's motives to ally with Statoil. Rather than a motive of organizational identity adaptation, BP was concerned with its "construed external image" (Dutton, Dukerich, and Harquail, 1994) and socially desired "projected image" (Gioia and Thomas, 1996). BP respondents were concerned about what they believed was their external image of being an old-fashioned, colonial, and imperialistic oil company. Though BP respondents felt that this assumed negative image was not aligned with their own "internally perceived identity" (Dutton, Dukerich, and Harquail, 1994), it was clear that allying with, and sometimes fronting, Statoil, perceived as a successful national oil company (NOC) from a politically neutral country, was an attempt to manage or project a more positive corporate identity and image. Inconsistency of identity and image is seen as a trigger for organizational identity adaptation through strategic action (Gioia and Thomas, 1996; Gioia, Schultz, and Corley 2000). In this case BP recognized that its identity and image beliefs and its construed external image were unacceptable, and for this reason it allied strategically with Statoil to project a more positive external image.

Whether or not BP or Statoil actually adapted their organizational identity through the alliance is not clear and outside the scope of the study. Though the vehicle for adaptation is ambiguous, some anecdotal evidence implies that Statoil had adapted its identity after the alliance was terminated. New Statoil-operated, large-scale exploration and production projects were undertaken at the same time as BP and Statoil competed for large projects in different international regions. Changes in the respect afforded to Statoil by BP respondents interviewed in 1995 and 2000 can be seen as changes in Statoil's identity and image. Respondents discussed that initially they had not truly understood the strengths of Statoil as an organization. They also discussed their perception that the company had developed and learned a great deal during the alliance period. Changes in Statoil's "perceived organizational identity" and "construed external image" are also well documented in interviews with Statoil respondents. Here, it is clear that there was a strong change from feelings of inferiority and out-group dynamics to feelings of superiority and "what do we need them for?" sentiments as the alliance progressed. This is supported by the fact that BP pulled out of the Statoil-operated Nigeria alliance project, leaving a self-confident, independent Statoil. Finally, the fact that Statoil was partially privatized on the Norwegian Stock Exchange in 2001 further supports the notion that its identity had changed from a small, domestic, national oil company to a successful, large, multinational oil company.

CONCLUSION

Changes in what the literature defines as "identity" (Albert and Whetten, 1985; Elsbach and Kramer, 1996; Gioia and Thomas, 1996), including both organizational self-conception and organizational image, were important motives for this alliance. For BP, this involved changing the organization's negatively construed external image in emerging nations through association with the more positively perceived national oil company Statoil. For Statoil, this involved adapting its identity beliefs and organizational image from primarily a domestic, state-owned company to an international, commercially oriented firm. This specific purpose was not printed in any official alliance documents examined, nor was it mentioned in either the press or internally in company materials. Furthermore, the term "identity" was not commonly mentioned in interviews. However, the wish to see and be seen differently organizationally was a dominant theme in the motive for this alliance. In the case of BP, the trigger for change can be understood as a discrepancy between identity and image, where respondents felt that BP had an unfairly negative image. For Statoil, the matter was not so much a discrepancy between identity and image but rather an "identity gap" (Reger et al., 1994) between current and aspired, or future desired identity (Gioia, Schultz, and Corley, 2000). Finally, Statoil was interested in joining the in-group of internationally recognized "major players." As a prototypical member of the aspired in-group, BP served as an organizational role model, and joint alliance teams served as the setting for emulation and imitation. The case also introduces organizational identity-based emulation and collaboration with a reputed role model as an important, additional, and complementary motive for alliance formation. We saw that BP was viewed as a prototypical member, suitable to be an organizational role model for the organization Statoil aspired to be.

The study also illustrates organizational identity in practice by showing that some organizations enter into alliances because of a desire to change their organizational identity. Organizational identity research has mostly been the study of individuals and groups within a firm or the individuals' identification with an organization. The present study of how a firm adapts its organizational identity, through the use of an organizational role model and interorganizational emulation, contributes to social identity and organizational identity theories by introducing the field of interfirm cooperation at a more macro, or industry, level. For individuals and social groups, the case illustrates that some organizations adapt their organizational identity through self-categorization and in-group/out-group dynamics among, for instance, industry-strategic reference groups (Elsbach and Kramer, 1996; Peteraf and Shanley, 1997). Further, joining the debates in the field of organizational identity, it provides support for arguments that there is a significant interdependence of the organization's own sense of self and its image (e.g., Dutton and Dukerich, 1991; Gioia, Schultz, and Corley, 2000). The case documents the "cognitive distress or identity dissonance" (Elsbach and Kramer, 1996) of BP – illustrated by its attempt to project a more socially sensitive image through an alliance with Statoil – and of Statoil by its attempt, through an alliance with BP, to project an image of being an international firm, thus attaining in-group membership. In this way, the cognitive dissonance between identity and image was in part a motive for alliance formation for both partners. This study also raises the issue of whether an organizational identity can be purposely adapted. An institutional perspective would argue that though organizational identity may change in a "convergent" and "evolutionary" manner (Greenwood and Hinings, 1996), manipulating or managing an organizational identity adaptation is not really possible. Rather, the view would be that organizations slowly change their identity and image through a more deterministic process accommodated by institutional expectations and contextual isomorphic convergence. We saw that BP entered the alliance in part to adapt its image, while Statoil wished to adapt both its identity and image. Whether or not the partners actually adapted their organizational identities is beyond the scope of this study, but their attempt to do so, through an organizational tool in the form of an alliance, is interesting in itself.

KEY QUESTIONS

1 As we saw in this case, how we define ourselves internally and how we are defined externally as an organization can be based on cognitively understood

perceptions rather than on more visible and tangible organizational structures alone. How are identity and "reality" linked?

2 BP and Statoil sought to project different, more advantageous images by allying with each other – BP by drawing on Statoil's national oil company image, and Statoil by drawing on BP's international "player" image. In what circumstances can this type of dual image projection be effective?

3 As Statoil learned through BP that it already possessed knowledge and expertise in running international operations, the organization adapted its identity and image to define itself as an "international" company. If acknowledging and understanding what we know defines who we are as an organization, does who we are define what we know? In other words, does being defined as an international company assume that we have international knowledge?

Chapter 8

Practice and identity

Using a brand symbol to construct organizational identity

Celia Virginia Harquail

INTRODUCTION

Organization members can take their cues about the organization's identity from a variety of sources. As discussed in the introductory section of this book about the sources of organizational identity cues, these cues can be internal and external, material and discursive, behavioral and conceptual. In the organization described in this case, members constructed their collective definition of the organization's identity by drawing on cues from a tool that they had developed for their brand. This tool, their brand icon, was a fictional character created expressly to personify and embody the attributes that they wanted to associate with their brand's identity. Features of the brand icon and her story, combined with organizational practices intended to help employees use the brand icon in marketing-related decisions, ultimately served as cues from which organization members constructed their beliefs about the identity of the organization itself.

The idea that organization members would draw identity cues from their marketing tools is interesting because we generally assume that members construct their organization's identity from cues related to the organization as a whole, in its entirety. Nevertheless, it is not altogether surprising that tools or practices related to branding the organization's products could be taken as cues for the organization's identity itself. Products are often believed to reflect or express the organization from which they come (see Chapters 10 and 11). For this reason it can be advantageous for organizations to blur the distinction between the organization's identity and the identity of their product brand, and organizations often explicitly enlist the organization's identity in constructing, reflecting, and legitimating the brand's identity for the consumer. Enlisting the organization's identity can add heft to the brand's identity claims by suggesting that the brand's attributes originate from the organization itself. At Kartell, for example, the organization's design philosophy (part of its organizational identity) is used to support their marketing claims that their brand of plastic furniture, although constructed from a mundane material, reflects very contemporary and highly sophisticated design (see Chapter 11).

While the distinction between them can be blurred, organizational identity and brand identity are very different constructs. Organizational identities emerge from members' collective values and experience, and help to provide the organization and its members with a deeper, broader reason for being. In contrast, brand identities are beliefs invented about a product to make it more desirable, to sell it, and to make a profit. Brand identities are largely "made up" to appeal to the desires and demands of a particular segment of potential customers (Aaker, 1996). Despite the fact that employees are able intellectually to distinguish between the identity of their organization and the identity of their brand, what is important is that *in practice* organization members often treat the organization's identity and the brand's identity as the same construct.

Blurring the line between the organization's identity and the brand's identity can be a savvy, effective marketing choice, especially when the brand's identity is difficult to substantiate, largely conceptual, and more rhetorical than real. However, reversing the direction of influence so that a somewhat fictional brand identity is used to construct the organization's identity invites questions about what is effective, what is authentic, and what is real.

The Heartland Corporation profiled in this case offers a vivid example of how the distinction between brand identity and organizational identity can be blurred and how the brand's identity can influence the collective definition of the organization. In practice, the Heartland Corporation used the attributes, tools, and beliefs they invented about their brand as resources for cues about their organization's identity. Their brand icon came to represent not only their beliefs about the brand's identity but also their beliefs about the organization's identity.

INTRODUCING THE HEARTLAND CORPORATION

The Heartland Corporation (a pseudonym)[1] is a 20-year-old, privately held business headquartered in a small city in Missouri, the "Heartland" of the United States. Heartland employs 500 full-time workers at its headquarters and about 20 employees at each of its 1,000 retail stores across the United States. The company sells its own name-brand gourmet foodstuffs, as well as unbranded gourmet kitchen implements and tabletop accessories. Heartland's target customers are

---

[1] Because of the sensitive nature of the strategic information shared with me, I agreed to preserve the anonymity of the organization by disguising identifying details. In my cover story, I have retained the central values of the organization, the symbolic attributes of the brand, the features of the organization's history, and the icon's personality and biography to reflect as accurately as possible the relationships between the organization, its brand, and the icon herself.

middle-class women who are interested in cooking and old-fashioned hospitality. Heartland's brand positioning focuses on food as a gift, cooking as a personal indulgence, hospitality, and honest goodness. Their foods are presented as being top quality, wholesome, and "good for you."

Branding practices at Heartland

Heartland has a simple, unified brand identity structure, where the organization and its product brands share the same name (Harquail, 2005; Cappetta and Gioia, 2005). As an organization, Heartland has a strong marketing orientation (Christensen, 1995): the organizational culture emphasizes the importance of marketing as a practice and the primacy of satisfying customers' desires. Heartland executives fully recognize that customers purchase Heartland products less for their function or material performance than for their ideational, symbolic aspects (Gobe, 2001). Therefore, to maximize their products' ideational, symbolic values, Heartland has become very skilled at branding. Branding is the practice of taking a more or less generic product and making it distinctive and desirable to consumers by associating the product with real and imagined attributes.

A commonly used tool in the practice of creating a brand identity is the brand icon. A brand icon is a character – fictitious or real, human or anthropomorphized – that an audience identifies with the brand and the brand's attributes. Well-known brand icons include KFC's Colonel Sanders, Virgin's Richard Branson, and Pillsbury's Dough Boy. To create a brand icon, marketers identify the attributes they want to associate with their product and invent or adopt a character who they define and depict as having those attributes. Sometimes marketers elaborate on the character's attributes by weaving them into a real or fictional life story. The character is then presented to the target audience as a symbol of these attributes. When a character is effectively created and communicated, the target audience not only recognizes the attributes the character is intended to convey but also connects both the character and its attributes with the brand. In this way, a brand icon symbolizes the brand and personifies the brand's identity.

Brand icons are most often thought of as tools for communicating with consumer audiences. However, brand icons can also be effective tools for communicating with an internal organizational audience. Internally, organization members can use the brand icon as a tool to help them elaborate upon or extend a brand's identity and to translate the brand identity into products, packaging and retail presentation, advertising, and so on. As a tool inside an organization, brand icons are increasingly common (Gobe, 2001; Schneider, 2002).

Heartland's brand icon

Inventing a brand icon

On an executive retreat early in the company's third year, Heartland's executive team decided to invent their own brand icon – a character whose personality and biography would help to organize, distill, and personify the identity of the Heartland brand. They wrote a story about Carrie King, the woman who founded Heartland, describing who she was, what she valued, how she came to start Heartland, and what she wanted for Heartland's customers. Executives hoped that employees throughout the organization would refer to the brand icon when they made decisions affecting the brand. In this way, they could align decisions about the brand across different organizational functions and strengthen the relationship between the product, the brand identity, and the presentation of the brand to achieve consistency across product lines and distribution points. The brand icon was intended for use only within the organization: it was never used as a public face to represent products to retail customers.

Describing Carrie King

Heartland's brand icon, Carrie King, is the thirty-something mother of Hannah and Max and the wife of Sam King. She was born in a farming town west of St Louis, Missouri. As a teen, Carrie earned pocket money selling her home-made jams, pies, and specialty breads at her family's produce market. As a young mother, Carrie started a small business, staffed by herself, her grandmother, and two other home-makers, selling "home-made" jams, sauces, spice mixes, and bread mixes under the Heartland brand name. The business was so successful that she opened her own stand-alone store, the Heartland Gourmet Shop. Four years later, when her business had grown to four stores and 35 employees, she sold it to a group of investors who expanded the business to 600 stores nationwide within the first ten years. Heartland continued to use Carrie's original recipes and retained the original brand positioning and retail store design. The company was relatively profitable, with very strong brand recognition, brand loyalty, and high market penetration.

Carrie is described by Heartland employees as being "everyone's friend":

> Carrie's virtues stand as an ideal. Honesty: Carrie is one of the most honest people you'll ever meet, and the way she sees it, truth is an ideal; it is an obligation. Carrie is truthful in the way she lives her life and the way she runs her business and in the way she expresses who she and her business are. Carrie is here always. Integrity: You can trust Carrie to do the right thing, and you can trust her products. Carrie stands for quality, pure and simple. Accountability: She stands behind her products because

she sees every one as an extension of who she is. Even if a product doesn't bear her name, it carries her reputation. Also, Carrie has humility. Carrie respects people and has the unique ability to appreciate them for who they are. In turn, people find her inspiring, motivating and kind.

Capturing, communicating, and using Carrie's story

To communicate the story of the brand icon easily and consistently throughout the organization, a marketing director summarized what had been developed at the retreat. The resulting ten-page booklet described how Carrie started the business, how she learned to cook, how she met her husband, why she moved back from New York City to St Louis, what she liked to eat and wear, and what values were important to her. The executive team worked to refine the story so that it captured, elaborated upon, and emphasized the attributes that they wanted for Heartland's brand identity. Later, this story was translated into a video that was shown at new employee orientation and at corporate events.

The booklet and the video were used as reference tools by product managers and creative staff. For example, the photo stylist at a product shoot was given the book to help her create visual imagery that would evoke the brand's desired identity. Similarly, at marketing meetings, product development discussions, and when discussing the retail presentation of products, executives and marketing staff referred to this document to help clarify and refine the Heartland brand attributes they were trying to express in the product, packaging, copy, and retail store.

Employees described using Carrie and her story to represent Heartland's brand attributes in their decision-making. As one product manager explained:

> Somebody had the idea that we should sign our customer service letters with Carrie's name – Carrie King. And I almost had a heart attack . . . I recall saying "Absolutely no way are we doing this," because to me that seems like the antithesis of what Carrie would do, if she were a real person. If Carrie were a real person and she had created a fictional founder, she'd never send customers a letter from a fictional person.

If consistency in product development, brand extensions, retail promotions, and strong overall business results are any indication, using Carrie King as a brand icon was a powerful branding tool.

CREATING A BRAND ICON: MARKETING AND ORGANIZATIONAL TACTICS

Establishing Carrie as an effective branding tool within Heartland required marketing tactics that developed the character and associated her with the brand, as well as organizational tactics that enabled every employee to recognize and potentially utilize what she represented for it. To link Carrie and the brand, Heartland used two marketing tactics: (1) cohering and explaining the brand's attributes through Carrie's story, and (2) positively elaborating Carrie's story. To establish Carrie as a symbol system shared throughout the organization, Heartland pursued two additional tactics: (3) brand training for all employees, and (4) ubiquitous co-presentation of Carrie and the brand. These tactics were interdependent in their execution, but are discussed separately here for theoretical clarity.

Linking Carrie with the brand's attributes

Creating a compelling personality and narrative

Heartland's marketers created a clear, coherent, and evocative personality and life story for Carrie. Carrie's personality was configured to create an explicit consonance between her personality and the attributes that marketers wanted to use to define Heartland brand's identity. Carrie was also given a personal narrative – a life story – to establish a connection between the set of attributes and the character and to explain why she was who she was. By creating a set of attributes for Carrie that matched the Heartland brand attributes, by cohering these attributes in Carrie's personality, and by explaining the source of these attributes in Carrie's narrative, Heartland made it possible for its internal audience – the organization's employees – to see Carrie as a representative of its brand.

> Have you seen the video? If you show the video to an associate [employee], it's like this transformation happens to them . . . they just get it. And so, suddenly, all these documents that talk about brand vision and pages and pages of what we stand for – it's like "I get it. I see it. I know what I have to do."

Marketing managers also elaborated on Carrie's narrative by inventing new episodes for her life story, sometimes to link Carrie with the brand as the brand identity evolved, and other times to embellish the reasoning behind business decisions made without initially considering Carrie or the brand identity (e.g., centralizing the distribution function). Between 1985 and 1992, the written story grew from 10 to 50 pages. As interpretations of Carrie evolved and as attributes in the brand identity evolved, the practice of elaborating Carrie's story helped to sustain a correspondence between what Carrie represented and what defined the brand's identity.

Creating a positive, elaborate character narrative

Heartland marketers created Carrie and her life story with only positive, attractive attributes. With no unhappy episodes in her story and no unpleasant characteristics in her personality, Carrie could represent only positive attributes of the brand. As one executive put it:

> We love the idea of using an imaginary person [to represent the brand] because of all the pitfalls of having to live with what a real person would be like.

Carrie's narrative was also very detailed and specific – this specificity helped the story make sense and seem convincing, allowing employees to visualize who Carrie was (Escalas, 2004; Hoorn and Konijn, 2003).

> The clearer the story is, the more you can engage around it . . . If the story is convincing enough, then anybody can embrace it. Just like you read a novel – "That character's not like me, but I can certainly picture it." I can imagine [Carrie] – what she would say, what she would do . . . They (any of the employees) could certainly engage around it because the story is just so convincing.

The richness of Carrie's story also enabled employees at Heartland to feel as if they actually knew her like a friend, inside and out:

> I think everybody in their life knows a Carrie. She's like your mother, or your best friend. You just know who she is. It's multicultural, it's ageless, she's easily understood.

The elaborate narrative created for Carrie allowed her audience to understand who she was, why she was who she was, and what she stood for – making her an easy and appealing tool to use.

Establishing Carrie as a shared symbol system

Employee brand training

Heartland used two organization-wide tactics – employee training and organizational décor – to spread an understanding of Carrie and to convey her importance to the entire organization. Through their new employee orientation, Heartland made sure that every employee knew the details of Carrie's story, could describe her personality, and could explain how Carrie represented what the Heartland brand was all about. New employees read a synopsis of Carrie's story and watched a seven-minute video that focused on her personality, depicted important episodes in her life, and talked about the values she wanted customers to experience with Heartland's products. Employees were taught how to use Carrie to evaluate brand-related issues. For example, they played a game called "Carrie or Not Carrie?" to evaluate whether a product idea was "on-brand" or "off-brand." Employees also were taught to act like Carrie in their interactions with customers and suppliers: "Carrie treats every customer like a friend, and you should too" (Employee Handbook). Through new employee training, staff were taught to recognize what Carrie represented and how to use her as a brand management tool.

Carrie's importance to the brand was regularly reinforced when marketing personnel invoked Carrie and her story. The question "What would Carrie do?" was raised in marketing discussions about all manner of brand issues, such as how to craft a product, how to position it, what to call it, and so on. This became such an important decision-making tool that banners asking "What would Carrie do?" were hung in the main conference room and in the employee training room. As every member of the Heartland Corporation recognized Carrie, knew exactly what she represented, and knew how and when to employ her as a guide for marketing decisions, Carrie was a symbol shared throughout the organization.

Organizational décor

To reinforce the relationship between Carrie, the brand attributes, and the Heartland brand – and to emphasize Carrie's importance – the company decorated their building with "dramaturgical props" (Goffman, 1959; Pratt and Rafaeli, 2001). Dramaturgical props are images, objects, words, artefacts, and other symbols that manipulate aspects of a physical setting to create a particular impression. Props were initially concentrated in the workspaces of the marketing department: brand meetings took place in the Hannah Conference Room and the Max Conference Room, where participants sat on wooden chairs painted to look antique, arranged around farm tables made of knotty pine, just as if they were sitting in Carrie's kitchen. In the product trend rooms, where marketing employees experimented with new visual imagery for the retail stores, props such as photos, objects, fabric swatches, typefaces, and potential products themselves reflected not only brand attributes (e.g., bins of grain and a hand-turned grist mill representing wholesomeness) but also elements of Carrie's personal story (e.g., 4-H posters, fabric swatches from "Carrie's kitchen curtains"). Bringing visual imagery from both the brand and the character together in the same places created a metonymic association between them and facilitated the perception that Carrie's story, the Heartland brand, and the brand attributes were all interconnected. Moreover, the ubiquity of these co-presentations kept Carrie and the brand identity salient in employees' minds (Ind, 2001). By combining traditional marketing tactics with organizationally targeted tactics, the company established Carrie as an internal brand icon that was recognized, understood, and used as a representative of Heartland's brand identity by everyone in the organization.

USING A BRAND ICON TO CONSTRUCT THE ORGANIZATION'S IDENTITY

Connecting the organization to the brand icon

Through additional practices intended to enhance their marketing effectiveness, Heartland's managers inadvertently made it possible for Carrie to symbolize not only Heartland's brand identity but also the identity of the corporation itself. Employees drew cues about their organization's defining characteristics from Carrie and her story, and Carrie came to personify and embody for the collective, internal audience some of the central, continuous, and enduring features that composed the organization's identity (Albert and Whetten, 1985).

The first step towards constructing their organization's identity using their brand icon occurred when Heartland organization members began collectively to see a connection between Carrie and the Heartland organization itself. This link was made possible by a foundation of similar attributes and was made desirable by the attractiveness to organization members of what Carrie represented. The second step evolved through Heartland's organization-wide efforts to enlist all employees in supporting the Heartland brand. These efforts, explicitly intended to get members to link Carrie to the brand, also encouraged them to link the organization to Carrie, because they implied that Carrie was relevant beyond the marketing function and throughout the organization.

A foundation of similar attributes

Although Carrie's personality and life story were created to express the brand's attributes, some of these attributes were also attributes of the Heartland Corporation. For example, Carrie's heartland and the Heartland Corporation were both located in the Midwest, both were informal and friendly places, and both were focused on creating a quality product that gave the customer good value. Like Carrie as a person, the Heartland Corporation was thought of by its employees and its competitors as a homegrown, local company that achieved national success by producing a high-quality product, by using honest business methods, and by capturing the imagination of the middle class with products that were neither snobby nor down-market. Heartland members perceived a similarity between Carrie's attributes and what defined the Heartland Corporation: "The values of Carrie are almost verbatim from what anyone will tell you are the values of the organization."

143

Although a complete overlap of the attributes of the brand and the attributes of the organization could not be inferred from cues such as material facts, social categories, strategic groups, and so on, this foundation of similar attributes made it possible for the organizational audience to believe that the brand icon and the organization shared key, defining attributes, and to view the brand icon as an expression of the organization's identity.

The attractiveness of the brand icon as a representation of the organization itself

Although consonance between brand attributes and organizational attributes makes it possible for organization members collectively to link the organization to the brand icon, it is the attractiveness of the brand icon as a potential representation of the organization that makes this linking desirable. For Heartland employees, two features of the brand icon made Carrie an attractive potential representation of the organization itself. First, Carrie appeared to be a plausible and legitimate representative of the Heartland Corporation; second, she offered Heartland employees an opportunity for collective, organizational "self-enhancement."

Plausibility, legitimacy, and the attractiveness of the icon

The idea that Carrie could be the founder of the Heartland Corporation and that she could embody what defined the organization seemed plausible and legitimate, as Carrie's story specifically describes her as the founder of the company. Organizational identities "bear the mark of the founder's imprint" (Whetten and Mackey, 2002). The idea that Carrie, as a founder, could define the corporation appears legitimate because it fits both scholars' and laypeople's beliefs about the influence of founders. Academic research demonstrates that founders have a profound impact on the norms, values, cultures, and identities of organizations (e.g., Deal and Kennedy, 1982; Schein, 1992; Whetten and Mackey, 2002). The popular press treats as a fact that organizations are stamped with defining features that are the direct result of the personalities and values of their founders. If "the culture of a business becomes, at least in part, an embodiment of the founder's personality" (Hollander and Ellman, 1988: 149), then using the story of a founder to clarify or represent an organization's identity fits expectations and thus seems legitimate. The founder and the founder's story – who she or he is and how he or she went about starting and growing the organization – are material traits that can be used as identity cues.

Carrie's story appeared to be a legitimate resource for identity cues, because stories about the organization are such a common way of constructing its organizational identity. Many scholars argue that it is through the construction of a narrative, by telling a story to themselves about their organization, that members develop and share an understanding of what defines their organization (Czarniawska, 1997; Whetten and Mackay, 2002). Narratives are extended identity claims and thus offer important identity cues. A narrative about the founding of Heartland is a legitimate resource for defining an organization's identity.

In addition, the content of Carrie's story – the material "facts" themselves – focuses on Carrie as the reason Heartland Corporation is the way it is. Carrie's story puts her personality, values, and biography at the center of collective attention and action. Her story tells the audience that she and her values defined the corporation. Because the details of her story appeared convincing, because her story seemed plausible, and because her relationship with Heartland appeared legitimate, Carrie's narrative was all the more attractive as a resource for identity cues to help members construct their collective definition of the Heartland Corporation identity.

It was plausible that a person like Carrie could have established certain attributes as important elements of the Heartland Corporation. Because her personality and story were plausible and realistic, the internal organizational audience could understand and trust the meaning of the story (Hoorn and Kinijn, 2003), and thus using Carrie as a cue to the organization's identity was attractive for organizational members.

The aspirational, "possible organizational self" and attractiveness

The attributes of Carrie and her story offered Heartland an appealing "possible self" (Markus and Nurius, 1986) that they could aspire to in the future and imagine and employ for themselves in the present. Just as an individual might identify with an organization in an effort to achieve an attractive "possible self" (Dutton, Dukerich, and Harquail, 1994), Heartland's members could enhance their collective self-definition by linking the company's organizational identity to the positive attributes that Carrie represented. Using Carrie to help to define Heartland's organizational identity offered company members as a group the opportunity to aspire to be all the positive things that Carrie and her story represented.

In addition, Carrie's story offered an appealing imaginary identity: one that explained Heartland's core values and attributes effectively but which was more romantic than the corporation's actual founding story, and in that sense was more attractive as an identity cue. The "real" story behind the Heartland Corporation was a perfectly respectable, even laudable story of a hard-working, millionaire businessman who saw a retail opportunity, hired talented executives, and worked with them to grow Heartland into a profitable national retail chain. Heartland's business success is the result of a strategy of quick and less expensive imitation of other specialty food companies' products. Heartland relies on sophisticated data mining and trend analysis to develop brand extensions, and their profits are helped by very strict cost controls. The company is a wholly owned subsidiary of a large international conglomerate.

In contrast to the actual founding story, Carrie's Heartland story explained the company's growth as the result of personal inspiration and creativity and established warmth, hospitality, and personal attention as dominant organizational features. Carrie herself is an appealing person: "Everybody wants to be Carrie, or if you're a man you want to marry her." Carrie's motivation for founding Heartland and the values she sought to instill in the company's products were themselves inspiring. Her story was attractive because it offered the organization an opportunity for "wishful identification" (Von Feilitzen and Linne, 1975), helping the organization overlook the ways in which they were unlike Carrie, as well as to visualize and focus on what they collectively thought would be a desirable "possible self."

Carrie's identity enhanced and highlighted Heartland's existing positive attributes, suggested that Heartland could be even better (perhaps even more welcoming, more honest, or with more integrity), and created a romantic fantasy about the source of the company's identity. The romantic, idealized identity also offered Heartland an opportunity to exaggerate its virtues, suggesting in this idealism that the organization was somehow special or unique (Wilkins, 1983). This sense of distinctiveness – that Carrie's Heartland was a unique place in terms of actual and aspirational values and attributes – also enhanced its attractiveness (Dutton, Dukerich, and Harquail, 1994). Allowing Carrie's story to substitute for or represent the actual story of the corporation accentuated all of Heartland's real attributes, suggested desirable additional ones, and imagined more attractive ones.

The irrelevance of fiction

It is important to recognize that Carrie's status as a fictional character was not an obstacle to seeing her as an attractive representation of the company's identity. Every organization member understood that Carrie's romantic, fantasy story was a fiction. Carrie did not exist, and they all knew that. Nonetheless, they felt that she was inspiring and that there was nothing harmful in acting as though her story were true. In their view, none of what Carrie represented led to anything undesirable; nor was it detrimental to how the organization functioned. Even though they acknowledged that Carrie was largely fictional, they still found her story collectively self-defining, aspirational, and appealing:

We'd like it if it *were* all true, but it's not as though it's *not* true.

In a jaded world, to think that there is even this fictional person who really cares about her customers and wants to be honest and wants to have integrity and says what she means and isn't lying, isn't giving you a product [with false] promises . . . You know, just to think there might even exist such a person! I really saw it in Carrie, and I believe that Carrie has a lot to do with how good our associates are and we [Heartland] are.

Implying a link between Carrie and the organization

The efforts of the marketing department to teach all employees about Carrie and how to use her were intended to get the entire organization to support the brand. Inadvertently, however, these brand-focused efforts also created an opportunity for employees to link the organization to Carrie, by suggesting this link symbolic-ally. By spreading symbols of a connection between the icon and the organization throughout their headquarters, and by creating new symbols that linked the organ-ization directly to Carrie, Heartland allowed the organization to appropriate Carrie's symbolic meaning for itself.

Carrie was present, symbolically, everywhere in the organization. For example, the entire wall behind the receptionists' desk at corporate headquarters was covered by a photographic mural depicting the farmhouse and fields where Heartland's original offices were purportedly located. In the cafeteria, each of the five food stations was decorated with a different fake storefront (e.g., a butcher's shop, a bakery) so that the cafeteria appeared to be a stylized replica of the main street of Carrie's hometown. Carrie even had a dog, Lucy, who had free run of the building and slept in her own doghouse in the reception area. To see Lucy, a living creature, roaming the corporate office created the illusion that Carrie was somewhere in the building too, and that she was really part of the corporation. The symbols of Carrie's presence throughout Heartland's corporate space led not only to a transfer and sharing of attributes between Carrie and the organization, but also to the perception that these attributes were characteristic throughout the organization and central to it.

Through a foundation of similar attributes, through the attractiveness of Carrie as a potential representative of the organization's identity, and through the organ-izational practices that implicitly connected the organization to Carrie, she and her story came to be used collectively throughout Heartland to represent what organization members believed to be the central, enduring, and distinctive attrib-utes of the organization. One demonstration that Carrie had become an organiza-tional icon was that every employee interviewed described Carrie as embodying characteristics and values that were important in defining the company. For example, as a product development executive explained:

Carrie in her own way is a legend. In twelve years, she built a two billion dollar company . . . Somebody had to have this great creative drive to be

147

able to do this . . . I think it's very important to have Carrie because she puts the human aspect into the company . . . even given the magnitude of our size, it [Heartland] never feels like a huge corporation. And it still amazes me when I talk about some of the numbers that we do, you just can't believe that this is how big we are, because we don't run like that. And Carrie is responsible for that. Carrie is responsible for the fact that we run more as a small-time company of people doing multiple jobs and multiple tasks. I think that keeping that [the small-time company feeling] is very unusual . . . Carrie has been responsible for that because everything that we have done, from the 4-H's of our company's values, which had been derived from Carrie, which put in the integrity, the respect, how we treated one another, hard work, good humor, whatever it might be. All those wholesome acts, so to speak, that you don't find in a corporation every day. That has been the responsibility or the outcome of Carrie. And I think that's why I directly link her as being the reason for our company being the way it is.

Or, as the CEO succinctly put it, "Carrie IS Heartland."

With Carrie as symbol of the organization, asking the question "What would Carrie do?" became a way of invoking the organization's identity when organization-wide issues were being considered. The idea that Carrie had come to represent what defined the organization itself was borne out in the ways that organization members appropriated Carrie and her story to explain their expectations of the organization and to explain organization-wide decisions that were not relevant to the brand or to marketing. For example, one organization member described her efforts to get the corporate cafeteria to use biodegradable paper cups:

You know, I'm waging a war in our cafeteria because they have Styrofoam cups, and I think that's just outrageous . . . I'm down there every week saying to [the cafeteria manager], "Carrie would not have Styrofoam; she cares about her earth."

In another example, Carrie was used to explain why the company cafeteria sold "carry out" dinners that employees could take home to their families, as well as why they had a dry cleaning facility and a nail salon at their headquarters:

Carrie understands what it's like to be a working mother – a working parent – and she wants to make it as easy as possible for all of us to take care of day-to-day things too. And, Carrie knows that sometimes you just need a nice manicure as a treat.

Having Carrie as an organizational icon gave Heartland a way to capture, make coherent, and begin to put into words the intrinsic and unexpressed attributes that defined their organization. It gave them something to talk about as they sought collectively to articulate and understand who they were as an organization. Carrie and her story functioned as a tool for constructing meaning, providing a "centering narrative" (Boyce, 1995) that enabled Heartland members to shape, revise, and enact their organizational identity.

DISCUSSION AND IMPLICATIONS

By providing members with several types of cues for construing the organization's identity, the brand icon was appropriated by members to represent their collective definition of the central, enduring, and distinctive attributes of the corporation. As Carrie came to symbolize Heartland's identity, she also influenced the company's identity-related practices. First, using Carrie and her story to represent their more abstract beliefs about what defined the corporation made it easier for Heartland members to evoke, articulate, and discuss their beliefs about the organization's identity. Once these beliefs were discussed, it was easier for Heartland members to implement these beliefs by translating them into behaviors, decisions, and operational strategies. Second, using Carrie to represent their organization's identity made it possible for every member of the organization to participate in discussions about its identity, because every member was familiar with Carrie and what she stood for. Third, using Carrie to represent the organization's identity facilitated conversations between different organizational functions, each working to put the company's identity into practice, and helped to keep all the functions aligned with each other.

The story of Carrie King and Heartland has several implications for our understanding of how organizational identity is put into practice and how it is constructed from practice. Most basic is the recognition that cues for constructing the organization's identity can be drawn from any part or any function of the organization. Specific functions or divisions, tools, and even products can become resources for constructing organizational identity. And, organizational identity can be shaped or influenced by activities that are not "about" the organization per se.

The idea that Heartland's brand structure, organizational structure, marketing orientation, and other features may have facilitated rather than impeded the use of a brand icon to represent the organization itself may make this an uncommon case. Nevertheless, although not every organization might identify with their brand or have their brand icon come to represent their collective self-definition, the case of Carrie and the Heartland Corporation encourages us to dig more deeply into the complex relationships between products, brands, brand icons, and organizational identity.

The Heartland story also suggests that we should consider whether identity cues and the conclusions drawn from them can be both factual and fictional. Collective fictions – in this case Carrie and her story – can represent collectively shared beliefs about the organization; fictional stories, embellished histories, and objective timelines can all provide cues from which organization members can construct their organization's identity. However, incorporating attributes that are fictional or embellished into an organization's identity can raise questions of authenticity and challenge members' collective meaning.

Heartland's experience helps us to understand the ways that organization members can connect their organization to a symbol and use this symbol in turn to influence how they define themselves collectively. By embodying Carrie King with brand attributes that resonated with important elements of the organization's actual story, with attributes that reflected an attractive potential collective self-image, and with a personality and biography that were familiar, plausible, romantic, and attractive, Heartland created in Carrie a symbol that potentially could reflect back on them all manner of desirable attributes – presently, potentially, and ideally. Through employee training that ensured organization-wide understanding of Carrie and what she represented, and by suggesting a link between Carrie and Heartland through stories, artefacts, and décor that presented her as central to the organization, the company facilitated the use of Carrie and her story as a source of cues about their collective sense of self. In this way, Heartland's marketing practices provided cues for the construction of their collective organizational identity.

KEY QUESTIONS

1 What are the potential advantages and disadvantages of representing an organization's identity with the same character that represents the organization's brand?
2 What is the appropriate relationship between an organization's identity and its products and brands?
3 What are the implications of drawing cues for organizational identity from stories, characters, and attributes that are largely fictional?
4 How might using Carrie to represent the organization's identity influence the thoughts, feelings, and behaviors of Heartland employees as individuals?
5 How do organization members' personalities, life stories, etc. offer cues for constructing organizational identity?

Part III

Projecting organizational identities

Lin Lerpold, Davide Ravasi, Johan van Rekom, and Guillaume Soenen

In the previous sections of this book we have seen how organizational identities affect major strategic decisions as well as everyday behavior in organizations. However, this is not the only way that organizational identities influence how organizations function and relate to external counterparts. Research in marketing and corporate communication has highlighted how internal beliefs about what the organization is and is about tend to influence, consciously or unconsciously, the images it projects to the outside world.

Building on the practice of graphic design consultancies (Olins, 1989), research in corporate communication has developed the concept of corporate identity, which refers largely to a relatively coordinated set of visible and tangible features of, within, or otherwise representing an organization or firm (e.g., logos, products, visual communication materials, building features, uniform designs). Research has shown also how the underlying choices may affect the formation of external impressions about the organization (van Riel, 1995; van Riel and Balmer, 1997). While different scholarly traditions seem to at least partly differ in the way they define and conceptualize corporate identity, most scholars tend to agree that corporate identities usually reflect and express underlying understandings of the organization (i.e., organizational identities).

Similarly, in marketing research brand scholars have observed how sound brand strategies ultimately rest on a deeply rooted understanding of what the organization is and is about. The concept of brand image has been advanced to indicate the range of associations that consumers attach to a given brand – understood as a name, sign, or combination of name and sign that identifies a specific good or service from its competitors (Keller, 2003). By brand identity, however, marketing scholars commonly refer to the set of associations that a brand manager wishes to create or maintain (Aaker, 1996). Some of these associations are peripheral and tend to change over time and across markets, others form a core set, which tends to remain constant even as brand policies evolve or the brand is applied to different products. According to brand scholar David Aaker, the core identity of a strong brand tends to rest on fundamental beliefs about what the organization behind the brand stands for and its unique values and competencies – in other words on the identity of the organization.

In this introduction to Part III we introduce concepts such as organizational image, corporate identity, and brand identity, and highlight the way that they reflect and are driven by organizational identities. The rest of the section includes four cases that examine how organizations may draw on different internal identity resources to build a coherent corporate identity and project attractive organizational images. Collectively, these cases highlight the importance of a clear and consistent organizational identity for the success of communication policies, and how these policies reflect back on organizational members, reinforcing or enriching the way they perceive and feel about their organization.

ORGANIZATIONAL (CORPORATE) IMAGES AND REPUTATION

Organizational and marketing scholars have not always used the terms "organizational image" or "corporate image" consistently over time or across different subfields (Gioia, Schultz, and Corley, 2000). In this book we refer to *organizational* (or *corporate*) *image* as a set of associations held about an organization by its stakeholders. In other words, while organizational identity refers to *internal* beliefs and understandings, organizational image refers to *external* perceptions and representations. Just as members of an organization may hold different views and beliefs about what their organization is about, external stakeholders also differ in their perceptions of the organization, leading to a multiplicity of organizational images.

Despite their intangible nature, organizational images may have tangible and substantial effects on the functioning of organizations. How an organization is perceived and represented by external stakeholders affects stakeholders' willingness to support the organization with funds, supplies, purchases, consensus, etc. (Dowling, 1986). Strategy and institutional theory scholars use the term *reputation* to refer to a relatively stable and broad assessment of the capacity of an organization to satisfy the needs and expectations of a particular category of stakeholders (Fombrun, 1996; Fombrun and van Riel, 2004). Broadly speaking, the reputation of an organization depends on its capacity to deliver high-quality offerings in a reliable, trustworthy and, possibly, responsible way. All other things being equal – if such conditions occur at all in the real world – highly reputed companies will be able to raise capital more easily and at lower cost (Stiglitz and Weiss, 1981), will attract a high-profile workforce (Gatewood, Gowan, and Lautenschlager, 1993), and will be able to charge high premiums on their products (Shapiro, 1983).

Different stakeholders, however, may emphasize different aspects of the conduct of an organization. For example, the same organization may enjoy an excellent reputation among the financial community for its ability to reward shareholders, but simultaneously a less positive reputation among the general public for its lack of social concern and care for the environment. This has been the case in the oil industry, for example.

How an organization is perceived and represented externally may also affect the way internal members feel about their organization. Some people also define themselves in terms of the organization they belong to – in other words they develop "social identities" connected to the organization (Ashforth and Mael, 1989; Dutton, Dukerich and Harquail, 1994) – and, occasionally, even develop an emotional attachment and sense of oneness and belongingness with it. Social psychologists refer to the outcome of this process as "identification" (Ashforth and Mael, 1989; Ellemers *et al.*, 2003) and highlight its positive influence on members' commitment and willingness to cooperate (Dukerich, Golden, and Shortell, 2002). Research further indicates that individuals tend to identify more strongly with highly reputed, prestigious organizations (Smidts, Pruyn, and van Riel, 2001). Spoiled or deteriorating images, in contrast, negatively affect individual self-esteem and are likely to trigger responses ranging from denial to distancing oneself from the organization (i.e., dis-identification).

More generally, previous research indicates that organizational members tend to perceive a discrepancy between external and internal perceptions as threatening or challenging (Elsbach and Kramer, 1996). A discrepancy between the way an organization is perceived by external stakeholders and the way its members perceive the organization, or wish it were perceived (its *desired image*), may lead to the adoption of various tactics aimed at regaining a favorable alignment between identity and image. Often these tactics rely on the manipulation of external images through corporate communication or impression management (Gioia, Schultz, and Corley, 2000).

CORPORATE IDENTITY

A comprehensive treatment of image management through corporate communication and impression management is beyond the scope of this book. However, among the various communication tools available to organizations, there are close links – to the point that the two concepts are often confused – between organizational identity and *corporate identity*.

As previously mentioned, the concept of corporate identity developed in the 1980s has become a widely used heuristic tool for uncovering various tangible and intangible elements of an organization, which, combined together, make it stand as relatively unique in the marketplace. The purpose of such analyses is often to prepare the ground for a carefully designed communication plan, aimed at visually presenting the organization to its various audiences through symbolism, communication, and behavior, and thus emphasizing the central ideas and values driving its policies (Birkigt, Stadler, and Funk, 2002).

In this book we adopt a conservative definition of corporate identity as a relatively coordinated set of visible and tangible features of an organization (logos, products, visual communication materials, building features, design of uniforms, etc.). In other words, we refer to more or less deliberate and conscious projections that influence how an organization is perceived externally. According to the organizational scholars Violina Rindova and Majken Schultz (1998), corporate identity is the material expression of the beliefs and understandings that are part of its organizational identity (see Figure 15). Corporate identities thus rely on the development and manipulation of symbols to produce a coherent image of the organization.

According to Rindova and Schultz (1998), while organizational identity primarily affects the identification and sense of belongingness of internal members, the purpose of a corporate identity plan focuses mainly on external audiences by supporting, at a symbolic level, organizational claims for differentiation. In fact, as the two scholars acknowledge, just as the emotional impact of organizational symbols can be felt even inside the organization (see, for instance, Chapters 8 and 11), the identity of an organization can provide a solid base for the development

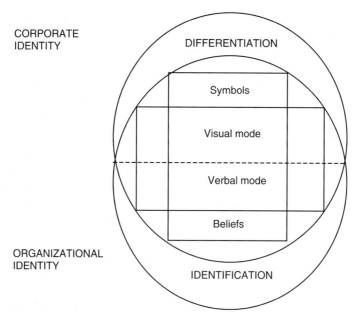

Figure 15 *Organizational identity and corporate identity*
Source: Rindova and Schultz (1998)

and implementation of communication policies aiming at differentiating the organization in the marketplace (see Chapter 12).

BRAND IMAGE AND BRAND IDENTITY

So far in the introduction to Part III, we have implicitly assumed a coincidence between an organization and the name under which its products or services are commercialized. Such is the case, for instance, for most financial institutions, many manufacturers (such as Sony, Renault, or Philips), transport companies (e.g., Air France, British Railways, Iberia), and producers of fashion or lifestyle products (Bang & Olufsen or Alessi). Just as frequently, however, large manufacturers of fast-moving consumer goods (e.g., Unilever, Procter & Gamble, Henkel) or consumer durables (Electrolux, Volkswagen, Matsushita) produce and sell products under numerous names – in other words, brands – often through relatively autonomous organizational units.

In these cases, it is likely that someone inside the company (usually a brand manager or brand strategist) will eventually develop what marketing scholars refer to as a *brand identity* – in other words, a formalized statement about the set of associations that she wants to be attached to the brand by external audiences. Brand identities are expected to shape communication and product-related policies, and ultimately the way that a brand and related products are perceived by consumers – i.e., its *brand image* (Aaker, 1996). Building on these notions, brand scholars have developed a broad range of practical tools and guidelines aimed at assisting brand managers in their efforts to build, preserve, and exploit brands (Aaker and Joachimstaler, 2000; de Chernatony, 2001; Kapferer, 2004; Keller, 2003).

While initially developed for promoting products, the concepts and principles of product branding have been increasingly applied to the organizations that produce and market those products. This has led to a growing body of work on what is called the *corporate brand* (Hatch and Schultz, 2001). Earlier research emphasized how a strong corporate brand – i.e., favorable organizational images resting on, or associated with, a high reputation for expertise, trustworthiness, and responsibility – positively influence product brands, which are enriched and reinforced by the explicit endorsement of the organization (Aaker, 1996; Keller, 2000). More recently, it has been recognized that corporate branding, as a set of practices aimed at aligning the image of the organization with its strategy and culture, may be strategically important in coordinating and standardizing corporate communication and reinforcing relationships with all its stakeholders (Schultz, Antorini, and Csaba, 2005).

The effects that corporate branding can have on multiple stakeholders form an important boundary condition, demanding a high degree of foresight from managers.

Collectively, the chapters in this section provide rich examples of how corporate branding strategies, firm strategies, and members' views of their organizations are interrelated, thus illustrating how managers can operate in this promising and intriguing field.

Chapter 9

Starbucks

Constructing a multiplex identity in the specialty coffee industry

Viólina Rindova

Organizations compete for and on the basis of interpretations as much as they compete for and on the basis of resources. The interpretations that develop inside and around organizations have significant implications for the competitive advantage and positions of firms, because resource allocations follow interpretations (Rindova and Fombrun, 1999; Rindova, Becerra, and Contrado, 2004).

Interpretations about the identity of a social actor play a defining role in the nature of the actor's exchanges with other social actors. Individuals develop interpretations about the identity of others based on a wide array of cues available during social encounters, including appearance, mannerisms, language, actions, content of statements, and social associations (Goffman, 1959). In seeking to develop relationships with their stakeholders, however, firms do not have the benefits of such co-presence as they are represented to stakeholders by organizational members and artefacts (Rindova and Schultz, 1998; Ravasi and Schultz, 2006). In an effort to manage their self-presentations further, firms issue various types of communications, such as advertising campaigns, product brochures and catalogs, and company-sponsored magazines and newsletters. While pragmatically many corporate communications are created to fulfill some business purpose other than expressing the firm's identity, communications can have far-reaching effects on the interpretations of observers through selective information provision, emphasis on particular topics, and the use of specific images to promote desired associations. For example, firms produce annual reports because they are required by law to disclose certain information to shareholders. However, annual reports also communicate images and ideas that extend beyond simple information disclosure (Preston, Wright, and Young, 1996). The annual report published by Nucor – a US steel manufacturer renowned for its low-cost strategy and egalitarian culture – lists all employees of the organization, in alphabetical order, on the front cover. This annual report, therefore, is a symbol conveying meanings about the values, and thus the identity, of Nucor as an organization. However, managers may not always take into account the identity implications of a certain communication, or may fail to take advantage of its identity-building potential.

In this chapter I emphasize the identity-constructing role of corporate communications. Corporate communications contain representations – explicit or implicit, intended or unintended – of organizational practices, resource allocations, and positions. As such they provide answers to the fundamental identity question, "Who are we?" In order to highlight the relevance of this question to both external and internal audiences, in the following discussion I depart from the oft-drawn distinction between identity as an internal construct and image or reputation as external constructs (see Rindova and Schultz, 1998; also Ravasi and Schultz, 2006, for a discussion of the relevance of the internal–external distinction). I also recognize that corporate communications reflect only the official, executive-sanctioned identity claims of an organization. However, despite this characteristic, and often because of it, corporate communications play an important identity-constructing role because they are carefully crafted self-presentations that reflect how an organization wishes to be viewed and treated. As such, they play an important role in defining the nature of exchanges between firms and their stakeholders (Scott and Lane, 2000; Rindova, Becerra, and Contrado, 2004).

CORPORATE COMMUNICATION AND THE EXPRESSION OF IDENTITY

Corporate communications conventionally fall in the domain of marketing. According to Kotler, who gives a summary of the various forms of communication, their purpose is to convey "some kind of benefit, motivation, identification, or reason why the audience should think about or investigate the product" (1991: 575). Consistent with traditional approaches, Kotler divides the forms of communication between advertising and public relations as the two main types of marketing activities. However, the emergence of the concept of integrated marketing has highlighted the fact that a wide range of communications issued for different purposes may influence observers' perceptions of an organization and its identity, and that organizations can benefit from a more integrated approach.

The integrated marketing approach converges with the strategic view of corporate communications, which is concerned with the overall representation of a firm across different functions and target audiences and the interrelatedness of corporate communications and strategic investments in the overall strategic efforts of firms (Rindova and Fombrun, 1999). Thus, from a strategic point of view the purpose of corporate communications is to provide information about the firm in a way that leads stakeholders to view the firm as a superior exchange partner and motivates stakeholders to exchange resources with it.

While strategic research is clear about the strategic goals of corporate communications, it is less clear about the means by which corporate communications achieve these goals. It is often assumed in organizational and strategy research and practice that the communication experts – whether an advertising or PR agency, the investor relations department, or a sole employee with the unenviable role of answering miscellaneous stakeholder inquiries about the organization – can draw on the knowledge in various communication disciplines to come up with communication strategies that achieve the desired goal, namely to represent the organization in a manner that motivates stakeholders to exchange resources with it and increase their support for it. In this chapter, however, I will argue that the question of how an organization is represented in its corporate communications is a strategic one, and that the content of corporate communications is closely intertwined with the strategic choices of a firm. By representing *these choices* in a manner that engages stakeholders, corporate communications perform their strategic function. The previous sentence emphasizes both the content of corporate communications in reflecting the relevant strategic choices of a firm and the discursive means employed to engage stakeholder audiences. These two elements represent the central emphases of this chapter – my goal is to explore the different discursive means available to firms to represent their strategic choices in order to construct what I call a "multiplex identity."

The idea of multiplex identity derives from my in-depth analysis of the corporate communications of the Starbucks Coffee Company and its nearest competitors in the specialty coffee industry in the US in the 1990s. A key observation from this analysis, discussed in the remainder of this chapter, is that Starbucks used a more diverse set of discursive means and constructed its identity using four different communication strategies: rational, social, emotional, and aesthetic. In contrast, its competitors relied primarily on rational communication strategies, focusing specifically on product benefits and advantages. While consistent with conventional marketing ideas about product advantages, communications that emphasize a firm's technology and the attendant product benefits may be too limited to achieve the strategic purpose of corporate communications – to present the strategic choices of the firm in a manner that enables stakeholders to develop preferences for the firm as an exchange partner. In contrast to the conventional approach, Starbucks' communication strategies represented the firm in a multifaceted manner and constructed its multiplex identity.

The concept of multiplex identity developed here builds on research on social relationships and social capital, which has argued that relationships that involve multiple overlapping roles are multiplex (i.e., they have many different facets). For example, a relationship in which one can be a spouse, a parent, and a friend is a multiplex relationship. Such relationships are argued to not only enable the efficient use of scarce time and energy but also to enhance the affective importance and meaning of the identities involved in these relationships (Thoits, 1983: 178). I extend these arguments to contend that identities that have multiple, overlapping dimensions are multiplex and that their varied facets enable the development of more nuanced, meaningful, rich, and engaged relationships as they stimulate more diverse exchanges among the participants in the relationship. As I describe later, a multiplex firm identity engages stakeholders on many levels – cognitive-rational, cognitive-normative, emotional, and aesthetic. As a result, stakeholder relationships with the firm may transcend conventional pragmatic considerations, and may also engender emotional attachment and aesthetic appreciation. As a consequence, firm–stakeholder interactions may become richer and more meaningful. In other words, multiplex identities may contribute to the development of multiplex relationships.

In the remainder of this chapter I provide some information about the research context and analysis on which the above ideas are based, and then develop in detail the four communication strategies that I identified as enabling firms to build multiplex identities. More specifically, to outline the distinct communication-based approach that Starbucks took and to highlight the different competitive outcomes that the various players obtained, I first discuss the emergence of the specialty coffee niche market and the growth strategies the focal firms adopted. Second, I discuss the four communication strategies that characterized Starbucks' corporate communications and their identity-constructing effects.

AN INDUSTRY BREWING

The specialty coffee niche emerged as a separate segment of the coffee industry in the 1960s. It developed as a reaction to the mainstream coffee industry in the US, which was dominated by the divisions of three international con-glomerates – Maxwell House (a division of General Foods), Folgers (a division of Procter & Gamble), and Nestlé. These three large players dominated the industry and competed on price and access to distribution channels, such as supermarkets. To keep costs low they bought the cheapest available coffee beans, roasted coffee in large commercial batches, and sold it in cans through the supermarket channel. While cost-efficient, most of these practices did little for the taste of the coffee, leading to a decline in demand. According to the National Coffee Association, between 1962 and 1991 coffee consumption in the US declined from 3.1 cups a day to 1.75. The large coffee companies attrib-uted these changes to growing health concerns and did little to improve their production practices.

However, it was their cost-oriented practices that systematically alienated con-sumers, in particular younger generations of consumers who grew up experi-encing coffee as a canned, undifferentiated product. In this impoverished market, small entrepreneurial firms began to emerge in the mid-1960s. They sought to build close relationships with local customers who were attracted to the carefully selected, freshly roasted coffee that these specialty coffee retailers offered. Specialty coffee retailers viewed themselves as operating in a small niche, where they could charge a premium price for a premium product. However, by the mid-1990s the specialty coffee sector had grown to 20 percent of the total revenues of the coffee industry (see Rindova and Fombrun, 1999, for further discussion). Although most companies in the industry remained relatively small, by the mid-1990s several had emerged as national chains with several hundred stores. In 1997, the four largest specialty coffee chains in the US were Starbucks (1,270 stores), Gloria Jean's Coffee Bean (267), the Coffee Beanery (190), and Barnie's Coffee Company (100). The first entrant in the specialty coffee niche – Peet's Coffee Company – operated 33 stores. In comparing the size of these chains, it is important to note that, of the five, only Starbucks operated as a public company; however, prior to going public in 1992, Starbucks was smaller than its nearest competitor, Gloria Jean's Coffee Bean, which in 1991 operated 124 stores as opposed to the 110 of Starbucks. These companies had chosen to compete as chains, and in doing so they had departed from the original model for specialty coffee retail based on a single store that sought to build local relationships with customers. However, they differed significantly in the means by which they sought to build relationships with their customers.

Peet's Coffee and Tea Company was founded in 1966 in Berkeley, California. Its founding is regarded as the official birth of the specialty coffee industry in the US. Peet's remained the model specialty coffee retailer and one that was widely regarded by other specialty coffee retailers as the quality leader of the industry. Although it has begun to expand, it has done so carefully, using an organic growth strategy to maintain personal contact with its customers. The personal contact between employees and immediate customers was Peet's primary communication strategy. The décor of its dark-brown, wood-rich stores with a few scattered coffee-related artefacts was aimed primarily at the already converted or at least the informed.

The Starbucks Coffee Company had a close birth link to Peet's, as the original founders of Starbucks were Berkeley graduates who received their coffee training from Peet's founder, Alfred Peet. Further, they sold Starbucks to Howard Schultz in the late 1980s to buy Peet's, which had come up for sale. Howard Schultz merged the original Starbucks Coffee Company with his own start-up Il Giornale, which sought to introduce the concept of the Italian coffee bar to the US. In 1987 Starbucks began a national expansion with a clearly stated goal of becoming the number one specialty coffee retailer. Unlike Peet's, Starbucks sought to build relationships with a large number of anonymous consumers, and although its employees were encouraged to develop one-to-one relationships with regular customers, the centerpiece of its growth strategy was a set of communication strategies that constructed an unusual and highly appealing identity for the company. Because of these characteristics, Starbucks has been chosen as the focal company of this study and an "exemplary case" best illustrating the phenomenon of interest; namely, the use of corporate communications to construct identity

(Yin, 1994). The other cases are used to refine the insights derived from the analysis of the focal company and to rule out alternative explanations, for instance that stakeholders' engagement with Starbucks could be explained primarily by its large size and ubiquitous market presence.

Gloria Jean's Coffee Bean is an example of a firm that pursued size advantages early on and became the first national chain of specialty coffee stores. As mentioned earlier, prior to Starbucks going public Gloria Jean's was the largest specialty coffee chain in the US. It was founded in 1979 by two entrepreneurs who converted an old gift shop into a shop specializing in specialty coffees. The success of the store led them to begin a national expansion through franchising. Communications and relationships with customers were not central to the firm's growth strategy as it grew opportunistically using a very "hands-off" approach to their franchisees. The Coffee Beanery had a similar history and followed the same growth logic as Gloria Jean's, though with fewer stores. It was therefore not used for further detailed analysis of communications.

Barnie's Coffee and Tea Company also sought rapid growth. It was founded in 1980 in Orlando, Florida, and two years after its creation had a dozen stores (by comparison Starbucks had 12 stores after 15 years of operations from 1971 to 1986). Barnie's also claimed a number of product innovations in the industry, including the first coffee chain, the first to use flavored coffees, the first to introduce decaf coffees, and the first to "develop an understanding that our stores would eventually be a brand, a product brand" (interview data). As such, Barnie's provides an example of and control for an alternative explanation of the stakeholder engagement with a firm as being driven by the introduction of novel products and features.

Together the four companies provided an excellent set of cases of companies confronting an environment in which their fundamental relationships with consumers and the dimensions along which value was created in the industry were changing. The four took different approaches to competing in the industry. Two of the companies – Gloria Jean's Coffee Bean and Barnie's Coffee Company – focused primarily on exploiting a growth opportunity they had identified. While they grew rapidly in the early years of the evolution of the specialty coffee sector, they were not able to create sustainable competitive positions, despite their ability to build sizeable chains of stores. Barnie's also sought to fuel the growth of the demand for specialty coffee by developing novel and "more specialty" product and service features. Yet product innovation alone was not sufficient to enable it to maintain a sustainable position in the industry. Starbucks, by contrast, while also seeking growth from the mid-1980s onwards, made the construction of a unique identity a centerpiece of its growth strategies. Its emphasis on communications as a growth strategy was viewed as a weakness by the industry, and some of its industry peers characterized it unflatteringly as "a marketing company, not a coffee company." As I argued earlier and will show later, such a dichotomy

between the "technological" aspect of a firm's identity as derived from the production technologies it controlled and mastered, and other aspects of an organizational identity that may be seen as less valuable by insiders due to their internal
focus on technology, may prevent firms from developing what I term a "multiplex
identity." In contrast, Starbucks' "marketing approach" was characterized by a
considerable attention to communications and the variety of meanings they can
be used to convey. The next section analyzes the company's communication
strategies in detail.

COMMUNICATION BLENDS: RATIONAL, SOCIAL, EMOTIONAL, AND AESTHETIC STRATEGIES

The rational communication strategy and a firm's identity as an economic actor

A rational communications strategy incorporates two subthemes: technical and
strategic presentations.

Technical presentations are concerned with communicating information about the
technologies a firm deploys and educating stakeholders about the relationship
between the use of a particular type of technology and the product attributes it
enables the firm to create. Through technical communications, firms can position
an innovative product as having higher levels of customer value by linking specific
product attributes to the firm's technological capabilities. In other words, these
communications focus on new features and functions that a company sees itself as
(or would like others to see it as) contributing in product markets.

In the case of specialty coffee, Starbucks and other leading specialty coffee
retailers placed great emphasis on articulating product dimensions along which
specialty coffee represented a significant improvement in value over traditional
commercial coffee. For example, they discussed the roasting process as an important technological aspect of their firms that enabled them to create variation in
coffee flavors, which was deemed a significant source of value:

> Dark roasts use coffees of varying geographic origins to provide a specific
> range of flavors, from the caramel spice of Espresso, to the smoky tang of
> Italian Roast, to the pungent roastiness of French Roast.
>
> (Product communication brochure, Starbucks Coffee Company)

By using technical communications, specialty coffee retailers provided consumers
with dimensions along which the value of coffee should be evaluated, as well as
with measures of quality on these dimensions.

In addition to highlighting the dimensions of quality along which their products
could be considered superior at the level of the product category, the companies

used technical communications to make *firm-specific statements about product quality*. These statements (and images) describe the specific characteristics of a firm's offerings that make them of superior value. Statements in this category were quite similar to the definitions of product value characteristics described above, but focused on specific attributes of the firm's products rather than on the product category. Whereas product descriptions at the category level position the firm's products relative to those of competitors in a broader competitive context, including substitute products or traditional products relative to which the firm is innovating, firm-specific quality descriptions position the firm relative to direct competitors using similar technologies and innovating along similar product dimensions.

The second type of presentations within the category of rational communication strategies are strategic presentations. *Strategic presentations* include descriptions of a firm's assets, success, and uniqueness. In statements in the first category, firms' communications covered both tangible resources, such as their plants and facilities, and intangible resources, such as brand recognition and employee expertise. Such statements can serve to reassure stakeholders about the ability of a firm to secure access to relevant resources. For example, the fourth largest coffee chain in the mid-1990s – Barnie's – reported in a product brochure that it had "120 locations in 18 states." This statement conveys information about the firm's asset base and its size. Although not required to disclose such information as private companies (with the exception of Starbucks, which went public in 1992, as stated earlier), specialty coffee chains chose to provide information about various aspects of performance including size, sales, growth rates, expansion, and strategic objectives that some of these firms had set for themselves.

Such information, and strategic presentations in general, is intended to portray the firm as a formidable competitor. It describes the degree to which a firm has developed a competitive advantage, both as a bundle of unique resources (Barney, 1991) and as a position in a product market (Porter, 1980). Strategic presentations convey the capability of a firm to compete successfully – backed up by resources and evidenced by results and a unique position.

Overall, the rational communication strategies serve to represent and develop the identity of the firm as an economic actor: as a producer of goods through technical presentations and as a user of resources through strategic presentations. These presentations of the firm are consistent with theories of the firm as developed in economic theory and the strategic research based on them. In general, rational communication strategies appeal to the audience's self-interest by emphasizing quality, economy, and value. At the firm level, rational communication strategies can build an attractive economic identity for the firm as possessing the potential to create value for both consumers and investors.

Rational strategies therefore engage stakeholders as exchange partners by suggesting benefits they can gain by transacting with the firm. Whereas technical presentations may be directed primarily toward consumers by emphasizing product attributes, they can also be useful to investors because they provide information about the product category and the different ways that firms competing in it seek to create value. Similarly, whereas strategic presentations may be directed primarily toward investors by emphasizing growth and performance, consumers may find them informative about how a firm compares to its competitors, enabling them to draw inferences about competing product offerings.

Overall, rational communication strategies address the main issues in evaluating firms – how they create value for customers (Porter, 1985; Moran and Goshal, 1999) and how effectively they compete for resources. Therefore, it is a strategy that tends to be used by the majority of firms competing in a market.

The social communication strategy and a firm's identity as an exchange partner

The second type of communication strategy is a social strategy. It comprises presentations of values, relationships, and standards.

Presentations of values explicitly state values or moral attributes that a firm seeks to associate itself with, such as honesty, integrity, and honoring of commitments. Such values express the moral sentiments that make social actors desirable exchange partners across a wide range of transactions (Jones, 1995). Actors who possess such characteristics are viewed as desirable partners because they can be trusted to do the right thing. In the case of the specialty coffee sector, specialty coffee retailers discuss integrity in bean selection and labeling, and commitment to product quality as a form of commitment to quality of life. In other words, statements of values provide observers with information about the principles that are intended to guide the actions, and even the overall strategy, of the firm. According to communications issued by the Starbucks Coffee Company, "Many of the specifics that make our company seem unique to others are, to our way of thinking, simply natural, even inevitable consequences of this core attitude and aspiration." In addition, presentations about values may create additional consumer value because some consumers value a congruence of brand values and their own personal values.

Presentations of value include statements (and images) that provide evidence about *how* a firm lives up to its values. These statements usually give examples and concretize professed values by linking them to specific practices. As such, they add texture and vividness, without which statements of values may be too abstract and declarative, and therefore less credible.

A second type of presentation that can be considered part of the social communication strategy of the firm are presentations of its *relationships with various stakeholders*. I observed several different types of presentations that described (and in a sense made visible) the relationships of a firm with different stakeholders.

Some presentations described the firm's *relationships as exchanges* — statements (or images) describing what resources different stakeholders give and receive in trans-acting with the firm. These described what a firm gives as well as receives from a given stakeholder group. In doing so, the firm is able to demonstrate that resources are being made available to it, thereby providing an example to other stakeholders. For example, in a product brochure Peet's Coffee Company communicated to its customers that:

> Peet's customers clearly appreciate our blends; over the years blends have become an increasingly greater part of our business, as customers discover that the complex flavors of a blend give them more pleasure than an individual coffee.

A second type of presentation about stakeholder relationships focused on the social capital that the firm had developed in its ongoing relationships, such as trust, respect, and cooperation (Nahapiet and Goshal, 1998). While social capital develops as a by-product of exchange over time, actors may make specific invest-ments to enhance it and use it as a resource. By explicitly discussing elements of the social capital it has developed, a firm (1) symbolically takes stock of this capital, thus validating its existence; (2) draws attention to the ongoing nature of relationships in contrast to one-off transactions; and (3) demonstrates that it understands the commitments associated with social capital and indicates that it is likely to honor them. Like the presentations of values, presentations of relation-ships as social capital build the identity of a firm as an exchange partner.

A third type of statement about relationships with stakeholders focused on their interdependence, describing either how the interests of one stakeholder group can be satisfied by taking care of the interests of another, or by emphasizing the embeddedness of a firm and its stakeholders in a community. Divergence of stakeholder interests makes stakeholder management a balancing act that firms perform to satisfy their often conflicting demands (Preston, Wright, and Young, 1996). However, in the specialty coffee sector Starbucks used communications to demonstrate interdependencies among various stakeholders and the outcomes they desire, as the following example from its communications indicates:

> We seek to seamlessly interweave variables that ensure quality for the customer with literal ownership in the company.

Marketing scholars tend to characterize social appeals as affective, in contrast to rational or cognitive appeals (Dube, Chattopadhyay, and Letrate, 1996). At the firm level, however, a social communication strategy enables a firm to represent itself as a participant in social relations and to construct its identity as an exchange partner and member of a social collective. Thus, like rational communication strategies, social communication strategies engage stakeholders as exchange partners. However, unlike rational communication strategies, which focus on the benefits of the exchange, social communication strategies establish the desirability of the firm as an exchange partner in terms of its moral character and ability to maintain equitable relationships. Jones (1995) argues that the expression of values has the potential to increase the desirability of social actors as exchange partners, because moral values indicate how participants in an exchange may treat each other in ways that depart from the expected self-interested behavior. Thus, social communication strategies enable the firm to differentiate itself on the basis not only of the economic value of its activities but also on the moral values that may underlie its relationships with stakeholders as exchange partners.

The emotional communication strategy and a firm's affective identity

Detailed analysis indicated that the communications of specialty coffee chains also varied in the extent to which they included references to emotions, or statements (and images) referring to or reflecting emotional states of organizational members or stakeholders. The vast majority of references to emotions were to positive emotions such as love, joy, and excitement. Such references build the affective identity of a firm by displaying the emotional experience of organizational members.

Building an affective identity through an emotional communication strategy achieves two types of results. First, the display of emotional behaviors leads to greater levels of affiliation and involvement with a social group (Plutchik, 1980). Emotional references invite observers to relate to the firm on an emotional level; for example, by making reference to the collective feeling and emotions of organizational members, Starbucks de-emphasizes the business aspect of exchanges and stresses the aspect of a shared human experience.

Second, displays of emotions serve to regulate the emotional responses of others. For example, positive expressions stimulate supportive, sharing, and expansive behaviors, whilst the display of negative emotions leads to distancing and avoidance (Reeve, 1992). Emotional expressions further facilitate social interaction, as the display of positive emotions, such as a smile, is considered a universal greeting. Communications with emotional content may trigger similar responses. At the organizational level an emotional communication strategy intended to display positive emotions may convey an open and welcoming attitude toward observers. In addition, to the extent that a positive affect encourages prosocial behavior, a display of positive emotions may stimulate supportive behaviors among stakeholders.

The emotional communication strategy just described differs from the emotional appeals used in product marketing, which are aimed at an audience's feelings of fear, guilt, shame, love, pride, and joy (Kotler, 1991). Rather than appealing to the emotions of observers, the emotional communication strategy presents the emotions of organizational members, thereby building the affective identity of the firm.

In considering an emotional communication strategy, it is important to bear in mind that a key issue that arises with the display of emotions is their authenticity. If observers perceive these references to be inauthentic (i.e., the firm is "faking it"), an emotional communication strategy may backfire. For example, Barnie's product brochure used an emotional reference to communicate an organization-wide attitude, and thus a potential quality guarantee: "At Barnie's our love for coffee has made all of us coffee perfectionists." However, the firm did not employ the highest coffee processing and production standards in the industry (as was the case with Peet's and Starbucks in the 1980s and early 1990s). As a result, customers could question the authenticity of the displayed emotions, and, by extension, the trustworthiness of the firm's communications more generally.

As this example indicates, this strategy should be used judiciously since observers may seek to verify the authenticity of emotional claims through contacts with employees or observation of organizational practices. In the case of Starbucks, for instance, the company benefited from its emotional communication strategy because early reviews of the firm's stores reported that employees conveyed a genuine enthusiasm for coffee. Overall, fewer competitors may be able to employ this communication strategy, unless they are confident that their emotion-laden statements to some extent reflect the underlying experiences of organizational members.

The aesthetic communication strategy and a firm's symbolic identity

A final dimension along which the communication strategies of the specialty coffee retailers differed was the degree to which they maintained a consistent linguistic and/or visual frame. A *visual frame* refers to the stylistic integrity of the images and artefacts associated with a firm, including graphic design, store design, use of photographs and paintings in the stores, and print communications. The visual frame is distinguished both by the *symbolic content in the form of images*, which elaborate on and embellish various aspects of the firm's activities, and by the coherent use of colors, textures, patterns, and shapes. The symbolic content generates the reflective effects of the visual frame and identity (i.e., the meanings they evoke). The colors, textures, patterns, and shapes a firm employs generate the visceral effects of its visual frame and identity, which determine which sensory experiences they trigger.

In a similar fashion, a *linguistic frame* encompasses linguistic stimuli, such as slogans, mottoes, terms and labels, stories, vignettes and metaphors, as well as statements accompanying visual stimuli, such as advertising copy. Like the visual frame, the linguistic frame comprises *symbolic content*, which includes story characters, metaphors, and other figures of speech that elaborate on and embellish various aspects of the firm, and a pattern of use of concepts, *metaphors, and other linguistic means* that generate a visceral response at the linguistic level. For example, Starbucks introduced and insisted on the use of Italian terms for various aspects of the coffee purchase and consumption process.

Deploying both linguistic and visual messages in building the symbolic identity of a firm is important because linguistic and visual stimuli are processed differently by the brain. Verbal messages are digital — they use combinations of letters and numbers to convey information; visual messages are iconic — they resemble what they represent (Pettersson, 1993). Perception of text is linear and slow perception of images is simultaneous, holistic, and fast. As a result, images are easier to grasp and remember. However, their interpretation is less consistent across subjects and situations and usually requires some framing through text. Visual stimuli show clearer effects on memory than linguistic stimuli with repeated exposure. Linguistic stimuli show effects with repeated exposure only if the message is cogent and the recipient processes it actively (Fiske and Taylor, 1991). As components of aesthetic communication strategies, both types of stimuli are used to create aesthetic value.

The question about what constitutes aesthetic value is debated in the field of philosophy (Schmitt and Simonson, 1997). Some philosophers have argued that aesthetic value derives from the fact that certain structural characteristics, such as unity or gestalt, appeal to people. Others have argued that it derives from the referential properties of aesthetic objects (i.e., because they symbolize other pleasing things). My analysis of corporate communications shows that aesthetic communication strategies rely on both. The structural component is created through the consistency of visual or linguistic cues. The referential component is created though the symbolic content of visual and linguistic images.

In sum, the use of aesthetic strategies also creates value for observers because of the inherent pleasantness of the aesthetic experience. In addition, an aesthetic communication strategy can differentiate firms by building their symbolic identity, combining sensory vividness with symbolic distinctiveness to transform the exchange experience into something that is beyond the everyday and the ordinary.

From diverse communication strategies to a multiplex identity

My analysis of the corporate communications of four leading specialty coffee retailers in the mid-1990s suggests four broad strategies that enable firms to construct multiple appeals across communication settings. I have argued that these diverse communication strategies enabled firms to build multiplex identities, i.e., identities with many facets that engage stakeholders in different ways — cognitively, emotionally, and aesthetically. While the idea of using different means to appeal to stakeholders is not entirely new, research shows that even in the area of product advertising the majority of corporate communications in the US rely on rational communication strategies (Dube, Chattopadhyay, and Letarte, 1996). Strictly rational communication strategies enable firms to establish only one type of identity – that as economic actors using resources more or less effectively to supply products of varying qualities. In contrast, firms that incorporate diverse communication strategies are able to develop multiplex identities to connect with their stakeholders in more diverse and more meaningful ways – they are able to build relationships that provide them with more lasting competitive positions, even in markets where consumer tastes change rapidly as new social trends and sentiments emerge. Through these communication strategies, firms, like individuals, construct their identity. By expressing these multiple aspects of self, firms can create multiplex identities, which enable multiple modes of engagement between the firm and its various stakeholders. Rational strategies appeal to observers who focus on the utility they derive from transactions with a firm. Social strategies appeal to observers' sense of identification with a social group. Emotional strategies appeal to observers' emotions. Aesthetic strategies appeal to observers' sense of beauty and/or taste for the arts. These strategies are complementary in that they present different selves of a firm and thus broaden its overall appeal to diverse observers. Rational strategies present the firm as an economic actor – a creator of value for customers and investors and a user of economic resources; social strategies present the firm as a member of a social group and a partner in an exchange process; emotional strategies present the firm as a source of emotional experiences; and aesthetic strategies present the company as a source of beautiful, extraordinary experiences.

Multiple modes of engagement create a multidimensional relationship where economic preferences, social commitments, and aesthetic appreciation may enhance, compensate for, or outweigh each other, as well as interact in other ways to affect stakeholders' interpretations of a firm.

Multiple modes of engagement also facilitate the meaning-making processes and therefore the development of favorable interpretations of firms. They appeal to different sides of observers, affecting not only how they understand but also how they feel about, accept, like, and ultimately prefer a firm and its offerings. Traditional approaches to communications rest on an information-processing perspective of cognition emphasizing issues relating to the amount, timing, and veracity of information (Heil and Robertson, 1991; Abernethy and Franke, 1996). Recent research in cognition has begun to demonstrate differences between an information-processing and a narrative mode of meaning-making (Brunner, 1990; Tenkasi and Boland, 1993). A story about a firm's strategy that presents it as an "epiphany" about changing people's lives (as in the case of Starbucks) affects the meanings observers associate with the firm differently than a statement of growth objectives. Research in marketing has shown that in making purchasing decisions, consumers rely on "symbolic meanings, hedonic responses, and aesthetic criteria"

(Holbrook and Hirschman, 1982: 132). Thus, the typology developed here shows how firms use different communication strategies to present multiplex identities and to stimulate different types of meaning-making processes.

Multiple communication strategies offer multiple cues. As such, they enable observers to develop more complex and elaborate schemas of the firm, which facilitate future information processing (Fiske and Taylor, 1991). With more developed schemas, observers can better evaluate each specific claim a firm makes as they have varied concepts and frameworks in which to place new cues.

Each communication strategy provides information, which observers may find useful and necessary. For example, rational strategies address one of the central problems in exchange – the problem of information asymmetries. Rational communication strategies may increase (or create an appearance of increased) transparency. Transparency means that the products, practices, and competitive position of a firm are made more apparent and comprehensible to observers. As a result, firms that use rational communication strategies may enjoy more cognitive legitimacy with resource holders (Aldrich and Fiol, 1994).

Social communication strategies address the problem of individual versus collective interests. They may increase or create the appearance of increased integration of the firm with the social group. Resource holders may feel more assured and the firm may enjoy higher sociopolitical legitimacy. Emotional strategies reduce the impersonality of exchange, and as a result resource holders may feel more involved. Aesthetic strategies make the firm more distinctive. As a consequence, resource holders may be more attracted to it. Therefore, all of these strategies may contribute to interpretations of uniqueness, which increase the attractiveness of a firm's identity (Dutton, Dukerich, and Harquil, 1994).

In addition to the specific effects of each of the strategies, multiple communication strategies may increase overall communication effectiveness through their interaction effects, i.e., the effects of communications of one type on the reception and interpretation of communications of another type. In discussing the development of cultures as shared understandings, Geertz (1973: 127) suggested that rational conceptions of the nature of the world justify the moral order by making it "intellectually reasonable by being shown to represent the way of life implied by the actual state of affairs which the world view describes"; similarly, the rational conceptions of the world are "made emotionally acceptable" by the moral order. Similar interplay may be at work with rational, social, emotional, and aesthetic communication strategies. Multiple communication strategies may be more effective because they represent many sides of a firm, enable it to engage observers in different modes, and possibly interact with each other in meaning-making.

In conclusion, it is important to remember that regardless of whether a firm uses communications purposefully to influence perceptions of itself, observers ascribe meanings to its actions and develop images of it. In other words, observers develop interpretations about firms irrespective of whether and how firms choose to engage in the process of influencing these interpretations. Firms that use communications purposefully to manage the interpretations that observers develop about them have greater influence over the process (Rindova and Fombrun, 1999). Furthermore, firms that use communications in a sophisticated manner to develop multiplex identities may enjoy relationships with stakeholders that are both more lasting and more meaningful. Such relationships are viewed by marketers, strategists, and organizational managers alike as some of the most (in)valuable assets companies can develop.

APPENDIX: RESEARCH DESIGN AND PROCESS

To address the lack of theory in extant strategy research on the strategic role of corporate communications, I used grounded theory building (Glaser and Strauss, 1967). Grounded theory methodology is suitable when substantial properties of a phenomenon of interest are not well understood. As Strauss and Corbin (1990: 191) explain: "The overall purpose of this approach is to describe the phenomenon as completely and with as much specificity as possible."

Data collection

I collected printed communications from different specialty coffee retailers both by visiting company stores and by requesting materials from their marketing departments. I also contacted the advertising and PR agencies that informants or media reports mentioned as having done some work for the focal firms. Informants from these agencies provided some archival materials and gave verbal accounts about the design and execution of communication campaigns for the firms. In addition, I conducted extensive interviews with founders of specialty coffee chains and several informants provided copies of their personal archives. The search generated a total of 103 documents consisting of approximately 300 pages of text and images. I also conducted store observation by visiting stores of the focal companies. I took pictures and used coding notes to record the content of in-store communications.

Data analysis and theory building

To analyze the data I used the coding procedures of grounded theory. I started by open coding and identifying key themes. Ideas and concepts were recorded in theoretical notes (Strauss and Corbin, 1990) that became the foundation of the emerging theory. Initially, I used within-case analysis for Starbucks' communications to develop categories for the content and form of communications (Elsbach, 1994). The result of this process was a typology of communication strategies, consisting of four main strategies with specific presentation themes in each. Having reached theoretical saturation (i.e., new data added no new concepts) and construct stability (i.e., repeated coding placed occurrences in the same categories), I analyzed the data to establish the degree of support for the theory.

Chapter 10

Projecting organizational identity through organizational dress at Air France, 1933–2005

Guillaume Soenen, Philippe Monin, and Audrey Rouzies

The choice of a uniform is both a delicate and exciting decision for every airline company. And when your name is Air France, it requires that extra something special . . . The uniform is a fantastic way to convey our image to our customers and a significant working tool for all the employees who wear it. For our passengers, it is a way of easily identifying Air France staff. It also carries a reassuring image of professionalism, competence, and proximity, while expressing a certain human warmth. Christian Lacroix's proposal fits perfectly within the history of Air France, which has worked with great names in French haute couture several times in the past. He was able to fully express all the values that we, as a company, want to convey, by translating a sense of openness to the world, along with a certain idea of modernity and innovation. Even more than a symbol of elegance representing the quality of service offered by a company, the uniform demonstrates the importance with which we consider our workforce, which forms the core of our company strategy.

(Air France CEO Jean-Cyril Spinetta's tribute to Christian Lacroix's
work, Fashion Show, Air France Headquarters, Roissy, Paris,
September 4, 2003)

INTRODUCTION

In service industries such as airlines with frequent and intensive contact encounters, employees' attire can be used to project an organization's identity. To illustrate this, we relate the evolution of Air France flight attendants' outfits since the company's creation in 1933 up to the release in 2005 of the latest organizational wardrobe, designed by Christian Lacroix. Our impetus for such an analysis is the following question: how can a single artefact such as flight attendants' outfits be tailored to reflect the complex identity(ies) of a large organization such as Air France?

THE EVOLUTION OF THE ORGANIZATIONAL IDENTITIES AND STRATEGIC CONTEXT OF AIR FRANCE, 1933–2005

Organizations often have multiple identities. Furthermore, organizational identities are composed of several facets. Soenen and Moingeon (2002) have proposed a system of five facets to understand identity dynamics in organizational settings: the projected, professed, manifested, attributed, and experienced identity facets. In this chapter, we focus on two of these. The *projected* identity facet refers to identity claims that are mediated and used to project a desired corporate identity (of which organizational dress is but one component, alongside logos, ad campaigns, etc.), while the *manifested* identity facet refers to those enduring elements that make up the technical core of an organization (Thomson, 1967; Larçon and Reitter, 1979).[1] Enduring elements include most notably organizational routines, technology, and achievements, but also relational systems and the demographic aspects of the workforce composition.

Based on Autier *et al.*'s (2001) in-depth analysis, we identified seven major changes in the projected and manifested aspects of Air France's identity: in 1933, 1945, 1970, 1977, 1988, 1993, and 2004. In order to help understand the changes in organizational identity facets we report on the industry dynamics and evolution of Air France's strategic context (Table 6); we then describe how the identity facets changed from one period to another (Table 7).

Since its creation in 1933, Air France has been a French emblem, if not a myth (Thibault, 2005). Before the Second World War the flagship company was associated with the heroes of the Aéropostale, the "flying madmen" like Mermoz, Daurat, and Saint-Exupéry who opened new routes and diffused news worldwide. After the Second World War the flight attendants of the company became a symbol of French elegance around the world. Air France went through several major rebirthing processes during its history. After the Second World War the company was nationalized, remaining a state-owned carrier for half a century. From the 1990s Air France was gradually privatized, with the share of the state decreasing from 100 percent in 1945 to 75 percent in 1999, 53 percent in 2003, and less than 20 percent in 2005. Air France had been — and still to some extent is

---

[1] The experienced identity refers to organizational members' beliefs about their organization's core, enduring, and distinctive features, while the professed identity refers to the identity claims that are orally professed by organizational subgroups when describing their organization: experience and discourse do not necessarily match. The attributed identity refers to the identity traits that are ascribed to the organization by its external publics (this is also referred to as corporate image or reputation).

Table 6 Industry dynamics and the evolution of Air France's strategic context

	1933	1945	1970	1977	1988	1993	2004
Industry dynamics and Air France's strategic context	The infancy of commercial aviation	Jet engine revolution Higher passenger capacity and reduced flying times	Growing traffic First oil crisis in 1973 Deregulation of the US market Joint monopoly: competition with Air Inter and UTA in the "sanctuary perimeter" (France)	Privatization in Europe (e.g., BA, KLM) *Hub-based* business model replaces *network-based* business model Second oil crisis in 1979 Government-led "Contrats de plans" from 1978 to prepare privatization of Air France	Stock exchange crash late 1987; numerous oil shocks (first Iraq War) Further deregulation worldwide End of shared monopoly (merger of Air France, Air Inter and UTA, 1990) but deregulation is rejected (Government change in France, early 1988; Gayssot, new communist French Minister of Transport, postpones privatization)	Bankruptcy of some major US airlines Second Iraq War September 11, 2001 Privatization ready in 1997, but again postponed as a result of government change Partial privatization 1998	Return to sustained growth and increased profits

Notes: All quotes are from Autier *et al.* (2001)

Table 7 Evolution of Air France's organizational identity facets

	1933	1945	1970	1977	1988	1993	2004
Projected identity toward the general public	Opening routes: the mystique of the line: "We are pioneers," and open new routes"	Technological excellence and security: technical paradigm, or the belief that technical perfection is primary, hence a focus on security Frenchness: "Diplomacy and the French Pavillon (flag)" "Public Service"	Commercial expansion and democratization	Market orientation	Troubled times, communication budget cuts, unclear projected identity, Air France close to financial abyss The times were not "propitious for imaginative undertakings"		Being the preferred company, focus on customers Seven words: openness, elegance, efficiency, movement, proximity, pleasure, and a "French touch"
Manifested identity *Routines, technology, and achievements*		Safety and Security Certificate (1955) "Growing hierarchy and bureaucracy following militarization"	First Boeing 747 at Air France in 1970 (seating capacity over 400)	First Concorde 1976 Multiple tariffs 1977 Business class and tourist class 1978	GDS Amadeus 1987	Bankruptcy 1993 Largest strike ever in 1993 First Air France president to resign in 1993 Roissy hub creation Skyteam founder Adoption of modern techniques (revenue optimization; yield management, etc.)	"Combination" then merger of Air France and KLM, achieving a major 80 per cent privatization
Relational systems, workforce composition, demography	Creation of the PCB derogatory category (Non-essential Extra in-flight staff). Only males below 60 kg (30 in 1939)	First female 1946 Marriage forbidden Aristocratic ("de") Recruitment from Red Cross and non-combatant military services Flight attendants eventually allowed to marry (1963)		New division of labor and shifting relations between "head" and "tail"		Working conditions deteriorate as productivity targets increase	

Notes: All quotes from Autier *et al.* (2001)

– a pure example of the "French model of corporate governance," where divergent stakeholders (the French state, workers' unions, employees, and the general management), coexisted and – practically speaking – shared the management of the company. After a series of domestic acquisitions (UTA and Air Inter in 1990) and the founding of the Skyteam Alliance in 2000, Air France eventually merged with KLM on May 5, 2004. In 2004, Air France–KLM was the leading airline company worldwide, with a turnover of 18.2 billion euros. Today, Air France *itself* is a major player in the air transport industry, with 71,000 employees, including 15,000 flight attendants, more than 200 destinations, 1,800 daily flights, 44 million passengers transported in 2004, and a fleet of 373 planes.

1933

Before the Second World War commercial aviation was still in its infancy. Air France was created in 1933 and the identity it projected (*projected* identity) was that of a "route opener." This was the period of the "mystique of the line": employees – pilots, co-pilots, or mechanics – were pioneers who opened up new "lines." The outfits of the flight attendants, however, convey symbols of luxury and service derived from bartenders' uniforms, which are not linked to the pioneering spirit. These are rather a reflection of the *manifested* identity. Indeed, at the time, flight attendants were barely "members" of the organization and on-board service was marginal: the first flight attendant was recruited in 1933 when the "Personnel Complementaire de Bord" category (or "Extra Inflight Staff") was created. Before 1939, only 30 attendants – all men under 60 kg – would be recruited: the weight restriction was to allow for heavy passengers. Often, Extra Inflight Staff would not even board because the aircraft was overloaded.

1945

With the jet engine revolution, flying times dropped significantly and passenger capacity increased. Air France *projected* identity changes: the pioneer era was over and the identity now emphasized technological excellence, security, and "Frenchness." Simultaneously, there was a change in the company's *manifested* identity. By this time, Air France had become the leading non-US carrier in size and number of routes. As regards organizational routines, Air France introduced the Security and Safety Certificate (1955), a compulsory certificate for professional cabin crew.[2] Other significant changes were the growing hierarchy and bureaucracy that was rooted in the militarization of the company from 1943 to 1945 and the

[2] Until 2005, very few companies considered this kind of certificate a prerequisite to fly; this issue was highlighted when Air France merged with KLM. Over the last few years, many have blamed US carriers for not imposing the certificate.

subsequent state ownership and centralized control. For flight attendants at this time, their status was low overall. The company now recruited female flight attendants, drawn from the Red Cross and similar non-combatant military services. Women with aristocratic origins were favored and were forbidden to marry.

1970

The first Boeing 747 was launched in 1969. With a seating capacity well over 400 (up to 569), it was almost triple the size of previous aircraft. With the jet revolution becoming a reality, Air France's *manifested* identity evolved significantly: the beginning of mass transportation led to exponential hiring of all kinds of personnel and the professionalization of flight attendants' missions, roles, and duties. While the core technology remained relatively similar, the organizational structure was profoundly altered and was now marked by greater diversity and an accompanying increase in coordination mechanisms (such as professional rules). Air France's *projected* identity also shifted – aside from security, which remained a concern, it now underscored commercial expansion and democratization, both a clear break from the former focus on technological excellence. The poster "Le petit François" (1970) symbolized this evolution: the image featured the silhouette of a *small* man looking like the *average Frenchman*, flying across the sky, his tie blowing in the wind and the legendary Air France case in his hand. At the time, Air France operated in a shared monopoly: competition was restricted to Air Inter and UTA.

1977

From this point on, Air France's *projected* identity showed a market orientation, while the corporate governance was transformed and the company slowly prepared for privatization. Changes in the *projected* identity went hand-in-hand with a major shift in the *manifested* identity. Indeed, this period was marked by the introduction of Concorde in 1976 and by multiple tariffs, notably business class in 1977 and holiday tariffs in 1978. A new division of labor was progressively implemented among flight attendants, leading to new hierarchical relations on-board between "head" and "tail."

1988

In May 1988, following the re-election of socialist François Mitterrand as president, the communist Gayssot was appointed the new Minister of Transport. The ongoing privatization of Air France was postponed *sine die*. This was a period of inertia, with little significant change in Air France's *manifested* identity, except for the creation of a new reservation system (AMADEUS) in collaboration with Iberia, Lufthansa, and SAS. However, flight attendants took an increasing role in the process of outfit design.

1993

Starting in 1990 a period of turbulence began, culminating in 1993 with the prospect of bankruptcy. Throughout this period, the company faced immense issues and was subject to sudden changes. In 1993 a new CEO, Christian Blanc, was appointed, who initiated a profound corporate transformation. As far as the *projected* identity was concerned, the company several times postponed updating flight attendants' outfits. As one executive put it, "Air France had more pressing concerns than the uniforms": merging with UTA and Air Inter in 1990 to create "Groupe Air France"; facing bankruptcy in 1993; building its own hub at Roissy (mid-1990s); privatization; and establishing the Skyteam Alliance network. During this period, the *projected* identity appeared unclear and blurred, and secondary to strategic issues and rebirthing processes. Oddly enough, the rapid expansion in mass airline transport coincided with a sudden break in the long history of creativity. Air France scaled back its communication strategy by limiting the themes to the tricolor ticket envelope, with only Concorde escaping this cultural desert. The dark years of the 1990s were not propitious to imaginative undertakings. In 1998, when Air France was back on its feet, it launched a brand image survey that pinpointed several problems: strikes, delays, disappointing meals, and unfriendly service. A second, more in-depth semiological study revealed an incoherent brand image. It was essential to start from scratch, and seven values emerged in 1998: *efficiency, movement, proximity, pleasure, openness, elegance*, and "*the French touch*." To translate these words into reality, Air France would use advertising and design as weapons, notably by hiring Christian Lacroix.

2004

Since 2004 the company has tried to *project* the above-mentioned seven values. In parallel, the *manifested* identity has profoundly altered: Air France merged with KLM and the share of the state decreased to less than 20 percent in 2005. In brief, over these 70 years, projected and manifested identity facets changed regularly. In the section below we examine the evolution of flight attendants' outfits over those same 70 years to see whether our core argument holds: if organizational dress reflects organizational identity, then changes in the former should follow changes in the latter.

Seventy years of organizational dress at Air France as *history of Air France*

Organizational dress includes the clothes *per se* (e.g., jacket, skirt, pants), but also accessories (e.g., name tag, jewelry) that employees of an organization wear while at work (Rafaeli and Pratt, 1993: 34). Organizational dress is but one category of artefacts. According to the *Collins Shorter Dictionary* (1995: 56), an artefact is "something made or given shape by man [sic] such as a tool or a work of art." Artefacts are always perceived by the senses and they express certain intentions; they are oriented toward the satisfaction of a need or a goal. Artefacts allow people to do things, and inspire people to feel or react in a certain way.

To study organizational dress, we use the framework developed by Vilnai-Yavetz and Rafaeli (2006). Beyond *symbolism*, organizational artefacts, notably dress, also have *instrumental* and *aesthetic* dimensions. Briefly defined, *symbolism* refers to the meanings or associations that an artefact elicits. Artefacts are multi-vocal: they have both intended and unintended symbolic consequences as viewers interpret them through their own lenses. *Instrumentality* captures the extent to which "the artefact, directly or indirectly, contributes to or hampers the performance of individual tasks and/or the accomplishment of individual or organizational goals" (Vilnai-Yavetz and Rafaeli, 2006: 12). Finally, *aesthetics* refers to the sensory experience that an artefact elicits. Aesthetics can have an effect on product or organizational performance that is separate from instrumentality. For instance, the evolution of cellular phone design demonstrates how aesthetic considerations override instrumental considerations: ergonomics calls for a certain angle for the telephone handset, but such an angle produces bulky and less aesthetic cellular phones.

According to Vilnai-Yavetz and Rafaeli (2006), artefacts cannot be fully described along one single dimension as they may display different qualities simultaneously, though with various intensities, i.e., *it is a matter of degree rather than of kind*. Consider, for instance, an image of a man on a door indicating the men's washroom. In most cases this has a low aesthetic value, but simultaneously a strong instrumental and functional value. In the following paragraphs, we analyze the evolution of flight attendants' dress along these three dimensions. While data come from multiple archival sources, the recent historical review by Thibault (2005), *Inflight Mythologies*, provides an important source of information. Based on this account, we identified seven generations of outfits, i.e., seven periods of roughly similar lengths. Table 8 summarizes the evolution of Air France flight attendants' outfits along the aesthetic, instrumental, and symbolic dimensions.

Symbolism in flight attendants' outfits

Symbolic content, or the meanings and values conveyed by artefacts, is often – as in this case – evident at first sight. Throughout the seven periods, the symbolic

Table 8 Symbolic, instrumental, and aesthetic dimensions of flight attendants' outfits

	1933–1939 (1st period)	1945–1962 (2nd period)	1962–1969 (3rd period)	1969–1978 (4th period)	1978–1987 (5th period)	1987–2003 (6th period)	2003 onwards (7th period)
Symbolism (meanings)	SERVICE AND LUXURY Bartender uniform *emulates* those of luxury hotels (Ritz) and transatlantic cruise lines	PROTECTION "The daunting lines of quasi-monastic outfits" "Uniforms protect flight attendants like medieval armor"	FASHION "This event marked the reconciliation of the world of fashion and AF"	CLASSICISM Return to military style of 1946	FREEDOM A multiform wardrobe is created for the first time. Rules for uniform use according to time and destination, no longer based on army calendar	ELEGANCE "reflect concerns about image and elegance"	ELEGANCE, PLEASURE and OPENNESS
					Tricolor logo appears		
Archetypal figure of flight attendant	None	Maternal stewardess, wartime nurses	Cover girls	Movie stars	Multiple figures (growing customer heterogeneity and in-flight hierarchy)	Multiple figures (growing customer heterogeneity and in-flight hierarchy)	*Corto Maltese* for men The *Parisienne* for women (half-model, half-aristocrat)
Instrumentality (contributes to or hampers performance – directly or indirectly)	NEGATIVE, but not important	INDIRECTLY POSITIVE (EMOTIONALLY REASSURING) Passengers, first-time flying business executives, feel protected	DIRECTLY POSITIVE (EFFICIENT: practical and light) Open, small jacket to greet boarding passengers	NEGATIVE (INEFFICIENT: not practical for working conditions)	POSITIVE (FREEDOM) Synthetic material for comfort and free movement First wardrobe with 17 pieces	POSITIVE (COMFORT) "Uniforms should (i) take account of crews' wishes, (ii) respond to the demands of the jobs"	POSITIVE (COMFORT, TAILOR-MADE) Largest wardrobe ever Resistance of the materials tested in real conditions

Aestheticism (sensory experience of flight attendants)	BORROWED BY DEFAULT	BORROWED BY CHOICE Years passed, and fashion completely bypassed flight attendants	POSITIVE Feeling like a top model	NEGATIVE "May '68 threw the idyll between the world of fashion and Air France into question once again"	POSITIVE Silk-like appearance of synthetic material (jersey, notably polyester) Stripes lengthen silhouettes	POSITIVE BUT DECLINING Air France and Air Inter uniforms coexist	POSITIVE
Fashion designer(s)	NONE The first "extra in-flight staff" – uniform established by default	LOW STATUS Georgette Rénal (1946), then Georgette de Trèzes (1951)	SINGLE HIGH STATUS Marc Bohan (1962, from Dior)	SINGLE HIGH STATUS C. Balenciaga	MULTIPLE HIGH STATUS J. Patou (Concorde 1976); Ricci, Grès, and Carven (1978)	MULTIPLE HIGH STATUS Ricci, Carven, and L. Féraud (1987)	SINGLE HIGH STATUS C. Lacroix (2005)

Notes: All quotes from Thibault (2005)

dimension is clear, and this is a remarkable result as this will contrast with instrumental and aesthetic dimensions. In the first period, the bartender uniform symbolized <u>Service and Luxury</u>. After the Second World War, the military style uniforms protected flight attendants like medieval armor – "the daunting lines of the quasi-monastic outfits" immediately evoke <u>Protection</u>. This trend relates to the first female recruitment, though according to a very specific profile: unmarried, aristocratic ("de") women hired directly from the Red Cross and non-combatant military services. The third period "marked the reconciliation between the world of fashion and Air France," and <u>Fashion</u> radiates from the uniforms designed by Marc Bohan (at the time the leading designer at Dior). The period after the May 1968 riots in France and de Gaulle's return to tight societal control constitute a very particular Zeitgeist, and Cristobal Balenciaga's return to the military style of 1946 is essentially a return to <u>Classicism</u>. These first four periods are *monotheistic*: along with one prominent symbol, the code is represented by one single archetypal figure: the Bartender (first period), the Maternal Stewardess/Wartime Nurse (second period), the Cover Girl (third period), and the Movie Star (fourth period).

The three last periods are *polytheistic*: outfits refer to multiple figures, and uniforms carry multiple symbols. In the fifth period, *Freedom* is paramount: the army's calendar that used to determine when and where each uniform had to be worn is discarded. The first multi-form wardrobe is created. Multiplicity also comes from the presence of multiple high-status fashion designers. In the sixth period, *Elegance* above Freedom adds to the symbolic content of the outfits. Finally, the seventh period is about *Pleasure* and *Openness*: "the clients who viewed them in test situations perceived Air France values: movement, efficiency, proximity, pleasure and openness" (Thibault, 2005: 96). In parallel, throughout these periods, the archetypal figure of the flight attendants evolved correspondingly. The shift from *monotheism* to *polytheism* is clear in 1978 with the introduction of multiple archetypal figures, which correspond to growing customer heterogeneity and in-flight hierarchy (as airplanes grew ever larger and the specialization of work increased). However, as a direct result, the symbols appear diluted throughout this period. In 2005, the design by Lacroix may be regarded as an attempt to rebuild clear archetypal figures:[3] for the men, Hugo Pratt's *Corto Maltese*, which evokes a detached stylish masculinity, voyage, dream, and mystery. For the women, it is the Parisienne, half model and half aristocrat. In brief, over 70 years and seven periods, the symbolic dimension is always present, and moves from *monotheism* (if not univocal as symbols are multi-vocal by definition) to *polytheism*.

---

[3] This is clear when one looks at Lacroix's original sketches in the early phases of the project.

Instrumentality in flight attendants' outfits

Answering the question whether uniforms hampered or contributed to the performance of flight attendants requires more in-depth analyses of flight attendants' discourses and studies of wardrobe, textiles, fabrics, and customers. Before the Second World War, the outfit certainly contributed negatively to the service, but at the time on-board service was very much marginal: often, it was the mechanics who played out the bartender role during the flight. The uniforms had been designed for ground (palaces) or sea conditions (transatlantic cruise lines), where bartenders benefited from ample volumes and storage capacity, which certainly was not the case in pre-war commercial flights.

The post-war military uniforms neither hampered nor contributed to practical performance directly. However, *indirectly*, passengers felt emotionally protected as the uniform reminded them of a combination of wartime nurse and maternal stewardess, and contributed positively to a feeling of security for the often first-time flyers. In the third period, the reconciliation of fashion and air travel brought *efficiency* to the fore: practical and light uniforms for the first time contributed directly and positively to the flight attendants' tasks. Notably, from then on stewardesses were allowed to keep their small jacket *open* while greeting boarding passengers. As another example, pockets appeared (for instance, the wide summer skirt received four box pleats). However, Cristobal Balenciaga interrupted this progress toward increased instrumentality, and in the fourth period the uniform was unanimously characterized as inefficient: it was not practical for working conditions and affected performance negatively and directly. With the movie star as ideal figure, "it was a magnificent dress for women stepping out of a Rolls Royce, but not for moving through the aisles of a Boeing airplane" (Thibault, 2005: 62). And Balenciaga completely missed the profound transformation of the industry that was underway: the development of larger aircraft and mass transportation that brought different working conditions.

Responding to the disenchantment of cabin crews, fashion designers in the fifth period leveraged technical progress in fabrics and textiles to introduce synthetic material for comfort and movement. Jersey and polyester reduced the weight of outfits. *Indirectly, psychologically*, the multi-form wardrobe further re-enforced *Freedom*. The sixth period explicitly built upon existing achievements, and for the first time in Air France history, the competition among designers was based on the following overarching principle: "Uniforms should account for crews' wishes, respond to the demands of the jobs, and reflect concerns about elegance" (interview at Air France, 2004). The last period witnessed an even stronger emphasis on *comfort*, as outfits became *tailor-made* to each employee's size and physical characteristics. Moreover, the wardrobe now includes more than a hundred pieces (the largest ever), and employees are allowed to combine elements according to general rules, giving 35 distinct possible attires. For the first time also, trials in real conditions were carried out to test the resistance of materials, notably wool, leather, and cotton. Accessories have become prominent over dresses (scarves, various handbags, and so forth).

In brief, while uniforms embodied strong – though shifting – symbols throughout the seven periods, and while symbolism was always an important dimension, instrumentality became only progressively important. Instrumentality first tapped the practical component – the direct and positive functional effect of for instance lightness and storage with pockets – then only consolidated with a psychological component – the indirect and positive psychological effect of feeling free to tailor one's uniform to one's tastes, hence reconciling the paradox of choosing one's wardrobe while being forced to wear the company uniform. Finally, the seventh period may be adequately termed the first period of "multi-form uniform."

The aesthetic in flight attendants' outfits

The sensory experiences of flight attendants, both directly and indirectly mirrored by the clients, tell us a lot about aesthetics. In the first two periods, the aesthetic experience was "borrowed": *borrowed by default* from palaces and cruise lines before the Second World War, and *purposely borrowed* from wartime immediately after the war. It was only in the third period that a specifically Air France aesthetic was developed, in the borrowing of French haute couture aesthetic values. The result was positive in 1962, as flight attendants felt like top models. However, "May 1968 [and the return to Classicism in 1969, 4th period] threw the idyll between the world of fashion and Air France into question once again" (Thibault, 2005: 51): flight attendants felt an incongruity between who they were (steward-esses serving an increasingly democratized clientele) and how they were dressed (impersonating classic movie stars).

The fifth period reconciled Air France with fashion, and the sensory experience was more positive than ever: synthetic materials had silk-like properties (such as softness), and newly introduced stripes lengthened silhouettes. The sixth period built upon the fifth, though numerous factors contributed to dull the aesthetic sense in the late 1990s. First, the merger of Air Inter and Air France led to a juxtaposition of different logics for uniforms. Second, the September 11 attacks in 2001 and subsequent crisis in the air transportation industry forced the company to twice postpone its project to rejuvenate the attire. The uniform looked outdated and frayed. At 20 years old, it was an all-time longevity record that could not continue without damaging the company's image. In brief, Air France had faced more pressing concerns than the uniform, which became misaligned with the identity it wished to project toward the public. As Carole Peytavin, project leader for the new uniform, put it once in discussing women's outfits (*Le Monde*, April 2, 2005): "Our challenge was to dress with style and elegance 25,000 women from 20 to 60 years old working in various climates."

In this second section, we have detailed the evolution of flight attendants' outfits along three dimensions: symbolism, instrumentality, and aestheticism. On several occasions we have already alluded to the roots of these changes. In the following section we discuss in-depth relations between organizational identity and organizational dress.

DISCUSSION: ARTICULATING IDENTITY FACETS AND ARTEFACT DIMENSIONS

An analysis of the Air France case shows that, as expected, changes in organizational dress often reflect changes in organizational identity facets, in this case in six out of eight instances. This supports the notion that organizational dress can be – and indeed is – used to project an organization's identity. As Table 9 indicates, a significant shift in one or more identity facets is reflected in evolving organizational dress in 1933, 1945, 1969/1970, 1977/1978, 1987/1988, and 2003/2004. In four cases, we observe a straight co-evolution of identity facets and organizational dress (1933, 1945, 1977/1978, and 2003/2004).

However, this relationship is not systematic. In 1969, the radical (re)turn to classicism by Cristobal Balenciaga fitted neither the projected identity, based on market orientation and democratization, nor the manifested identity, calling for the instrumental uniforms and comfort necessitated by growing aircraft size. Interestingly, however, the rigorous classicism fitted well with management's imperatives, calling for greater productivity and profitability alongside the long-standing priority on security and safety. In this case, fashion designers chose to express the management's most pressing issues rather than portray the organization's identity.

In 1987, a co-evolution of organizational identity and organizational dress intended by management failed to be implemented. A new uniform was launched and the forthcoming privatization announced, but at the last moment the socialist coalition took over from the right-wing government and privatization was postponed *sine die*.

Finally, as shown in Table 9, we observe in 1962 one case of organizational dress evolution without a related obvious or radical organizational identity change, and one opposite case, in 1993, of a large and salient organizational identity change without evolution in organizational dress. In 1962 there was a highly significant change in organizational dress with the launch of Dior's uniform and the celebration of the alliance between Air France and the fashion world, while no significant shift in any identity facets emerges. Conversely, in 1993 there was a highly significant change in Air France's organizational identity – bankruptcy, the

187

Table 9 *Co-evolution of organizational dress and organizational identity*

Identity change/ dress change	Fit intended by management	Fit realized	Comments
1933/1934	Yes	Yes	—
1945/1946	Yes	Yes	—
Up to 1962	No	No	Change in dress unconnected to any significant identity change
1969/1970	? (No)	Yes	Evolution of organizational dress follows changes in management concerns, but is misaligned with both projected identity and manifested identity
1977/1978	Yes	yes	—
1987/1988	Yes	No	Extraorganizational factors (political shifts) lead to postponement of privatization
1993 to date	No	No	Acute crises (bankruptcy, strikes, and resignation of president) divert managerial attention from issues related to organizational dress
2003/2004	Yes	Yes	—

largest strike ever, and resignation of the president, which led to a profound corporate transformation – without adaptation in dress. In that case, the attention of top management (Ocasio, 1997) was directed toward crisis issues – survival was in question and alignment of identity and dress was a minor issue by comparison.

Fashion designers as identity architects

The historical review of the Air France case reveals the role of fashion designers as identity architects. On the one hand, after the Second World War fashion designers took an increasing role in creating outfits. Two trends are notable: first, *the status of the fashion designers employed increased progressively* – from low-status Georgette Rénal and Georgette de Trèzes (second period) to higher status Marc Bohan (following Yves Saint Laurent at Dior, third period) and Cristobal Balenciaga (fourth period),[4] then high-status Patou, Ricci, Grès, Carven, Féraud, and finally Christian Lacroix for the fifth, sixth, and seventh periods.

Second, the number of fashion designers involved varied over time. Up until 1978 (the end of the fourth period), individual designers created the outfits for flight attendants, who wore the clothes, worked in standard and homogeneous situations, and had little input in the process (see pp. 193–196). In the fifth and sixth periods, Air France recognized that heterogeneity increased with stratification of flight attendants' classifications and with increasingly diverse products (practices and services in Concorde differed from practices and services in short-haul economy flights). Moreover, Air France progressively dressed ground staff.

[4] Balenciaga's campaign for Air France was his swan song as he went bankrupt in 1969 and lost his legendary touch.

To satisfy these multiple requirements, the company called upon multiple high-status fashion designers: Jean Patou for outfits for Concorde (1976), and Ricci, Carven, and Grès jointly for flight attendants in 1978. Later, in 1987, again Ricci, Carven, and this time Louis Féraud shared the design of multiple uniforms. In 2005, Air France's return to one single high-status artist, Christian Lacroix, reflects a dual synthesis: the synthesis of the personnel categories – when for the first time a single fashion designer conceived the outfits for all employees wearing a uniform (ground personnel at sales and check-in as well as ground personnel on the tarmac; cabin crew: flight attendants and pilots) – and the synthesis of the "product range," where one single collection should cover the great diversity of codes related to differentiated offers (products and services, lounge access, and so forth). In brief, the status and diversity of selected fashion designers reflected fundamental identity issues at Air France, today notably that of inclusion.

Flight attendants' growing involvement in outfit design

Finally, the historical review of the Air France case highlights the growing involvement of the employees who wear the outfits. The flight attendant profession underwent substantial changes over 70 years, and the professionalization of flight attendants, itself the result of profound industrial transformations, explains the progressive emergence, then consolidation of instrumentality as a core dimension of uniforms as artefacts.

In airlines, dress has an obvious instrumental dimension: it protects from the weather, provides storage, identifies flight crews to passengers and, more subtly, indicates the roles and functions within the highly hierarchical crew; finally, it distinguishes between the person and the role, helping to reduce the stress felt by cabin crews in conflict situations with passengers. However, these apparently obvious functions have not always been addressed, even less so fulfilled, by successive uniforms. Two prominent dimensions – the rising status of flight attendants as a profession within airlines, notably at Air France, and changes in the conditions of operation of international airlines – notably the evolution of aircraft sizes and the consequent division of work – explain why these apparently obvious dimensions were only progressively taken into account in uniform design (see Table 8).

During the first period, flight attendants were officially described as a non-essential category (French PCB = *Personnel Complémentaire de Bord*), and outfits were not the result of a deliberate design process. After the Second World War, Air France realized that it had to catch up with competing airlines, notably Swiss Air and Lufthansa. The identity of flight attendants changed in 1946, but marriage remained forbidden, and young aristocratic women who served in non-combatant military services were favored. The third period starts with a *coup d'état*: the elimination of the provision against married flight attendants — against Air France's will — following the ruling by the French Conseil d'Etat, the country's highest court. The secretary-general of the Union for Flight Attendants married a colleague — who was immediately fired — but he filed an appeal with the Conseil d'Etat who ruled in his favor. This ruling merely echoed the increased freedom in French society: an increasing number of candidates applied, as the adventurer mystique declined and travel and fashion became attractive values for modernizing France. Throughout these three periods, however, flight attendants had no say in uniform design.

Nevertheless, other categories of personnel than flight attendants cared about their performance, and uniforms progressively incorporated instrumental components: in the second period, the uniform indirectly served a psychological role of reassuring passengers. It was not until the third period that efficiency came to the forefront, with practicality and lightness directly and positively contributing to performance. This was a period where fashion and efficiency coexisted well.

The fourth period is an anomaly in this long process of increased positive instrumentality. At the beginning of the period, flight attendants began to claim a role in the design of uniforms, but their claims were denied. An anonymous Air France executive went so far as to say, "We are not at La Sorbonne, they have no place protesting," in a dramatic comparison with the May 1968 riots and the students' demand for freedom to choose their curriculum. Further, Balenciaga's uniform disrupted the coexistence of fashion and functionality, fashion playing against practicality.

From that fourth period, Air France decided to make instrumentality a core concern, and inputs by flight attendants increased progressively. With mass transportation and larger aircraft, a hierarchy developed within crews, with regular crew members, principal cabin crew members, and chief cabin crews. Moreover, with economy cabins, aisles became narrower and more passengers had to be served (i.e., catered for), with movement more constrained. Preparing the fifth uniform, Air France recognized these new work-related requirements, and for the first time flight attendants participated in the process of design. As a result, flight attendants were fully satisfied with growing individual freedom (multiple uniforms) and free movement (through silk-like synthetic materials). Flight attendants even took the lead in preparing the sixth set of uniforms, selecting a set of designers through a democratic internal poll, with 52 percent contributing their views. Eventually, as a prelude to the seventh period, flight attendants led and organized a more sophisticated process than an individual poll, with instrumentality reaching a new level: tailor-made uniforms that all flight and ground crew, men and women, received simultaneously from one designer. For men, Christian Lacroix was inspired by *Corto Maltese* as the ideal figure, with the half-aristocratic, half-model "Parisienne" best representing the ideal feminine figure.

CONCLUSION

Based on historical data, our analysis suggests that changes in organizational dress may reflect changes in some facets of organizational identity. Notably, organizational dress may be changed to reflect changes in identity claims (the *professed* identity), to accompany changes in the corporate identity (the *projected* identity), or as a result of changes in the organization's technical core (the *manifested* identity). However, the relationship is not systematically bidirectional: at times of crisis, there may be changes in some aspects of organizational identity without changes in organizational dress, as strategic or survival issues capture available managerial attention. In addition, some changes in organizational dress occur without obvious or radical organizational identity changes, which should in theory be linked. Finally, the historical review of Air France highlights the role of fashion designers and the growing involvement in the design process of those wearing the outfits. From a managerial standpoint, in service organizations where organizational identity and corporate identity must be tightly aligned, it seems important to pay attention to all stakeholders: managers may push designers in a direction that reflects the interest of their own division or subgroup rather than expressing the positioning, and hence the identity, of the organization. Designers, on the other hand, especially those of international renown, evolve in a world of their own: they may cling to aesthetic values that do not match the requirements originating from projected or manifested identity facets. Finally, as organizational democratization increases, employees play an increasing role in the design process.

KEY QUESTIONS

1 The case builds on a conceptualization of organizational identity as a dynamic system composed of five facets. What are the advantages and drawbacks of such an approach? Taking one organization you are familiar with, try to describe the various facets of its identity.

2 Mergers and acquisitions are common practice nowadays, and personnel from diverse, sometimes adverse companies are merged. Consequently, diverse outfits may remain side by side, as evidenced by the merger of Air France and Air Inter. For external reasons, Air France's top management could not devote attention to this issue in the early 1990s. Had you been in charge of organizational dress at that time, and had you been given one year and a suitable budget, what would you have invented and implemented?

3 Organizational identity facets sometimes diverge, as evidenced in the fourth period. Designers then have difficulties aligning organizational dress with all identity facets, and must choose one or some of the facets. What external factors and internal contingencies could determine uniform designers' choices of relevant identity facets to align organizational outfits?

4 Optimal Distinctiveness Theory (ODT) suggests that in many situations, individuals try to be optimally distinct from relevant others: they want their uniqueness to be recognized, yet also desire to be part of collectives as sources of attachment and belonging. Uniforms certainly promote similarity and prevent uniqueness. Christian Lacroix's "Multi-form Uniform" is an ambitious attempt to put into practice this optimal distinctiveness principle. However, recent interviews by the authors suggest that at least a minority of flight attendants are unhappy with variety, and some even describe it as anarchy when cabin crew members on board the same aircraft all display differences in their outfits. Given your understanding of what a uniform should be, what guidelines/principles would you establish for the individualization versus standardization of organizational dress?

5 As shown in the case study, those employees who wore the organizational dress claimed an increasing role in its design. However, dress also conveys the organization's identity to external audiences, meaning that top management is logically entitled to control the process. Considering three sectors of your choice (for instance, bank tellers in the finance industry, waiters/waitresses in top restaurants, faculty members of universities and/or business schools, and so forth), what relative roles in the design process would you expect from, and provide to, top management and/or employees actually wearing the uniform?

APPENDIX: THE EVOLUTION OF ORGANIZATIONAL DRESS AT AIR FRANCE, 1933–2005

The illustrations on the following pages are by courtesy of Air France, *Collection Musée Air France.DR*

1945–1962: Georgette Rénal and Georgette de Trèzes

1933–1939: The Ritz barman

1969–1978: Balenciaga

1962–1969: Dior

■ *1978–1989: Patou, Ricci, and Carven*

■ *1987–2003: Carven, Ricci, and Féraud*

2005 onwards: Lacroix

Chapter 11

Organizational artefacts and the expression of identity in corporate museums at Alfa-Romeo, Kartell, and Piaggio

Ileana Stigliani and Davide Ravasi

INTRODUCTION

In Chapter 1 we saw how the unique shape of Scania's trucks was central to managers' conceptualization of their company. Similarly, at Bang & Olufsen, in the face of rising challenges to the identity of the organization, old logos, product milestones, and visuals from past campaigns were widely used to make sense of what the organization was really about (see Chapter 6).

In organizations, a variety of objects, ranging from uniforms, logos, stationery, visuals, buildings, and the products themselves, provide cues about how members perceive their organization or – as exemplified by the changing uniforms of Air France flight attendants (see Chapter 10) – would like it to be perceived externally (Olins, 1989). Management scholars commonly refer to these objects as *artefacts*, and observe how they may be used by organizational members to express professional or group identities (e.g., Pratt and Rafaeli, 1997) or to construct or preserve a common sense of self (e.g., Ravasi and Schultz, 2006).

What the cases of Scania and Bang & Olufsen share, however, is the explicit connection that members traced between these objects and a claimed *corporate heritage* – a web of cultural expressions (myths, artefacts, traditions, etc.) that are perceived as a manifestation and legacy of a shared past, and as central to the identity of the organization. At Scania and Bang & Olufsen, references were occasionally made to the corporate heritage in response to internal debate on different courses of action. Other organizations, however, invest time, money, and attention to produce a visible and tangible display of their corporate heritage in what are commonly called *corporate museums*, and they use them as platforms for the projection of organizational and corporate identity.

What are corporate museums?

A corporate museum is an exhibit-based facility, owned and operated by a company, collecting and displaying objects (products, visuals, photographs, prototypes, and other material from the corporate archives) illustrating the history of the company itself (its roots, milestones, achievements, leading figures, etc.) and/ or its operations to employees, guests, customers, or other visitors (Danilov, 1992; Nissley and Casey, 2002). Such museums are often hosted inside corporate facilities or located near the company's headquarters. They are usually run by the companies themselves or by foundations to which companies donate the objects to be displayed. Admittance policies vary considerably: while some museums have a commercial intent and charge visitors an entrance fee, in many others entry is free, even though an appointment may be required. In rare cases, entrance may be restricted to the employees of the company and to selected guests.

The origins of corporate museums can be traced to the early 1900s, when a number of companies in Europe and the USA began to preserve tangible records of their own history and operations, as well as of their industry. Pioneers of corporate museums include the Wedgwood Museum (ceramics), founded in the United Kingdom in 1906, the Daimler Motor Company Museum (automobiles), established in Germany around 1911, and the Union Pacific Museum (railways), opened in 1923. Only in the second half of the twentieth century, however, did corporate museums begin to enjoy increasing popularity all over the world. In fact, it is calculated that about half of the corporate museums existing today were founded in the 1970s or 1980s. Now, such museums can be found in a variety of industries ranging from automobiles to furniture, cosmetics to food and beverages, and fashion to home appliances.

At the beginning of the 1990s, about half of all corporate museums were in Italy (Danilov, 1992). The diffusion of corporate museums in Italy, however, is a fairly recent phenomenon, as the first corporate collections and archives date only to the second half of last century. This gap can be explained by the relatively late development of Italian industry. In fact, Great Britain, France, Germany, and the United States were struck by the wave of industrialization and by growing interest in the exhibition of technical products and technological know-how already from the end of the eighteenth century. At the time of the Great Exhibition of industrial products in England in 1851, followed by the opening of what is thought to be the first industrial museum in the world, the South Kensington Museum, Italian firms still lagged behind on the road to industrialization.

In the period after the Second World War, however, the lack of planning for the reorganization of the military industry encouraged the growth of small and medium-sized firms, who tried to bridge the technological gap that separated them from their foreign competitors. They did this by emphasizing the symbolic values of industrial objects. What became known as "Italian Design" was born, along with the diffusion of new "mass icons" such as Alfa-Romeo and Ferrari cars, Artemide lamps, and the Vespa motorcycle by Piaggio. These contributed to redefine the concept of "Made in Italy" in the collective imagery.

In the 1960s, in the wake of the English experience, the Association of Italian Designers (ADI) began to emphasize the importance of industrial design and the need to create a permanent exhibition of the production of the most important Italian firms. However, at that time the absence of solid and specific educational and institutional infrastructures delayed the foundation of such a museum, conceived as the means to train the future creators of everyday objects. In fact, in that period, house magazines of leading Italian companies, such as *Zodiac* by Olivetti, *Edilizia moderna* by Pirelli, and *Qualità* by Kartell, played an important role in the diffusion of a culture of industrial design.

In the early 1970s, while foreign exhibitions acknowledged the increasing international relevance of Italian design, at home its legacy still lacked proper institutional recognition. In the absence of official appreciation by museum institutions of the importance of the products of industrial design, an increasing number of Italian firms established corporate collections and archives within their facilities to preserve a tangible record of their achievements and to record the development of their industries. In time, these collections evolved in genuine corporate museums, where selected items were combined and displayed in appropriate facilities in order to illustrate the histories of the companies through various manifestations of their past.

Thirty years on, Alfa-Romeo, Kartell, and Piaggio are among the best known and most active corporate museums in Italy. In the following sections, after a brief introduction on each, we will use evidence from comparative field research to illustrate how identity-related issues may underlie the conscious selection, preservation, and display of corporate artefacts.[1]

Alfa-Romeo Museum: technology, design, and sport

Founded in 1910, the "Anonima Lombarda Fabbrica Automobili," or ALFA, was later named Alfa-Romeo after one of its owners, Nicola Romeo. Since its beginning, Alfa-Romeo combined car production with participation in races. Indeed, the first car produced by ALFA, the 24 HP, made its debut in the most important

[1] The following sections report findings from a study of three corporate museums. The sample selection was based on a mix of critical informants and snowballing techniques, as our key informants in each organization were asked to indicate other instructive cases. Data collection relied on in-depth interviews with museum curators and other employees of the company, direct observation (part of the interviews included a visit to the museum), and archival data (brochures, corporate websites, corporate biographies, and other internal documents). Data analysis relied on grounded theory building to uncover common themes across cases.

Italian race of the time, Targa Florio, in 1911. From then on the company became deeply involved in many Italian and international races, such as Mille Miglia (11 times winner, a record), Targa Florio (ten times winner), Le Mans 24 hours (four times), the Formula 1 World Championship (champions in 1950 and 1951), and several European and World Touring Car Championships from 1960 to 2004. Thanks to its numerous successes in these competitions, Alfa-Romeo built what according to Alfa supporters is considered to be "its extraordinary sporting legend."

In the same way, the company promoted technological experimentation and the search for forms and stylistic details consistent with Alfa's philosophy of "sustaining beauty," based on a balance of form and engineering. This continuous search for a coherent link between "technical essence" and "formal essence" is represented in some of Alfa's product milestones, such as the "1900" four-cylinder engine saloon, the Giulietta in the "Sprint," saloon, and "Spider" versions – emblematic products of the concept "Made in Italy" during the 1950s and the 1960s – the production and competition Giulias, launched in the early 1960s, and the most recent Alfa 147, Alfa 159, Brera and 8C Competizione.

The Alfa-Romeo Historical Museum was officially opened in 1976. According to Antonio Magro, who participated in the founding of the museum, and is now curator:

> The idea of opening a museum, suggested for the first time by Orazio Satta Puliga [one of the three most influential of Alfa's chief designers, together with Giuseppe Merosi and Vittorio Jano] was inspired by the strong affection that was felt for the brand by so-called "Alfisti" inside and outside the company.

While the core of the collection consists of vintage cars that have been preserved or acquired by the company, employees contributed substantially to the enrichment of the historical archives by donating old brochures, visuals, photographs, and even vehicles. As the museum curator recalled:

> In our employees' view, throwing away even a corporate catalogue was unimaginable . . . Almost everybody had kept something. A person even donated an Alfa-Romeo fridge produced during the War – something almost everybody had forgotten about!

The museum now covers an area of 4,800 square meters and is divided into four main sections. The first section is devoted to production and competition cars and includes over a hundred vehicles, two chassis, and twenty-two engines. The second is dedicated to design and "milestones" in the company's production. Alfa-Romeo's activities in the aviation industry are the theme of the third section, while the fourth section displays models of Alfa-Romeo cars and the trophies won in a hundred years of motor sport.

The exhibition is arranged in chronological order and, in order to emphasize the close links between the evolution of the motor car and changes in the Italian way of life, each exhibit is accompanied by ample documentation, including photographs and reproductions of old advertising campaigns enabling the visitor to place each car in its correct historical context.

As the corporate website reads, the exhibition is arranged so that visitors are able to grasp the main themes that make up the history of the firm:

- *Passion*: witnessed by the evolution of the Alfa-Romeo brand, by the representation of the company in a parallel journey through the evolution of Italian and international customs, and by the role of Alfa-Romeo in books and film as an object of desire, a status symbol, an image of beauty, and of Italian technology.
- *Cars*: from the first "A.L.F.A." car, the 1910 24 HP, to the first torpedo with the "ALFA-ROMEO" logo, the "20–30 ES" to the "Duetto," the 1600 Spider launched in 1966 by way of the Giulietta, the museum shows the "unforgettable" products – "technological masterpieces" from the epic age of the motorcar that captured the imagination of car lovers all over the world.
- *Races*: Alfa-Romeo has taken part in competitions since the early days, "by vocation, by necessity, and by conviction." The museum therefore shows the extraordinary run of success on the track, all under the name Alfa-Romeo.
- *Personalities*: represented by the men who contributed to the creation of the Alfa-Romeo legend, from Alfa's technical managers such as Giuseppe Merosi, Vittorio Jano, Wifredo Ricart, and Orazio Satta Puliga, and the chairman of the company in the 1960s, Giuseppe Luraghi, to top drivers such as Tazio Nuvolari, Giuseppe Campari, Achille Varzi, and Juan Manuel Fangio, and Sports Division General Manager Enzo Ferrari, including famous Italian "carrozzieri" such as Touring, Castagna, Zagato, Pininfarina, Bertone, and Giugiaro, whose memory is preserved in their artefacts and pictures.
- *The company*: rather than simply telling the story of the company as an institution, the museum relates Alfa-Romeo's adventure, from the early years of the last century to the present day, in a historical journey across products, sports trophies, and historical records.

Initially conceived as a sort of display of the "family jewels," the museum became increasingly used for communication purposes. At the beginning of the new millennium it intensified its synergy with the marketing department to support communication events and campaigns, as well as to host internal events such as presentations of new cars to the sales force. In addition, the museum has traditionally been linked to Centro Stile Alfa, the internal design centre. Thanks to its physical proximity to the centre, the collaboration between these two structures is intense.

The KartellMuseum: a tradition and culture of design

Founded in 1949 by the chemical engineer Giulio Castelli, Kartell is an internationally renowned leader in design using plastic materials, and one of the flagships of Italian design.

From the 1950s to the 1980s, under Giulio Castelli's management, the production of the company gradually expanded from car accessories to lamps and household items, and finally to furniture and objects for laboratories. Nowadays the Habitat and Labware divisions constitute the core business of the firm. In 1988 Claudio Luti, Giulio Castelli's son-in-law and former business partner of fashion designer Gianni Versace, became the new president and owner of the firm. Two years later, Luti promoted the foundation of the KartellMuseum. As Simona Romano, the museum curator, observed:

> [Luti's goal] was to create a way to communicate the unique identity and personality of the company internally and externally . . . The aim was to illustrate the challenges that Kartell took on in experimenting with innovative applications of plastic material to design objects.

At the KartellMuseum, the history of the company is illustrated over a 2,000-square-meter area through more than 1,000 products, displayed in chronological order and divided by decade from the 1950s to the 1990s. Official commentaries, printed on the walls, follow four different perspectives through each decade: key corporate events, design choices, technological advances, and communication efforts. All the objects are linked by what Simona Romano describes as "a consistent thread representing the identity of the company."

According to the exhibit, products created in the 1950s witness Kartell's twofold challenge, "to bring plastic into every Italian home" and "to substitute glass with plastic in laboratories." These represent the outcomes of Kartell's approach to production, characterized by the involvement of famous Italian designers and architects, and by continual technological experimentation. The collection from the 1960s emphasizes the official recognition of the design world, with five "Compasso d'Oro," and the first revolutionary products marking the entrance of the firm into the furniture industry, such as Marco Zanuso's chair made entirely from plastic, followed by Joe Colombo's chair in ABS, the first human-scale plastic chair produced using injection molding, and by Anna Castelli Ferrieri's line of containers, the first examples of modular plastic furnishings produced using injection molding.

The 1970s bear witness to Kartell's aim of a leading role in the promotion of

Italian design worldwide (in 1972, the company was part of the exhibition "Italy: The New Domestic Landscape. Achievements and Problems of Italian Design" at MOMA), as well as the company's efforts towards consolidation and specialization in furnishings. The 1980s show how Kartell concentrated its efforts in the Labware and Habitat divisions and dedicated itself to research and experimentation in the ergonomic field, paying increasing attention to the functional aspects of objects. Finally, the production of the 1990s is influenced by the change in leadership in 1988. Claudio Luti's desire to renew Kartell's production prompted him to contact designers of international renown and to ask them to re-interpret Kartell's style, though respecting what the company itself considers its core values: "originality in design, high technological levels for its reproduction on an industrial scale, the originality and quality of the materials, value for money." In this period, Kartell began to use other materials, such as wood and aluminum, together with plastics; it also extended its range of colors to include primary and secondary colors, and created products with not only rounded but also squared forms.

At the KartellMuseum, visitors – exclusively designers, architects, journalists, researchers, and students – can also access a database with detailed information on the company, its products, and designers. The museum is also responsible for the physical rearrangement and cataloging of pictures, cataloges, prototypes, objects, and drawings. As curator Simona Romano observed, one of the purposes of the museum is to bring order to the "historical and artistic heritage" of the company.

This proves to be particularly important when Kartell is asked to loan artefacts to international exhibitions:

> We receive several requests of objects for exhibitions . . . Our press office cannot manage these requests, because it knows the present but it does not know the past of the organization . . . It is fundamental to lend the right objects at the right time; to do this it is important to bring order to our historical and artistic heritage.
>
> (Simona Romano, museum curator)

Museo Piaggio: innovation, creativity, and technological excellence

Founded in 1884 by Rinaldo Piaggio, today the Piaggio Group is one of the world's leading manufacturers of motorized two-wheel vehicles (including scooters, motorcycles, and mopeds under the Piaggio, Vespa, Gilera, and Derbi brands). In Europe it is the market leader. Inaugurated in 2000 and located in one of the company's oldest buildings in Pontedera, the Museo Piaggio forms part of a wider project to reconstruct Piaggio's history. The project was launched by

Giovanni Alberto Agnelli, Rinaldo Piaggio's great-grandson, who had taken on the leadership of the company at the age of 28. As Professor Tommaso Fanfani, a business historian at the University of Siena, now museum curator and chair of the Piaggio foundation, recalled:

> In 1992 he [Alberto Agnelli] called to ask whether there were any undergraduate students who wanted to write their dissertations on the history of Piaggio. I answered that we could not do that without histor- ical archives. He replied that they did not have any archives. So the first step was to gather archival material from all around the company . . . Then he told me: "Why don't we consider establishing a collection of objects illustrating the most important phases of our company in terms of innovation, creativity, and corporate success?"

As Professor Fanfani told us, the museum was eventually founded with the aims of "preserving the historical memory of the most important engineering com- panies in the center of Italy" and of "becoming an example of the harmonious conversion of an industrial area for cultural purposes." As he described the con- tent of the collection, he observed how:

> [t]hese extraordinary objects show transport in all its forms . . . there- fore, the museum tells the history of products that represent excellence in creativity and technological competence, while paying tribute to the entrepreneurial capabilities of the people who designed and produced them.

The 3,000-square-meter site displays the products of the creativity of famous Italian designers such as Giovanni Casiraghi, Luigi Pegna, and Corradino D'As- canio, and the work of generations of men and women employed in the company.

The museum's halls display Vespa and Gilera collections alongside the most significant of Piaggio's numerous products. The Vespas on display are among the rarest of their kind, including the prestigious Vespa Dalì, the very first piece of the collection donated by Giovanni Alberto Agnelli, or the record-breaking Vespas, such as the first Vespa 125 produced in 1948 – the Vespa used by Gregory Peck and Audrey Hepburn in *Roman Holiday*. The museum also displays the Vespa Siluro 125 with opposing pistons – used by the Italian pilot Dino Mazzoncini to break the world record for the flying kilometer in 1951 – and the Vespa Alpha, a one-off model made for the 1967 movie *Dick Smart, Agent 2007*.

Alongside the various Vespa models the museum also displays other classic mopeds, such as Ciao and Sì, and the multi-functional Ape, the small three- wheeled truck appreciated by generations of Italian artisans, farmers, and retailers for its versatility. Furthermore, the museum exhibits some of what are considered the most beautiful motorcycles from the two-ring Gilera brand, including 1950s models like the Saturno and the Gilera 500 that kindled the dreams of an entire generation of sports enthusiasts.

The Piaggio historical archives – a collection of over 4,000 files tracing every aspect of the company's history, and including drawings, designs, and films of advertising campaigns from the 1930s to the present day – are also located inside the museum.

Finally, many of the Piaggio Foundation's activities take place on the museum premises. The Foundation was established in 1994 by Giovanni Alberto Agnelli, by the officials of Pontedera municipality, and by the Pisa provincial administration. The aim, Professor Fanfani told us, was to retrace "the historical memory of the company and of the society in which Piaggio operated" and to become "a reference point in the local and national debate on business, culture, and society" through the organization of events such as conferences and modern art exhibitions.

> "Company – culture" and "company – territory" formed the binomial from which the triad composing the cultural project promoted by Piaggio – namely the Foundation, the Museum, and the Archives – took shape. Its objective was to become a reference point in the local and national debate on some of the most current themes.
>
> (Professor Tommaso Fanfani, Chair of the Piaggio Foundation)

Corporate museums and the projection of corporate identity

Corporate museums are a powerful means of communication. Although their external reach is somewhat limited to interested visitors or occasional guests, they can be among the most powerful symbols that corporate leaders can use to influence how the organization and its products are perceived and represented within and without. They can also be used as a platform for a whole range of communication events and initiatives aimed at promoting and preserving the identity and image of the organization.

The cases of Alfa-Romeo, Kartell, and Piaggio that we have summarized illustrate different ways in which organizations may leverage their corporate heritage to garner and consolidate the support of their constituencies around an attractive organizational and corporate identity (see Table 10 and Figure 16).

Inspiring corporate identity management

A corporate museum is primarily a repository of tangible and visible manifestations of the organizational history, including products, photographs, drafts,

Table 10 *Identity-related processes in corporate museums*

	Alfa-Romeo	Kartell	Piaggio
Inspiring corporate identity management	Designers at the nearby Centro Stile – the industrial design center – are among the most frequent visitors to the museum, as they look for inspiration when developing new concepts. Observation of old models helps them to preserve consistency in the core stylistic traits that characterize Alfa-Romeo cars	The museum collection is considered an expression of the values and identity of the company and a tangible set of guidelines to generate new ideas and innovative projects	The museum premises host training courses and workshops for new designers. Design teams often browse the collection and the archives, which contain detailed documentation on all the past models. Old materials preserved in the archives are increasingly used in marketing communications
Enriching corporate and brand images	The Alfa-Romeo Museum celebrates a glorious past in racing dating back to the early days of the company. With its thorough reconstruction of past accomplishments in motor sport, vividly illustrated through photographs and old models, the museum is expected to provide credible support to the traditional positioning of the brand, summarized in the old tagline "Cuore sportivo" ("Sporting heart")	At the Kartell Museum, objects are not merely displayed: a guided tour and detailed comments are meant to reveal to visitors the philosophy underlying design choices, and to emphasize the pioneering role of the company in industrial design and plastic technologies. A video illustrates the complexity of the process involved in the manufacture of the most popular products	The selection of items on display at the Museo Piaggio (products, photographs, press clippings, etc.) emphasizes the interrelation between the company and some of its products and the evolution of lifestyle and personal transportation in Italy. Reclaiming the central role of products like the Vespa in the evolution of culture and society is meant to enrich the corporate brand and image with the charm and prestige of the corporate heritage
Reinforcing identification inside and outside the organization	The museum was initially conceived as a collection of the "family jewels." Numerous employees contributed to the inaugural collection. The museum is credited for reinforcing a sense of family and identification. Today, numerous events involve some of the one thousand Alfa-Romeo clubs from all over the world (far more than any other car brand) and purposefully support the activities of these brand communities	The Kartell Museum is used to introduce new employees to the heritage and core values of the company in detail, and to strengthen their sense of belonging. For international sales managers and distributors, visits to the museum are used to spread awareness of what the company is and what it stands for	One of the purposes of the Museo Piaggio is to reinforce a sense of belonging among employees as well as the local community of Pontedera, as witnessed by the numerous cultural events intended for local audiences. More than 800 Vespa clubs around the world interact with the museum through visits, donations, etc.

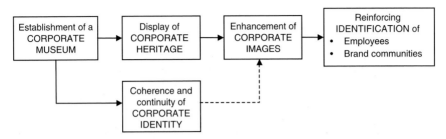

Figure 16 *Corporate museums as a platform for corporate branding policies*

prototypes, and other historical documents. As such, it may become a reservoir of cues to inspire communication choices manifested in all the components of corporate identity: logo, visuals, products, buildings, and so on.

Internal coherence among all these elements is central to the effective management of *corporate identity* (Olins, 1989; van Riel and Balmer, 1997). For this reason, corporate communication policies ranging from advertising to the design of products and visuals should rest on a shared understanding of what the company is and stands for – or, in other words, its organizational identity. In many organizations, coherence is pursued by visual identity manuals containing detailed graphic prescriptions for logos, letterheads, stationery, and sometimes even uniforms or buildings. Formal statements about the "essence" or "identity" of the brand – as managerial aspirations about brand positioning are commonly referred to – are expected to coordinate marketing efforts across the organization. To date, however, few companies seem to have developed detailed, formal policies explicitly addressing identity issues as manifested in product and communication choices and ensuring coherence between managerial aspirations, corporate claims, and widespread beliefs. In this respect, establishing a corporate museum may constitute a visible and tangible reference point for marketers, designers, public relations managers, and any other employee engaged in identity-related activities.

Research on identity management has shown how tangible manifestations of a collective past help organizational members to construct or preserve a sense of what their organization is about (Ravasi and Schultz, 2006). In corporate museums, the mere preservation of artefacts reflecting the history of the organization, its aspirations, efforts, achievements – and sometimes its failures – provides marketers and designers with a source of inspiration that draws on the heritage of the company, embodied in hundreds or thousands of products, prototypes, ads and photographs preserved in its archives.

At Alfa-Romeo, for instance, internal designers are among the most assiduous visitors to the museum, as they analyze and compare the design of old models in order to preserve a continuity and distinctiveness of style. As Antonio Magro, the curator of the museum, observed:

Designers at Centro Stile come here to find inspiration and to try to preserve continuity in our product lines. There are always old models, details, elements that are reproduced in newer models, possibly re-interpreting them in a more current light . . . This could be a logo or any other element . . . The link between the museum and the design center is very important in carrying on the tradition of the company.

The director of the design center, Wolfgang Egger, expressed the same view:

During the development of a new concept the role of our museum is fundamental, because going through the evolution of Alfa's products, we are able to understand the thread and the underlying logic, and to develop a concept with a certain continuity with the past . . . The role of the museum is crucial in maintaining continuity in the stylistic identity of products.

Similarly at Piaggio, designers, product developers, marketers, and advertisers often visit the museums in order to find inspiration for identity-based marketing campaigns and identity-coherent product innovation:

Piaggio designers do visit both the museum and the archives to pick up ideas for future products. Often they decide to take some stylistic elements of past vehicles and re-interpret them in the new ones. [Also] the marketing and communication offices often use the archive materials to create advertising campaigns – they study pictures, logos, and earlier advertising materials.

In 2005, for instance, designers at the Piaggio design center repeatedly visited the museum to familiarize themselves with the early Vespa models – their key features, their most popular colors, and the details that distinguished Vespa from other scooters. Their efforts eventually led to the development of a new line that tried to recapture the flavor of the early Vespas as faithfully as possible, combined with advanced mechanics. These were released a year later as Vespa Vintage.

Enriching corporate and brand images

Over the last ten years, corporations have increased their efforts to manage the overall perceptions of a company in the mind of its various constituents – in other words, to manage its *corporate images* (Dowling, 1986). Corporate identity policies, therefore, are increasingly aimed at supporting communication efforts by making the core values of the company and its brands visible through graphic, product, and environmental design (Olins, 1989).

Indeed, as previously discussed, corporate museums are often used to support communication strategies and events aimed at leveraging the heritage of the company – its technological achievements, product milestones, leading personalities, and its role in the development of industry or society – in order to enrich corporate associations and establish or reinforce the foundation of its corporate and product brands.

At Piaggio, for instance, great emphasis is placed on the early decades of the company when, under the leadership of Rinaldo Piaggio, it pioneered technology development in railroad and air transportation as well as experiments in industrial democracy (corporate housing, schooling, etc.). Through the display of old press clippings, photographs, and excerpts from various forms of cultural expression (art, cinema, etc.), a separate exhibition traces explicit connections between the huge popularity of the Vespa motorcycle and the changing lifestyle and transportation habits in Italy. As the communication officer, Paolo Pezzini, observed:

> Everything we use now – pictures, posters, the Dolce Vita, John Wayne on a Vespa, etc. – comes from the historical archive . . . Now that we are celebrating Vespa's sixtieth anniversary, magazines from all over the world are requesting pictures, stories, and anecdotes. And to me the archive is a precious source – Vespa could not be what it is today if we had not set up the archive and the museum.

Collectively, these exhibits project the image of the organization as an agent of cultural changes at the societal level by celebrating the company's role in the history of the social, industrial, or technological field. "After all," Paolo Pezzini told us "we are the ones who invented the scooter."

As Professor Fanfani, Chair of the Piaggio Foundation, declared:

> [The objective of the museum] is to narrate the history of Piaggio and, through it, of the development of Italian industry, the Italian economy, and Italian society. This is done by exhibiting some of the company's best-known, most representative products. These extraordinary objects show transport in all its forms . . . All the artefacts we have gathered over time have become a fundamental means of communication not only of who we are, but also of our continuous cultural commitment . . . For our firm, recovering our own history represents an effective means of giving value to our brands and to the corporate image, and to increase the gap between us and our competitors.

Similarly, at Alfa-Romeo the celebration of the company's illustrious past is meant to preserve and revive the prestige of a brand name, which, in many consumers' minds, is still associated with winning races. Museum exhibits, however, go beyond sports, as they also illustrate the industrial and technological achievements of the company. As Antonio Magro explained:

> Our firm has certainly contributed to, if not pioneered, the birth, the growth, and the improvement of the Italian car industry . . . Our strategy is to use our past to support the new . . . The role of our museum is to become a bridge between the historic and cultural heritage of one of the most prestigious car brands worldwide and our future projects.

More generally, as Pasquale Oliveri, head of Automobilismo Storico, the organizational unit running the museum and the archive, remarked:

> Alfas are cars that made the history of a nation and a history of primacy; the history of a nation that got back on its feet after two world wars; and a history of an Italian nation that works and wins.

In these museums, the savvy display of corporate artefacts and their stated connection to broader changes in society, industry, and culture is meant to position companies as "cultural producers" as well as to support a credible and meaningful narrative around the company, its cultural values, and practices. At Kartell, the display of objects is intended to let the public grasp the "cultural world" behind the company's products: its continuous technological experimentation and its design philosophy. As the museum curator states:

> The KartellMuseum has a dual function: to communicate the identity and the cultural mission of the company . . . The museum tells the history of the design philosophy of Kartell, which represents one of the most interesting and significant chapters of Italian design . . . Kartell's products are born with a high cultural content, in terms of research and meaning . . . Our corporate museum may be a powerful tool to let this differential emerge.

In doing this, communication and branding efforts aim at increasing the symbolic value of products, as these are embedded in a corporate narrative that draws considerably on the company's heritage to increase the meaningfulness of the company and its products to external constituencies.

Reinforcing identification in and around the organization

Communication efforts leveraging on the heritage of the company may have also another purpose, namely to reinforce the *identification* of some of its constituencies with the company and/or its products, hence to garner their support. The concept of identification – conceived as the degree to which individuals define themselves in terms of an organization they are somehow related to (Ashforth and Mael, 1989) – was initially developed in order to understand the relationships between employees and their work organization: strong organizational identification is generally associated with a higher level of intraorganizational cooperation, commitment, and citizenship (Dukerich, Golden, and Shortell, 2002).

Members' identification with their work organization is influenced by their beliefs about what outsiders think about the organization (Dutton, Dukerich, and Harquail, 1994). Other things being equal, then, members will show a higher level of identification in organizations that enjoy a higher level of prestige, status, and social recognition. Therefore, it is not surprising that much corporate communication apparently directed to external audiences is in fact aimed at projecting favorable images of the organization to and strengthening the identification of its members. In this process, organizational artefacts, such as products, logos, or advertising campaigns, may play a pivotal role (Olins, 1989).

Of all the organizational artefacts, the company's products are perhaps those that exert the greatest influence on external and internal perceptions of what the organization is and is about (Bergami, 1994). Internally, products represent the most visible and tangible outcome of members' work, a concrete reflection of working practices and organizational values. Externally, products are frequently the sole way that an organization is known – and judged – by external audiences, who make inferences about an organization's values, competences, and attributes based on the physical and technical characteristics of its products, their design, performance, originality, quality, etc. Almost inevitably, then, product images will tend to affect organizational images, as the relative prestige of a company will be influenced by the social recognition of its products.

In corporate museums, therefore, communication is directed towards both external and internal audiences, as the display of the most significant products – those that marked substantial innovations in design or technology, or gained exceptional commercial success and social recognition – is frequently used to support the celebration of collective accomplishments and to instill or reinforce pride and a sense of belongingness in organizational members.

As Simona Romano, curator of the KartellMuseum, observed:

> Our museum helps to create a strong "sense of belonging," as employees are more conscious of the world they work in and really feel tied to it . . . Exhibitions and other events involve organizational members coming from different functional areas . . . the result is an exchange of competences, a stronger identification in the firm, and the pride of being part of this firm.

In fact, Kartell and Piaggio both systematically organize guided tours during the initial training period of new recruits. At Kartell, a visit to the museum is considered an important step in the socialization of employees at the head-quarters, as well as international dealers and sales managers. As Simona Romano remarks:

> Being Kartell, an international brand, international sales managers and dealers are invited to visit the museum, as it represents a powerful means of communicating Kartell's complex identity . . . In international firms like Kartell, it is difficult to spread and strengthen a sense of cohesive-ness; in this respect the museum is particularly helpful.

Similarly, managers at the Automobilismo Storico Alfa-Romeo took the responsibility for producing internal documents and for organizing visits, events, and exhibitions that would help new recruits in sales and marketing understand what made the company's products and the brands unique. As Pasquale Oliveri observed:

> We had to help all these new managers who move from company to company familiarize themselves with our culture. It was very important for us, so we produced a small booklet that we gave to all the new sales staff and marketing people . . . Each page explained the history and pride about being Alfa-Romeo . . . because if you are inconsistent with what you've been in the past, people who have always bought Alfa might no longer identify with the new products and start buying other competi-tors' models. This is how we turn our history into one of our strategic assets: a competitive advantage for the brand, acknowledged by our competitors and by our customers – particularly the "Alfisti."

Recent developments, however, suggest that identification may even cross the boundaries of the organization. Consumer behaviorists, for instance, have observed how particular groups of customers may come to define themselves in terms of a product or a producer. "Mac users" (Muniz and O'Guinn, 2001; Belk and Tumbat, 2005) or Harley-Davidson "bikers" (Schouten and McAlexander, 1995) are some of the most widely cited examples of this phenomenon. Research in marketing has developed the term *brand communities* to identify groups of consumers sharing a high identification with an object of consumption – i.e., a product or a brand (McAlexander, Schouten, and Koenig, 2002).

It is still unclear how and why brand communities arise and whether companies can artificially stimulate their formation. However, given established com-munities, corporate museums may help to preserve or reinforce the emotional attachment and identification between community members and the company. In fact, with geographically dispersed communities, museums may come to represent a locus of aggregation, a physical location where "cult" objects are preserved and displayed to devoted "acolytes." In the cases of Alfa-Romeo and Piaggio, for example, hundreds of clubs – more than a thousand for Alfa-Romeo and more than eight hundred for Piaggio – bring together enthusiast customers (called respectively "Alfisti" and "Vespisti") from all over the world.

Indeed, religious metaphors are frequently used to describe the attitude and behavior of these customers. Oliveri described the members of the global community of "Alfisti" in this way:

> We Alfisti are all equal, united under a faith and a flag . . . By winning all over the world, everywhere you find offspring of the Alfa myth . . . In 1968 I went to the Caribbean and I found a guy driving a Spider: we understood each other immediately – we were thinking and talking exactly in the same way! It's a passion, a way of being, a way of suffering and winning . . . And you can't really call yourself an Alfista if you have never visited the Museum. The Museum is like a Mecca.

In both cases, corporate museums have become platforms for a number of initiatives and events aimed at celebrating the heritage of the companies, affirming their unique identity, and revamping their mythology among the respective brand communities.

CONCLUSIONS

Our research indicates how, by selecting and displaying a variety of organizational artefacts (products, visuals, photographs, etc.), presented as tangible evidence of a shared past, corporate museums may play an important role in expressing organizational identity, as grounded in the collective history of its members and in its tangible manifestations, and projecting rich and attractive corporate images.

In the companies we have observed, corporate museums reflect the intention to create a link between past, present, and future conceptualizations of the organizations – connecting "what we have been, what we are and what we will be as an organization." In this respect, corporate museums help organizations simultaneously address identity-related needs for *continuity* – by reclaiming a corporate past to give sense to future action – and for *differentiation* – by emphasizing the uniqueness and qualities that distinguish the organization and its products from competitors.

Essential to this endeavor, however, seems to be the possession of a distinctive *corporate heritage* – understood as a web of traditions, values, and practices that underpin a distinct role in the development of the industry, technologies, society, and culture – and embodied in organizational artefacts (products, buildings, and other manifestations of the organization and of the work of its members) that are perceived internally and externally as central to the organization's identity. By selectively highlighting and displaying elements of the corporate heritage, then, museums help managers use the corporate past to increase the current appeal of the organization and its products to their audiences, and to provide a direction for future growth. As one of our contacts at Piaggio put it: "A museum makes you aware of what you are and where you want to go. If you don't know your past, you can't design your future."

KEY QUESTIONS

1 Could any company establish a corporate museum? Antonio Magro, curator of the Alfa-Romeo Museum, claims that a prestigious brand and an old tradition are fundamental to set up and manage a corporate museum effectively. But is a rich cultural heritage really necessary for the establishment of such a museum?

2 Simona Romano, curator of the KartellMuseum, states: "A corporate museum is justified as long as a company has something to tell; communicating a fake identity may be a very risky undertaking." To what extent is it possible to "manufacture" cultural heritage? Can effective corporate rhetoric or sophisticated arrangements of corporate records compensate for a blurred organizational identity and an opaque history?

3 Some museums are centered on products; others make extensive use of photographs and other visual documents. Is it possible to trace a connection between the prevailing role assigned to the museum (fostering identification, enriching associations, etc.) and the criteria followed in the selection and display of objects?

4 What is the most appropriate profile for a museum curator? What is her/his most appropriate position? To whom should s/he report? What are her/his goals and job description?

Chapter 12

Crafting an Inter-National identity

The Nordea case

Eero Vaara, Janne Tienari, and Olivier Irrmann

INTRODUCTION

Internationalization poses specific challenges for organizational identities. These challenges are accentuated in situations such as cross-border mergers and acquisitions, which imply radical changes for the organizations and people involved. We argue that a key issue in such contexts is how corporate management succeeds in handling the needs for national identification on the one hand, and the requirement to construct a joint international identity on the other. Corporate image-building campaigns are one means for such identity management, and they can potentially have a major impact on how people identify with the organization. Unfortunately, we seem to know little of the specific problematics related to international identity-building efforts, and there appears to be a paucity of knowledge concerning the use of national or international symbols in such campaigns.

This chapter presents a discursive[1] perspective on an international identity-building program in a financial services company. Our point of departure is to view identities as constructions drawing from various kinds of texts and visual images such as symbols and icons. Texts and visual images may, however, carry stereotypes and myths that are ambiguous or even loaded with negative sentiments. This makes purposeful organizational identity building a challenging endeavor.

We focus on an identity-building program carried out in a leading North European financial services group, now called Nordea. This organization was formed through a series of cross-border mergers and acquisitions in Finland,

[1] We see "discourse" as a linguistically mediated representation of reality. In this view, discourse is not simply "language" or "communication," but an essential part of the social practices through which we socially enact reality as we experience it. Discourse thus not only reflects but also constitutes our social world.

Sweden, Denmark, and Norway in the period 1997–2000, and through subsequent smaller acquisitions in Poland and the Baltic states. To craft a new common identity, the financial services group was named Nordea at the end of 2000. This name is derived from "Nordic" and "Ideas", highlighting the intended Nordic identity of the company. The new company logo depicts a blue sail, said to allude to the Baltic Sea.

Identity-building efforts at Nordea have in many ways been successful. The company has established its position in the market, and its financial performance has been satisfactory. Identity building at Nordea has, however, also included controversial elements. In our analysis we concentrate on the mobilization of Nordic identity through four key dimensions: naturalness versus artificiality, uniqueness versus banality, positive versus negative self-esteem, and enabling versus constraining future orientation. While the Nordea case has unique features, we argue that the points raised in this chapter are central in international identity-building programs more generally.

The Nordic ideas campaign

Nordea is the outcome of a series of domestic and cross-border mergers and acquisitions. In October 1997, the Finnish Merita Bank and Swedish Nordbanken, both themselves products of earlier domestic mergers, joined forces in an unprecedented cross-border merger in the European financial services sector. Already at this stage the representatives of the new MeritaNordbanken group announced their intention to proceed with mergers and acquisitions in other Nordic countries. In March 2000 it was announced that MeritaNordbanken was to merge with Danish Unidanmark, a group created around a year earlier by a merger between leading Danish banking and insurance companies. Already before the Finnish–Swedish–Danish stage, however, MeritaNordbanken had made a first public offer for the Norwegian Christiania Bank og Kreditkasse (CBK), which was eventually acquired in October 2000 after lengthy negotiations. This completed the basic Nordic constellation. Figure 17 summarizes key events in the restructuring of the Nordic financial services sector leading to the creation of Nordea.

The Nordic region

The Nordic region consists of Denmark, Finland, Iceland, Norway, and Sweden as well as the autonomous regions of the Åland Islands (Finland), Greenland and the Faroe Islands (Denmark). With a population of almost nine million, Sweden is the largest of the Nordic countries. It is also the largest in area. Denmark, Finland, and Norway all have populations of approximately five million. Denmark is, however, markedly smaller in area than Finland and Norway. In a number of ways,

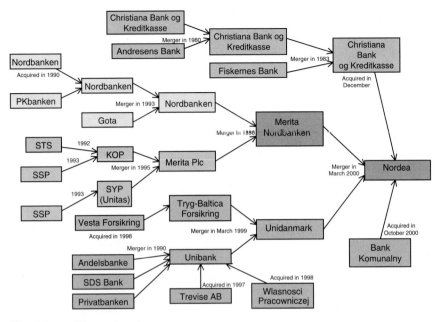

Figure 17 Nordea's history

the Nordic countries share a web of common histories. While Sweden and Denmark are old nations, however, Norway gained its independence in 1905 and Finland in 1917.

Gustav I Vasa, King of Sweden from 1520 to 1560, is generally considered the creator of the centralized Swedish state. A strong military power during the seventeenth century, Sweden has not gone to war for almost two centuries. Sweden also managed to preserve its non-alignment in both world wars, while Denmark and Norway were occupied by the Germans during the Second World War. Finland fought two wars against the Soviet Union (1939–1940 and 1942–1944) and one against Germany (1944–1945), and managed to stay independent throughout, albeit ceding part of its eastern region to the Soviet Union in 1945.

The Danish kingdom was once a major North European power reigning over areas that now belong to the UK, Germany, Iceland, Norway, and Sweden. In the late seventeenth century, Sweden conquered rich agricultural areas from Denmark, today constituting the southern regions of Sweden. As a result of the Napoleonic wars, Denmark lost its hegemony over Norway in 1814. The southern regions of the Danish kingdom, Schleswig and Holstein, were conquered by the Prussians in the late nineteenth century. These events weakened Denmark as an economic and political power.

In 1397, Norway was absorbed into a union with Denmark that was to last for more than four centuries. In 1814, Norwegians resisted the cession of their country to Sweden and adopted a new constitution. As part of the Peace of Vienna, following the Napoleonic Wars, Norway entered into a union with Sweden, which nevertheless agreed to allow Norway to keep its constitution in return for accepting union under a Swedish king. Rising nationalism in the nineteenth century led to a 1905 referendum granting Norway independence as a kingdom. The new Norwegian king was called from the Danish royal family.

With Finland, the web of historical relations becomes even more complex. Already in 1150, King Erik of Sweden led a crusade to what is today the south-western part of Finland. From the peace treaty of 1323 until 1809, Finland was a dukedom in the Kingdom of Sweden. In 1809, Finland was incorporated as a Grand Duchy within Imperial Russia. In 1917, Finland gained its independence for the first time. A republic was formed after heated discussions, but a kingdom had, in fact, been a serious option.

In general, geographical proximity and the web of common histories mean that the Nordic nations appear to share particular traits. Many of the institutions and traditions have the same origins. The legislation in the four countries is relatively harmonized. Denmark, Finland, Norway, and Sweden also have common charac-teristics in terms of their form of government and social welfare offered to their citizens. Nordic societies are deeply rooted democracies and (at least until recently) developed welfare states.

Furthermore, the Nordic countries have – especially since the Second World War – worked consciously to create institutions and procedures that foster Nordic cooperation and values. The Nordic Council was established in 1952 as a public institution for collaboration between the Nordic parliaments and governments. Since 1954, Nordic citizens have been able to move freely across their borders without a passport, and in the same year the Nordic countries decided to form a common labor market.

The Nordic ideas ad campaign

In late 2000, after having been given permission to acquire the Norwegian Chris-tiania Bank og Kreditkassen, the corporate management of the new financial services group faced several challenges. These included the distribution of key management positions and respective responsibilities, integration of organiza-tional structures and processes, creation of synergy and value, ensuring motivation and commitment, and convincing investors and other external stakeholders. The new financial services group also lacked a name. In internal discussions, investing in a new corporate identity was seen as a major means to tackle not only the identity issues *per se* but also the other challenges already mentioned.

After weighing up various alternatives, the corporate management decided to tap into Nordic imagery. Introduced in spring 2001, the Nordea brand – as stated, derived from "Nordic" and "ideas" – was gradually to replace the existing bank

Figure 18 *Nordea's brands*

brands, as shown in Figure 18. It was to serve as the basis for a new common identity for the group and its various units.

The new Nordea brand was implemented at a different pace in various parts of the new organization. It began to be used at group level (so-called concentrated functions) and in cross-border operations in business units such as corporate and institutional banking and asset management. In operations such as retail banking, country-based brands (bank names) were maintained for some time, depending on the country organization and unit in question. However, by and large, Nordea had replaced the old brands by the end of the year.

The identity-building program at Nordea included both internal and external activities: sociocultural integration within the organization (for internal audiences: the employees) and an extensive international ad campaign (for external audiences: customers and investors). Internally, integration activities within the organization were implemented to develop a new cultural identity; these included establishing and communicating new corporate values and their translation into common standards and daily practices (for a detailed discussion of these efforts, see Søderberg and Björkman, 2003). Externally, the Nordea brand and the intended Nordic identity were introduced to the public in spring 2001 through advertisements in major newspapers in the various Nordic countries and in international media such as *The Economist*. These advertisements were developed in collaboration with consultants and ad agencies.

In this ad campaign, an international Nordic identity was crafted to provide a meaningful basis for developing a common future for the multinational financial services company. An important part of this was to avoid national confrontation between Swedes, Finns, Danes, and Norwegians – united and divided by the common histories we have already described. The idea was also to make use of distinctive positive images related to the Nordic countries.

The Nordea advertisements published in major newspapers in the Nordic countries introduced a set of six images and slogans: *Nordic simplicity, Nordic opportunities, Nordic security, Nordic flexibility, Nordic freedom*, and *Nordic individuality*. The central point or image in each ad was accompanied with the text "Nordic idea" (see Figures 19 and 20).

The Nordea advertisements published in targeted international media such as *The Economist* introduced a similar message, but with different images and slogans: *Nordic modesty, Nordic clarity*, and *Nordic ideas* (this last slogan thus provided an explicit connection between the two sets of ads). As an example, one of the advertisements is reproduced in Figure 21.

A discursive perspective on international organizational identity building

Our starting point here is to draw on the interpretative tradition, which emphasizes the role of meanings and constructions in identity building. According to this perspective, identities are in flux as they are constantly negotiated and (re)constructed in social interaction. Consequently, people may have multiple identities that may also involve ambiguity and contradiction. This is the case with organizational identities too. It also means that people as individuals or groups can pursue specific "identitarian" strategies; that is, to purposefully identify with and consequently convey the image of belonging to a specific social category. In corporate settings this is often called "corporate image building." Such campaigns frequently target both the external and internal audiences. In fact, much market-related communication is characterized by "auto-communication," i.e., communication through which the organization reinforces its own identity by the promotion of specific values and use of particular symbols.

When studying national and international identity building one is unavoidably dealing with nationalism (Anderson, 1983; Hobsbawm, 1990). For our purposes, it is meaningful to view nationalism as a discourse based on shared understandings of history and continuity. This echoes Anderson's (1983) idea of nations as imagined communities rather than stable ahistorical institutions. As Hobsbawm (1990) has emphasized, symbols, icons, stereotypes, and myths play a central role in constructions of nations. In this context, it is particularly interesting to note the central role of what Billig (1995) has called "banal nationalism" in contemporary society. According to this view, the construct of nationality is often reproduced in mundane habits of language, thought, and symbolism in everyday life. It is, for example, easy to talk casually about "us Finns" or "us Swedes" and make the distinctions "those Swedes" or "those Finns." Such nation talk can also be more purposeful. Wodak *et al.* (1999) provide an analysis of the various discursive

En nordisk idé

Nordisk säkerhet

"Varför skulle 1900-talets fortskaffningsmedel No 1 inte anpassas till vägbanans kondition på vintern lika väl som på sommaren?" Så tänkte naturligtvis den finländare, som uppfann dubbdäcket. Ett bra exempel på en nordisk idé, som skapade möjligheter där andra nog mest såg problem.
Vi på Nordea har samma sätt att tänka. Vi är en kombination av några av de främsta bankerna och försäk-ringsbolagen i Norden. Vi vill ge dig store säkerhet i livet, så att du får större chans att utveckla dina idéer, förändra dina affärer, genomföra dina livsprojekt. När du når dina mål, når vi våra.

Nordea

Nordeakoncernen består av Merita Bank, Nordbanken, Unibank, Christiania Bank og Kreditkasse, Tryg-Baltica, Vesta, Merita Life, Livia och ArosMaizels. Du möter oss under våra vanliga namn även i fortsättningen – i kombination med Nordea. Våra expanderande verksamheter i de baltiska staterna bär dock redan nu namnet Nordea, liksom affärsområdena Corporate and Institutional Banking och Asset Management. **www.nordea.com**

Figure 19 Nordic security

strategies used in these processes. Particularly important are strategies of assimilation and dissimilation. Assimilation strategies linguistically create a sense of similarity and homogeneity. Dissimilation strategies, in turn, lead to a sense of

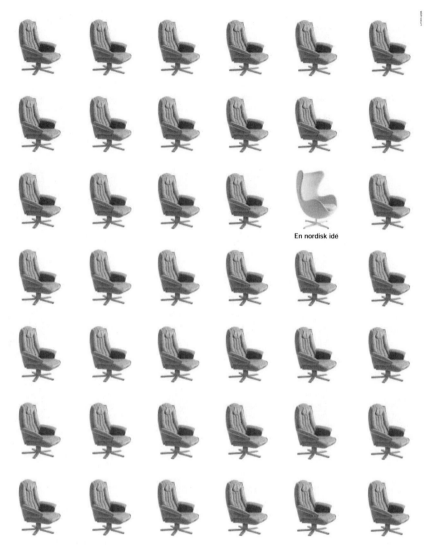

En nordisk idé

Nordisk individualitet.

Den danska äggfåtöljens design kan verka avvikande. Men vem sa, att en fåtölj bara är till för att sitta i. Jacobsens fåtölj ger en god bild av vårt nordiska sätt att tänka och några av våra viktigaste ideal; individualitet, kreativitet, ökad livskvalitet. Nordea bärs upp av samma ideér. Vi är en kombination av några av de främsta bankerna och försäkringsbolagen i Norden. Vi vill, att livet ska bli enklare och mer innehållsrikt för just dig. Vi vill, att du ska få större chans att.utveckla dina idéer, förändra dina affärer, genomföra dina livsprojekt. För när du når dina mål, når vi våra mål.

Nordea

Figure 20 Nordic individualism

Nordic ideas

Believe it or not, this man is busy harvesting our greatest natural resource and it isn't fish - it's ideas. We love ideas, the wealth of our region is founded upon ideas the and ability to realise those ideas. The future will be built upon ideas and we encourage our customers and our employees to dream. We will partner our customers, helping them to realise their ambitions and dream up new ideas.

We are a reflection of our region and its most important natural resource, ideas. We bring a clear Nordic outlook and approach to the market places of the world.

We are looking forward to doing business with you ... the Nordic way.

Nordea AB is a world leader in Internet banking with 2 million e-customers. We have total assets of EUR 230 billion. Six business areas serve 9 million personal and 700,000 corporate and institutional customers. We have 1,260 bank branches, 125 insurance service centres, telephone and e-banking services. We have operations in 18 countries outside our region. With EUR 107 billion under management, Nordea holds a leading position in the Nordic asset management market. Nordea comprises Merita Bank, Nordbanken, Unibank, Christiania Bank og Kreditkasse, ArosMaizels, Tryg-Baltica, Vesta, Merita Life and Livia. www.nordea.com

Figure 21 *Nordic ideas*

difference or heterogeneity. Both of these strategies can then be constructive, justifying, transformative, or destructive in nature.

While most organizations have national origins, national identification is subject to change in processes of internationalization. In cross-border mergers and acquisitions, the people involved face a struggle between instinctive or banal national identification on the one hand, and international or "global" identification on the other. For corporate management, this implies specific challenges to support positive identification while avoiding problems related to identity conflicts. In practice, corporate managers typically end up promoting an international or even "global" identity. One reason is the obvious need to combat confrontation between representatives of different nations, which can have dysfunctional effects on organizational performance. Another may in some contexts be the progressive image related to "internationalization" or "globalization."

Studying such processes is not uncomplicated, and we propose a particular kind of discursive perspective. According to this perspective, specific discursive resources are essential means through which specific conceptions of organizational identity are created and re-created. These include symbols, icons, stereotypes, and myths that can be mobilized for specific purposes. This mobilization takes place through specific identitarian strategies. Of the various kinds of discursive identity-building strategies, particularly important for our purposes are strategies of assimilation and dissimilation. The former strategies create a temporal, interpersonal, or spatial similarity and homogeneity; the latter in turn construct a temporal, interpersonal, or territorial difference or heterogeneity. In practice, there exists a variety of means to create, use, or manipulate images for collective organizational identity.

The effectiveness of specific identity-building efforts is, however, difficult to evaluate – for example, because identification is by its very nature often ambiguous and contradictory. Yet most students of organizational identity tend to agree that (tenable) identities are characterized by features such as authenticity, distinctiveness, self-esteem, and efficacy (e.g., Hogg and Terry, 2000). These are important aspects of social and organizational identity that need to be examined to better understand the problems and challenges in specific identity-building projects. In such settings, special emphasis must be based on the future, and therefore we consider future orientation as a specifically important aspect related to efficacy. These characteristics form a basis for our analysis of intentional corporate identity building in the Nordea case. Figure 22 summarizes our theoretical framework.

Nordea as a constructed identity

To provide a more in-depth understanding of the discursive construction processes involved in the Nordic ideas campaign, we will now examine the identity constructions *vis-à-vis* the following key dimensions: authenticity, distinctiveness, self-esteem, and future orientation. To be effective a constructed organizational identity needs to be authentic ("we" share something that is real) and distinctive ("we" are unique), related to positive self-esteem ("we" achieve positive things together), and create an enabling outlook for the future ("we" can do more in the future).

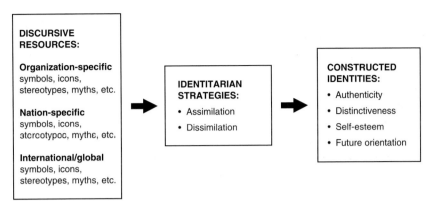

Figure 22 *A discursive perspective on organizational identity building*

Authenticity

In many ways, the use of the Nordic symbols and icons by Nordea provided an *authentic* basis for identification. The Nordic countries share a common history, as we have described. This joint history provides a meaningful historical basis for identity building that can be traced back to the Viking era. The Nordic countries also have similar institutions, such as legal systems as previously mentioned. In addition, Swedish, Danish, and Norwegian belong to the same language group and are mutually intelligible. Approximately 6 percent of the Finnish population has Swedish as their mother tongue, with Swedish the second official language of the country.

The specific icons used as unifying symbols in the press campaign within the Nordic countries on the one hand, and the stereotypical images used in *The Economist* on the other, are concrete and compelling examples of Nordic characteristics and achievements. Our particular examples – Nordic security, Nordic individualism, and Nordic ideas – all feature elements that may relatively easily be associated with being Nordic. Providing security for all citizens is a key element of the Nordic welfare society model, individual initiative is valued and respected, and the man ice-fishing in the Nordic ideas ad (Figure 21) illustrates the sometimes harsh conditions that lead Nordic people to think up practical ideas to make life a little easier for all.

However, the construction of the Nordic identity at Nordea may also be viewed as *artificial*. In fact, it hides essential differences between the Nordic countries. In spite of similarities, there are important cultural differences between Denmark, Finland, Norway, and Sweden. Further, the economies of the Nordic countries differ, which has a direct bearing on banking activities. In brief, Sweden and Finland have a number of large industrial groups operating in various sectors, whilst the Danish economy is much more entrepreneurially oriented. The Norwegian economy is to a large extent based on oil resources. Consequently, for those in financial services, the common Nordic platform is not self-evident. There are different emphases and aspirations especially in relation to corporate clients.

In using national symbols, it is also problematic that the nationalism of each of the countries – in particular Norway and Finland – has been based on the creation of specific mythologies that distinguish these nations from their neighbors. For example, in Finland the nationalist imagery has, to a large extent, been based on old Karelian myths and sagas and the institutionalization of the Finnish language as an alternative to Swedish from the nineteenth century onwards. In Norway, there is a specific language, called "Nynorsk" or "New Norwegian," that was developed as an alternative to the Danish-based language. Finland and Norway are so-called new nations, whereas Sweden and Denmark represent old ones (Gellner, 1983). In fact, the relationship of Finland to Sweden and of Norway to both Denmark and Sweden can be seen as involving post-colonial features. Against this background the focus on the Nordic is at odds with the instinctive tendencies of Finns and Norwegians in particular to distinguish themselves from Swedes or Danes.

Importantly, the icons used in the campaign in the Nordic newspapers are not Nordic but, at best, national emblems. This may be considered a natural choice in view of the difficulties in finding any specific joint "Nordic" achievements, if the Nordic institutions referred to above are not considered as such. All of the six icons used (Figures 19 and 20 provide two examples) are inventions by specific individuals who are most often seen as national figures. Although these icons are examples that may be widely known in their "homeland," this does not make them particularly Nordic in the eyes of others.

In the *Nordic security* ad (Figure 19), "that Finn" ("den finländare" in the Swedish text in the ad) who invented the studded winter tire brings an obscure flavor to the whole. Does the inventor not have a name? Why is it irrelevant here? The text in the ad introduces the studded winter tire as a Nordic idea "that created opportunities where others mostly saw problems." While many people undoubtedly see the link to Nordic conditions, many may also wonder why the exact origins of this innovation are disguised. The *Nordic individualism* ad (Figure 20), centering on the chair designed by Arne Jacobsen, presents a markedly Danish icon. This is in spite of the fact that Jacobsen originally designed the chair for the SAS (Scandinavian Airlines System) Hotel in Copenhagen. So what is authentically Nordic in the ad? An English translation of text below the visual image states that "Jacobsen's chair gives a good example of our Nordic way of thinking and some of our most important ideals: individualism, creativity, increasing quality of life. Nordea is based on the same ideas." However, the Danish icon of individualism, presented here as an example of being Nordic, may puzzle non-Danes. Swedes, for example, are well known for their communitarian, consensus-seeking society – the "People's Home" – and they may not agree that Danish individualism is an adequate representation of being "Nordic."

The campaign in *The Economist*, in turn, reproduced specific myths and stereotypes about the Nordic countries and their peoples without relying on specific icons. Here, it is interesting to note that not all the images used fit all the Nordic countries: ice-fishing in our example – the *Nordic ideas* ad (Figure 21) – is mostly a Finnish or Swedish winter pastime, not something that is popular or even possible in Denmark. Viewed in this way, it is again an artificial representation of the Nordic. The text in the ad claims: "Believe it or not, this man is busy harvesting our greatest natural resource and it isn't fish – it's ideas. We love ideas, the wealth of our region is founded upon ideas the and ability to realise those ideas" (misprint in the original). For Danes, it would require a stretch of the imagination to consider the ice-fishing metaphor to be representative of a "Nordic" they can share.

Distinctiveness

The Nordic imagery used provided in many ways a basis for a unique identity at Nordea. The Nordic ideas campaign underscored the fact that this was the first ever pan-Nordic financial services company – and, indeed, one of the first pan-Nordic companies in any industry. This *distinctiveness* was emphasized to the extent that it could be presented as a competitive advantage for Nordea. Importantly, this distinctive identity was claimed for audiences both in the Nordic countries and elsewhere.

Our examples – Nordic security, Nordic individualism, and Nordic ideas – all feature elements that are distinct or even unique to the Nordic context. Studded winter tires are used in the harsh Nordic winters; Arne Jacobsen's chair was conceived in a Nordic country; ice-fishing is extremely difficult to associate with non-Nordic countries, with the exception of parts of Russia and Canada. "Harvesting ideas" with a kick sled, borer, and a short rod *is* in many senses distinctive.

Like authenticity, this distinctiveness can, however, be questioned. The Nordic ideas campaign did not say much about what it means to be a *pan*-Nordic financial services group compared to other banks or insurance companies operating in the Nordic countries. Most of the icons in the first campaign (in the Nordic press) or the stereotypical images reflecting specific values in the second (*The Economist*) could, in fact, have been used by many if not all banks in Finland, Sweden, Denmark, or Norway to promote their "Nordic" identity. The icons and stereotypes used are not distinctly Nordea. Some of Nordea's competitors – such as the Sweden-based Handelsbanken, which has grown by greenfield investments and acquisitions in the other Nordic countries – could in theory have used the same symbols to run a similar campaign. However, Handelsbanken has chosen not to refer to "Nordic" in its identity building (see Chapter 4). In Finland, for example, it has run an interesting ad campaign dealing with its Swedishness in a humorous way.

The theme of ideas running through the Nordea ads aimed at underscoring the ability of Nordea to transfer ideas (practices, services, or products) developed in some parts (countries) of the company to other parts (countries). This is specific to a *pan*-Nordic organization, and special efforts were made to identify so-called best practices and to transfer them across the country organizations (Vaara, Tienari, and Björkman, 2003). However, in the Nordic Ideas campaign this particular theme remained relatively weak, something that was mentioned in the text rather than in the visual elements of the ads. No concrete examples of transferring ideas were given in the ads. In internal communications at Nordea, however, the corporate management promoted examples of successful knowledge transfer. The Solo electronic banking concept, originally developed in Finland and then transferred to other Nordic countries, was an early example of this.

Self-esteem

A successful organizational identity gives a positive sense of self-esteem. This was also the intention with the Nordic Ideas campaign. The icons used are achievements that Nordic people can be proud of: Arne Jacobsen's chair, for example, is a design classic that can hardly provoke anything other than positive feelings of association. The ice-fishing image can even be thought to convey gentle humor in presenting the "Nordic" as something positively peculiar. The imagery is definitely not aggressive; it may even appear boring. The wo/man "harvesting ideas" is clearly minding her/his own business. Notably, ice-fishing is something that everyone can do; it conveys democracy and equality. All these features relate to the fact that many contemporary Nordic people are proud of the peaceful and equality nurturing nature of their societies.

What was problematic with this campaign, however, is that the Nordic imagery could be turned into a handicap by competitors. Not surprisingly, some competitors in the domestic markets worked on their national and/or local image. Norwegian competitors had already drawn on the Norwegian national identity to try to prevent the "foreign" acquisition of CBK (Tienari, Vaara, and Björkman, 2003). In their communications, Finnish and Swedish competitors emphasized their Finnishness or Swedishness to underscore a difference to Nordea. Handelsbanken in Sweden is one example of this. At the same time, in the international scene, being Nordic could be interpreted as "not international" or "not global." And this was indeed seen as a major issue by those in charge of international operations at Nordea. In other words, being Nordic could be interpreted as parochial in the increasingly global banking business.

The self-esteem of Nordea employees in Estonia, Latvia, Lithuania, and Poland is another potentially problematic element in the Nordic ideas campaign. Are they not a source of ideas at Nordea? Or, conversely, should "being Nordic" be considered a state of mind that Estonians, Latvians, Lithuanians, and Poles identify with?

Future orientation

In terms of the future, the Nordic construction provides an enabling platform for Nordea in many ways. In particular, the campaigns in Nordic newspapers and *The Economist* promoted integration by offering a joint or "umbrella" identity, which seems to have made it possible for different stakeholders to retain their national identities. In effect, "being Nordic" does not exclude being Danish, Finnish, Norwegian, or Swedish.

In cross-border mergers and acquisitions, dominance by any party is a key issue, which is frequently viewed in terms of national balance (Søderberg and Vaara, 2003). A distorted balance is often interpreted by organizational members and the media as a sign of winning or losing for the nations involved. Fears of losing one's national identity may be a constant threat in an internationalizing organization. The Nordic identity offered by Nordea's campaign worked to circumvent such threats. Furthermore, the Nordic construction promoted equality, which was another important means of preventing confrontation between nations, which is a frequent problem in such settings.

By focusing on "ideas," the campaign specifically promoted the transfer of knowledge and capabilities across borders. Interestingly, all this meant that integration was constructed as a process of symbiosis or partnership rather then takeover, absorption, or standardization. A joint, international future was envisioned for Nordea. This proved to have a positive impact on the employees' attitudes in the integration process in the chain of cross-border mergers and acquisitions.

However, the Nordic ideas campaign also involved constraining elements. Despite the apparent focus on equality, some people could read underlying dominance tendencies in the Nordic imagery used. For example, some Norwegians associated the name "Nordea" with Nordbanken (the Swedish root of Nordea, literally "North Bank"). Consequently, Nordea's equality could be interpreted as disguised dominance by Swedes. At the time of writing, the Swedish state remains the single largest shareholder in Nordea with approximately 19 percent, whereas all other individual shareholders each own less than 5 percent. Further, the imagery emphasized and identity crafted in the Nordic ideas campaign did not support the integration of operations in the Baltic States and Poland, where Nordea has attempted to build significant presence in recent years.

Finally, the emphasis on Nordic identity can also be seen as ambiguous or even problematic in view of future mergers and acquisitions in financial services in Europe. Nordea was close to merging with an international banking group based in the Netherlands only a year after the campaign discussed in this chapter. There have also been constant rumors of other forays into mergers and acquisitions. Should they materialize, they would probably require a completely new kind of identity-building program for Nordea. How would the "Nordic" fit in a Dutch-based or German-based multinational? Would the Nordic brand be maintained or discarded? In any case, Nordea is now positioned in a particular way for the coming European consolidation in financial services.

CONCLUSION

Corporate organizations face specific challenges with respect to international identity management. These challenges are accentuated in situations such as cross-border mergers and acquisitions. We have suggested in this chapter that these challenges often revolve around national identification on the one hand and international or global identification on the other. In such settings, management of the transition towards an international corporate identity is particularly tricky, and can usually be controlled by corporate managers only to some extent. Nevertheless, corporate brand-building campaigns have potentially great effects on these identification processes. The Nordea case is an interesting example of such intentional identity-building efforts. We have concentrated on their Nordic ideas campaign, which can be seen as a particularly revealing example involving the mobilization of Nordic symbols and icons as well as myths and stereotypes for the construction of a new organizational identity.

By and large, Nordea's ad campaign can be seen as a successful example of corporate identity building (see, however, Søderberg and Björkman, 2003, for a more critical analysis of Nordea's internal communications). As discussed previously, the campaign seemed to help in the construction of an authentic, distinctive, positive, and enabling organizational identity. Succeeding in this kind of setting is far from certain, and one can only speculate what might have happened without such a campaign. Would MeritaNordbankenUnidanmarkKreditkassen (MNUK) have been a better choice? We doubt it.

What is particularly interesting in the Nordea case is the crafting of an umbrella-like Nordic identity under which specific national identities could still coexist. Such an international (here regional) identity is a novel means of tackling the challenges related to internationalization. It is more concrete than vague attempts to portray an internationalizing corporation simply as "global." The parallel to conscious attempts to construct European identities is obvious (Breakwell and Lyons, 1996). However, we argue that the Nordic identity involves less contradictory elements than a pan-European one.

The coexistence of national identities under a broad Nordic umbrella seems to be a particularly insightful approach *vis-à-vis* the challenges encountered in cross-border mergers and acquisitions. This framework enables the people involved to retain their national identities while becoming committed to a joint future symbolized by the Nordic. The fact that Nordic is often associated with democracy and equality may also help to play down concerns about dominance. This should be taken seriously in corporate settings that involve historical rivalry and post-colonial relationships.

This is not to say that the Nordic identity is uncomplicated. Indeed, like any constructed supranational identity it involves in-built tensions between different national identities. In the Nordic setting the rivalry between the four nations, and in particular the post-colonial relationships involved, brings with it specific difficulties in envisioning a totally harmonious and equal Nordic basis. In the Nordic ideas project, the unusual feature is that the first campaign drew on explicit national icons. One reason for this is that it is hard to find exciting and compelling icons that are purely Nordic. In this sense the campaign contained a paradox: trying to deal with the problematic aspects of nationalism by mobilizing national icons.

In all, what the Nordea case shows is that any international identity building is complex and involves inherent problematics that relate to authenticity, distinctiveness, self-esteem, and future orientation. The point is that the meanings created through specific ads or other communication means are often ambiguous and even contradictory. In the case of the Nordic identity, the images created are particularly tricky. What is taken as genuine can soon be interpreted as artificial. What is seen as a virtue may quickly turn into hypocrisy or banality. What may appear as equal can suddenly be interpreted as dominance. Yet, without such support for corporate identity building, the future of the organization would remain even more vague and the associations created could be much more problematic.

Part IV

Conclusion

Chapter 13

Analyzing organizational identities

Some guidelines for practice

Lin Lerpold, Davide Ravasi, Johan van Rekom, and Guillaume Soenen

In this book, we have collected a number of cases illustrating how organizational identities influence the functioning of organizations, how members make decisions, how they react to and deal with environmental changes, how they relate to external audiences, and how they try to project attractive images. Together, these cases suggest the importance of organizational identity issues for the survival of an organization and the well-being of its members. They illustrate how notions of "who we are" influence how members make decisions and behave in daily organizational life, and they highlight the need for appropriate tools to support managerial action on organizational identities.

Some of the cases show how identity-related issues may catch managers unaware or act subconsciously, as happened with managers at Statoil, Scania, or some of the "Baby Bells." Others, such as the cases of Bang & Olufsen, Nordea, Industrifonden, or Air France, show managers trying to make sense of the identity of their organization and attempting to influence internal and external audiences' notions of what their organization is and stands for. Not all of these attempts were equally successful. Their mixed success suggests the need for a more complete toolkit with which issues of organizational identity can be tackled.

Several tools and frameworks have been proposed to analyze, diagnose, revise, and reformulate organizational identities. In this concluding chapter, we have selected four that, in our view, are both coherent with the overall conceptual approach to the analysis of organizational identity and cover the most critical aspects of identity dynamics:

- The *identification of core, distinctive, and enduring traits* that can plausibly and legitimately justify identity beliefs and support identity claims (Whetten's CED framework and Collins and Porras's articulation of core ideology).
- The *assessment of potential inconsistency between various elements of the identity* of an organization (Soenen and Moingeon's five-facet framework).

- The *definition of an internally coherent platform for the projection of a credible and appealing corporate image* (Hatch and Schultz's Corporate Branding Tool Kit).

This chapter is intended as a guide for further reading. For each model, we summarize the fundamental goal, core tenets, and main methodological steps. Interested readers are encouraged to turn to the original publications referred in the text of this chapter for further details on using the models in analyzing organizational identities.

WHETTEN'S CED FRAMEWORK

The idea of organizational identity as a set of core, enduring and distinctive features is as old as the concept itself (Albert and Whetten, 1985). For decades, however, while most articles on this subject have cited this definition few have attempted to use it as a guide for distinguishing organizational identity from related concepts or to develop valid measures.

Recently, David Whetten (2006) proposed a set of guidelines aimed at identifying those features of the organization that can be legitimately used as referents for identity claims, or, in other words as *"distinguishing organizational features"* (Whetten, 2006: 221; italics in original). The proposed framework aims primarily at providing guidance to organizational scholars and at increasing the validity of empirical research on organizational identity. However, we believe that the elements of Whetten's model can also be of great use to managers engaged in reflections about what is central, enduring and distinctive about their organization.

In this respect, organizational members might be encouraged to nominate what they consider to be their organization's "identifying features." This list could then be scrutinized further, using the CED definition as a three-part parsing tool for distinguishing between bona fide organizational features and bona fide organizational identity referents/claims. This analysis might take the following form.

- *Central.* Is the feature central to survival? Does it reflect what is required and/or ideal for that type of organization? Would the organization become something else without it? Does it reflect the organization's highest values? Would members feel that the organization acted "out of character" if strategic decisions were made that were inconsistent with this feature? Is this feature of the organization considered to be "essential knowledge" for those expected to act or speak on behalf of the organization?
- *Distinctive.* Is this feature used as a way of distinguishing the organization from similar others? Does it reflect the organization's distinctive strategic preferences and competences? Is it a real or potential source of competitive advantage?

- *Enduring*. Has this organizational feature withstood the "test of time"? Is it reflected in the organization's core programs, policies, and procedures? Does it reflect its highest priorities? Is it experienced as an "irreversible commitment"? Is it celebrated in the organizational lore? Is it considered sacrosanct? Would members react with heated emotions to its loss or violation?

According to Whetten (2006), proper identification of valid identity referents becomes especially crucial in times of organizational transition or upheaval. In these situations, identifying attributes serve as clarion reminders of what constitutes "in-character" choices – being true to the organization's distinctive history and acting in accordance with organization-type defining practices and expectations. The logical consequence of acting out of character is that the organization risks becoming "indistinguishable, unrecognizable, unknown" (2006: 224), and hence, unpredictable and untrustworthy. This is the fate of organizations that, in response to pressure and turmoil, lose their sense of "who we are as an organization." Left unchecked, a growing loss of "self-recognition," what Whetten (2006: 223) refers to as the potentially fatal state of confused or mistaken identity, undercuts the organizational actor's capacity for self-governance and self-direction.

COLLINS AND PORRAS'S CORE IDEOLOGY

While they do not mention organizational identity explicitly, James Collins and Jerry Porras are among the first scholars to provide extensive evidence of the relationships between long-term success and a stable set of core values. Their comparative study of companies that had achieved enduring leadership in their respective industries – Johnson & Johnson, Procter & Gamble, Sony, 3M, and others – led them to the conclusion that:

> Companies that enjoy enduring success have core values and a core purpose that remain fixed while their business strategies and practices endlessly adapt to a changing world.
>
> (Collins and Porras, 1996: 65)

Based on their extensive research, the two scholars have developed a set of guidelines to support the efforts of top managers in detecting and preserving the values that have underpinned past success and to provide a bedrock for future growth. Their recommendations, discussed extensively in their book (Collins and Porras, 1994) and in a *Harvard Business Review* article (Collins and Porras, 1996), provide a useful complement to Whetten's framework. They can be summarized as follows.

1 *Assemble a "Mars Group."* Top managers should select five to seven people that they would trust for "recreating the very best attributes of the organization on another planet." People should be selected based on their understanding of the organization, their credibility with their peers, and their personal competence.

2 *Identify core values.* Group members should make an effort to define honestly what values are truly central to their organization. No more than five or six values should be identified, paying attention not to confuse them with practices, policies, and cultural norms. The following questions might help members' discussions:

- What values do you personally bring to your work?
- What would you tell your children are the core values that you hold at work and that you hope they will hold when they become adults?
- Would you bring them to a new organization, regardless of its industry?

3 *Establish endurance and commitment.* Group members should interrogate them-selves on the relative (and prospective) endurance of the preliminary set of values identified in the previous step. Core values should have withstood the test of time and should be expected to continue to do so in the future. In this respect, members might ask themselves questions such as:

- Can we envision this value as valid even a hundred years from now?
- If circumstances changed and penalized us for holding this core value, would we still retain it?
- Would we hold on to this value even if it were to become a source of competitive disadvantage?

4 *Define a core purpose.* Finally, group members should try to identify a funda-mental purpose providing an idealistic motivation to people in the organization. According to the authors, the core purpose should go beyond target customers or operating goals – rather, it should capture "the soul" of the organization. Collins and Porras suggest that a good method to arrive at the core purpose that inspires – or should inspire – organizational action is what they call "The five why's." Group members should start with a descriptive statement of the organization such as "We make X products," and then ask themselves "Why is that important?" five times – an exercise that will eventually bring them to the fundamental reason of being of the organization.

In Collins and Porras's terminology, core values and core purpose constitute what they call *core ideology*; in other words:

> the enduring character of an organization – a consistent *identity* [italics added] that transcends product or market life cycles, technological breakthroughs, management fads, and individual leaders.
>
> (Collins and Porras, 1996: 66)

238

According to the two authors, core ideology defines "what we stand for and why we exist" (1996: 66), and represents a fundamental source of guidance and inspiration for managers' aspirations, condensed in an *envisioned future*.

SOENEN AND MOINGEON'S FIVE FACETS

The model developed by Moingeon and Soenen is based on a decoupling of organizational identity into five analytical dimensions or facets, which together create what they refer to as "the organizational identity system." In their view, top management needs to become aware of both the content and the dynamics of their organization's identity system as this has profound implications for performance. When the identity system reaches a dynamic equilibrium, it contributes to organizational performance by harmonizing strategic intent, collective behaviors, and external perceptions. In other words, identity aspirations, beliefs, and claims are aligned. When in disequilibrium, the identity system generates tensions, incoherence, and ultimately underperformance. Furthermore, even when the system is in equilibrium, it has its own inertia and may become disconnected from the organization's strategic needs. Therefore, an absence of any apparent "identity issues" in an organization is not necessarily a sign that all is well. For organizational identity to be a strategic enabler, it needs to be aligned with the organization's strategy.

As previously stated, the organizational identity system is composed of five facets. For each, the criteria of centrality, distinctiveness, and enduringness (see pp. 234–235) apply:

- The *professed* identity: the identity traits that top management, or other powerful groups, use to define their organization's identity, notably in terms of its positioning with respect to competition, its core competencies, its values, and boundaries. The professed identity is often future-oriented; thus, it usually corresponds to identity aspirations.
- The *projected* identity: the identity traits the organization projects through various media (such as advertising, PR, product and office design) towards its many audiences. While by definition multifaceted and adapted to specific target audiences, the projected identity may, or may not, carry a coherent underlying identity. This aspect of firms' identity is often referred to as "corporate identity."
- The *experienced* identity: the organizational traits that members believe represent their organization's identity. In practice, identity beliefs may be pre-conscious or even subconscious.
- The *manifested* identity: the organizational traits that are at the core of the organization's routines, rites, and achievements.
- The *attributed* identity: this corresponds to the identity that is attributed to the organization by its many audiences. This is often referred to as organizational

image, but should be distinguished from the construed organizational image, which refers to what members believe others attribute to their organization (in this five-facet framework, this aspect is subsumed under the experienced identity category).

To conduct an audit of an organizational identity, Soenen and Moingeon advocate a three-step process. The first step consists of making explicit the content of each facet: for each, there are specific sources of information and data collection techniques, as well as specific points of vigilance that need to be addressed.

Professed identity:
- Data collection: interviews with managers to assess how they define their organization's identity, including its strategic positioning, core values, core competencies, and boundaries.
- Points of vigilance: including questions such as is management discourse about the firm's identity clear and articulate? Is there substantial consensus or are there divergences among powerful organizational actors? Is the professed identity the result of sound strategic analysis or is it merely replication of the established, "historical" identity?

Projected identity:
- Data collection: systematic collection of representative samples of the organization's communications, from advertisements to product packaging, logos, uniforms, and so on. Such data can be sorted using techniques such as content analysis, semantic analysis, or semiotic analysis.
- Points of vigilance: including questions such as is there a coherent underlying identity to all these projections? For service industries, do employees' behaviors align with the identity traits put forward in formal communications? From a visual standpoint, are the various communications coherent, taking into account the branding structure of the firm?

Experienced identity
- Data collection: interviews, focus groups, or surveys of employees. There are several alternative models of data analysis ranging from content analysis to more interpretive techniques.
- Points of vigilance: are the identity beliefs largely shared? Is there a single coherent set of beliefs or are there several? How strongly are these beliefs held?

Manifested identity
- Data collection technique: this facet of identity is difficult to assess on its own. It is better first to clarify the content of the *professed* identity, and then to observe the organization's routines, resources, and achievements (both current and historical) in order to outline, by contrast, the features of this facet of identity. Industry benchmarks may be useful.

- Points of vigilance: do the various resources and routines contributing to the organization's value creation processes show common identity features? How distinct are these from the competition?

Attributed identity

- Data collection technique: external surveys.
- Points of vigilance: how distinct is the firm from competitors? Is the identity attributed to the firm the same among its different audiences?

The second step of the audit is to analyze the interactions between the facets. This analysis must assess whether the system is in equilibrium or whether there are wide discrepancies between the facets. The third step is to decide whether the gaps that have been identified above foster or degrade the firm's performance. For example, in many instances a gap between the projected identity and the attributed identity is a concern. This means that the positioning that the organization is trying to achieve in the minds of its stakeholders has not been achieved. However, in most other cases, whether a gap is positive or negative is context-specific. For instance, if the firm is undergoing a period of radical transformation, a gap between the professed and projected identity, on the one hand, and the manifested and experienced identity, on the other, is bound to develop. Whether the gap is too wide is a matter of managerial judgment: there needs to be an optimal tension between members' current identity beliefs and the aspirations of its leaders. Too little gap and members will not bother engaging with change, while too wide a gap may create too much resistance and may lead to paralysis.

HATCH AND SCHULTZ'S CORPORATE BRANDING TOOL KIT

One of the key issues raised by Soenen and Moingeon's model is the importance of internal coherence of various aspects of the organization's identity. Similarly, Hatch and Schultz (2001) observe how the projection of an effective corporate brand (see further the introduction to Part III) rests on the alignment of three essential elements: culture, image, and vision. The concepts of "culture" and "image" have already been introduced in this book. By vision, Hatch and Schultz (2001) refer to top managers' aspirations for the company – a concept close to what we have called identity aspirations.

According to Hatch and Schultz, it is not uncommon for inconsistencies to develop between these three elements, undermining the effectiveness of corporate branding policies, i.e., the capacity of an organization to project an appealing image. In order to identify potential misalignments between culture, image, and identity, Hatch and Schultz have developed what they call the Corporate Branding Tool Kit: a set of questions that aim to guide managers' analyses as they collect information from corporate leaders, employees, and key stakeholders in order to identify potential gaps:

- *The vision–culture gap.* A vision–culture gap occurs whenever the ambitions of senior managers – possibly reflected in corporate communication – are not shared by the rest of the organization, either because employees do not understand them or because they clash with their own values and beliefs. The result is that corporate claims may not be supported by reality. Do employees practice the values promoted in corporate rhetoric? Do all the various subcultures of the company (engineers, salespeople, researchers, etc.) share the same vision of top managers? These are some of the questions managers need to ask themselves in order to diagnose and compensate for possible inconsistencies between leaders' aspirations and employees' beliefs and values.

- *The image–culture gap.* At times, external impressions and expectations about what a company is and stands for may not truly reflect (or may no longer reflect) the values and beliefs that inspire organizational action. Results may vary from unfulfilled expectations and deteriorating images to internal frustrations about the lack of external appreciation for organizational efforts. In order to identify image–culture gaps, then, managers should periodically assess how the organization is perceived externally and internally, asking themselves questions such as: what images do stakeholders associate with the company? How do employees feel about these images? How does communication about the organization flow between departments, and between them and external audiences?

- *The image–vision gap.* Finally, top managers' aspirations may be inconsistent with external impressions and expectations. Even carefully crafted strategic visions may fail if they do not take into account what key stakeholders expect from the company. Who are really your stakeholders? What do they want from your company? Are you effectively conveying your ambitions? As top managers begin to interrogate themselves about these issues, it is not uncommon for the data they collect to reveal that the reality is somewhat different from what they assumed.

The aim of the Corporate Branding Tool Kit is to sensitize managers to the importance of aligning what managers want their organization to be (vision) with external impressions and expectations (image) and employees' values and practices (culture). In a later work, Majken Schultz (2005) observes how effective corporate brands tend to be underpinned by a clear organizational identity, which acts as a platform for aligning vision, image, and culture – ensuring that managers' ambitions, reflected in corporate claims, are supported by employees' values and practices and are coherent with external impressions and expectations.

We believe that the conceptual models we have summarized – Whetten's CED framework, Collins and Porras's core ideology approach, Soenen and Moingeon's five facets, and Hatch and Schultz's Corporate Branding Tool Kit – can be potentially valuable tools to address the identity issues highlighted in the chapters in this book. This is not to say, however, that these are the only tools available to practitioners and scholars interested in the analysis of organizational identities and related concepts. For reasons of space and simplicity we have selected those that seemed most consistent with the specific focus and conceptual approach of this book.

Readers interested in further stimuli and suggestions, or other points of view, may refer to broader overviews (e.g., van Riel and Fombrun, 2004). As the practical approaches summarized in this chapter and the rich cases collected in earlier chapters show, the field of organizational identity is a promising and appealing one for both scholars and practitioners.

CONCLUSION: ORGANIZATIONAL IDENTITY ANALYSIS AND STRATEGIC MANAGEMENT

The models reviewed in this concluding chapter are based on a common assumption, illustrated in several case studies presented in this book (see notably the introduction to Part II); namely, that organizational identity influences both strategy formulation and strategy implementation. Therefore leaders should understand their organization's identity – indeed, whether actively managed or not, organizational identity will influence the functioning of the organization. Strategy should thus build on organizational identity, otherwise it may generate significant resistance; for example, should the strategy challenge deeply held identity beliefs? Furthermore, as the Bang & Olufsen case shows, organizational identity can be at the heart of strategy when a link is established between organizational and corporate identity and it is made a key differentiator valued by the customers.

We would like to draw the attention of readers to one potential pitfall that may result from a narrow understanding of the assumption we have just described. That strategy is influenced by organizational identity in the actual functioning of organizations is a fact, clearly illustrated in this book. However, this should not be understood to mean that organizational identity should always constitute the bedrock of strategy formulation. Indeed, there are many instances when the role of top management is to introduce a strategic reorientation that runs exactly counter to the historically established organizational identity. Such a departure may primarily concern the projected identity, as illustrated in the Air France case, where this happened on several occasions in the organization's history. However, the departure may also be tight to the internal aspects of organizational identity and concern identity beliefs or/and identity claims.

For example, the French postal organization La Poste is having to transform itself from a state-owned monopoly operating solely domestically into a for-profit organization competing at European level. This strategic reorientation is made necessary by changes in the regulatory and competitive landscape in Europe. For the leaders of La Poste, one key element is their ability to implement a strategy to relinquish a significant portion of the current organizational identity. For the firm to be able to compete at European level, many identity beliefs deeply and widely shared among members of the organization must change. Furthermore, the identity claims put forward by the organization to its many stakeholders also need to change radically – something that, given the corporate governance in place, may prove difficult. Should the leadership of La Poste allow the current organizational identity to continue shaping behaviors and, notably, strategy formulation and strategy implementation, the necessary transformation will not take place and the future of the organization may be jeopardized.

In conclusion, we believe that practitioners should become cognizant with the dual nature of organizational identity. Like a double-edged sword, identity can be a strategic enabler or a core of rigidity. In all cases, however, managers need to be aware of their organization's identity: its content, its tensions, its various facets, its dynamics, and so on. The models we have briefly summarized in this chapter provide useful tools to delve into this complex but strategic aspect of organizational life.

Bibliography

Aaker, D. R. (1996) *Building Strong Brands*. New York: Free Press.

Aaker, D. R. and Joachimsthaler, E. (2000) *Brand Leadership*. New York: Free Press.

Abernethy, A.M. and Franke, G.R. (1996) "The information content of advertising: a meta-analysis." *Journal of Advertising*, 25(2): 1–17.

Aguilar, F. (1967) *Scanning the Business Environment*. New York: Macmillan.

Albert, S. (1998) "The definition and meta-definition of identity." In D. A. Whetten and P. C. Godfrey (eds), *Identity in Organizations. Building Theory Through Conversations*. Thousand Oaks, Calif.: Sage, 1–13.

Albert, S. and Whetten, D. A. (1985) "Organizational identity." In B. M. Staw and L. L. Cummings (eds), *Research in Organizational Behavior*, 7: 263–295. Greenwich, Conn.: JAI Press.

Aldrich, H. E. (1999) *Organizations Evolving*. London: Sage.

Aldrich, H. E. and Fiol, C. M. (1994) "Fools rush in – the institutional context of industry creation." *Academy of Management Review*, 19(4): 645–670.

Alvesson, M. (1994) "Talking in organizations: managing identity and impressions in an advertising agency." *Organization Studies*, 15(4): 535–563.

Anderson, B. (1983) *Imagined Communities; Reflections on the Origin and Spread of Nationalism*. London: Verso Editions and NLB.

Andrews, K. (1971) *The Concept of Corporate Strategy*. Homewood, Ill.: Irwin.

Anon. (1999) "SEBs nya guldägg. Internetbanken skulle vara värd 25 miljarder på Wall Street." *Dagens Industri*, March 18.

Ashforth, B. E. (1998) "What does the concept of identity add to organizational science." In D. A. Whetten and P. C. Godfrey (eds), *Identity in Organizations: Building Theory Through Conversations*. Thousand Oaks, Calif.: Sage: 273–291.

Ashforth, B. E. (2001) *Role Transitions in Organizational Life: An Identity Based Perspective*. Hillsdale, N.J.: Erlbaum.

Ashforth, B. E. and Johnson, S. A. (2001) "Which hat to wear? The relative salience of multiple identities in organizational contexts." In M. A. Hogg and D. J. Terry (eds), *Social Identity Processes in Organizational Contexts*. London and New York: Routledge, 31–48.

Ashforth, B. E. and Mael, F. (1989) "Social identity theory and the organization." *Academy of Management Review*, 14(1): 20–39.

Ashforth, B. E. and Mael, F. (1996) "Organizational identity and strategy as a context for the individual." *Advances in Strategic Management*, 13: 19–64.

AT&T (2006) "AT&T, BellSouth to Merge." Press release, 5 March 2006. Available: http://att.sbc-

.com/gen/press-room?pid=4800&cdvn=news&newsarticleid=22140&phase=check   (accessed March 20, 2006).

Autier, F., Corcos, G., and Trépo, G. (2001) *Air France, des années héroïques à la refondation*. Paris: Vuibert.

Balmer, J. and Soenen, G. (1998) *A New Approach to Corporate Identity Management*. International Centre for Corporate Identity Studies Working Paper Series, University of Strathclyde.

Balmer, J. M. T. and Soenen, G. B. (1999) "The acid test of corporate identity management." *Journal of Marketing Management*, 14: 69–92.

Bang, J. and Palshøy, J. (2000) *Bang and Olufsen, Vision and Legend*. Copenhagen: Danish Design Center.

Bargh, J. A. and Chartrand, T. L. (1999) "The unbearable automaticity of being." *American Psychologist*, 54: 462–479.

Barnes, J. H. J. (1984) "Cognitive biases and their impact on strategic planning." *Strategic Management Journal*, 5: 129–137.

Barney, J. B. (1991) "Firm resources and sustained competitive advantage." *Journal of Management*, 17: 99–120.

Barney, J. B., Bunderson, J. S., Foreman, P., Gustafson, L. T., Huff, A., Martins, L. L., Reger, R. K., Sarason, Y., and Stimpert, J. L. (1998) "A strategy conversation on the topic of organization identity." In D. A. Whetten and P. C. Godfrey (eds), *Identity in Organizations: Developing Theory through Conversations*. Thousand Oaks, Calif.: Sage, 46–51.

Bateson, G. (1972) *Steps to an Ecology of Mind*. San Francisco, Calif.: Chandler Publishing Co.

Belk, R. (1988) "Possession and the extended self." *Journal of Consumer Research*, 15: 139–168.

Belk, R. and Tumbat, G. (2005) "The cult of Mac." *Consumption, Markets and Culture*, 8: 205–218.

Berg, P. O. (1985) "Organization change as a symbolic transformation process." In P. Frost, L. Moore, M. R. Louis, C. Lundberg, and J. Martin (eds), *Reframing Organizational Culture*. Beverly Hills, Calif.: Sage, 281–300.

Bergami, M. (1994) "Identificazione organizzativa e immagine del prodotto." *Economia & Management*, 6: 9–23.

Bernstein, D. (1984) *Company Image and Reality: A Critique of Corporate Communications*. Eastbourne: Holt, Rinehart & Winston.

Billing, M. (1995) *Banal Nationalism*. London: Sage.

Birkigt, K., Stadler, M. M., and Funck, H. J. (eds) (2002) *Corporate Identity: Grundlagen, Funktionen, Fallbeispiele* [Corporate Identity: Premises, Purposes, Case Examples], 11th edn. Landsberg: Verlag Moderne Industrie.

Bouchiki, H. and Kimberly, J. R. (2003) "Escaping the identity trap." *MIT Sloan Management Review*, 44(3): 20–26.

Boyce, M. E. (1995) "Collective centering and collective sense-making in the storytelling of one organization." *Organization Studies*, 16(1): 107–136.

Breakwell, G. M. and Lyons, E. (eds) (1996) *Changing European Identities. Social Psychological Analyses of Social Change*. Cornwall: Butterworth Heinemann.

Brewer, M. B. and Gardner, W. (1996) "Who is this we? Levels of collective identity and self representations." *Journal of Personality and Social Psychology*, 71: 83–93.

Brown, A. B. and Starkey, K. (2000) "Organizational identity and learning: a psychodynamic perspective." *Academy of Management*, 25(1): 102–121.

Brown, J. S. and Duguid, P. (1991) "Organizational learning and communities of practice: toward a unified view of working, learning and innovation." *Organization Science*, 2: 40–57.

Brown, T. and Dacin, P. (1997) "The company and the product: corporate associations and consumer product responses." *Journal of Marketing*, 61: 68–84.

Brunner, J. (1990) *Acts of Meaning*. Cambridge, Mass.: Harvard University Press.

Cappetta, R. and Gioia, D. (2005) "Fine fashion: using symbolic artefacts, sense-making, and sense-giving to construct identity and image." In A. Rafaeli and M. G. Pratt (eds), *Artefacts and Organizations: Beyond Mere Symbolism*. Mahwah, N.J.: Lawrence Erlbaum Associates, 199–222.

Cauley, L. (2005) *End of the Line. The Rise and Fall of AT&T*. New York: Free Press.

Chreim, S. (2005) "The continuity–change duality in narrative texts of organizational identity." *Journal of Management Studies*, 42: 567–593.

Christensen, L. T. (1995) "Marketing culture." *Organization Studies*, 16(4): 651–672.

Cinnirella, M. (1998) "Exploring temporal aspects of social identity: the concept of possible social identities." *European Journal of Social Psychology*, 28: 227–248.

Collins, J. C. and Porras, J. L. (1994) *Built to Last: Successful Habits of Visionary Companies*. New York: HarperCollins.

Collins, J. C. and Porras, J. L. (1996) "Building your company's vision." *Harvard Business Review* (September–October): 65–77.

Cooley. C. H. (1902) *Human Nature and the Social Order*. New York: Scribner.

Corley, K. G. (2004) "Defined by our strategy or our culture? Hierarchical differences in perceptions of organizational identity and change." *Human Relations*, 57(9): 1145–1177.

Corley, K. G. and Gioia, D. A. (2004) "Identity ambiguity and change in the wake of a corporate spin-off." *Administrative Science Quarterly*, 49: 73–208.

Corley, K., Harquail, C. V., Pratt, M., Glynn, M. A., Fiol, M., and Hatch, M. J. (2006) "Guiding organizational identity through aged adolescence." *Journal of Management Inquiry*, 15: 373–390.

Creutzer, A. (1998) "Årets bank 1998: Största utbud: SEB – Stort utbud men höga avgifter." *Privata Affärer* (December).

Czarniawska, B. (1997) *Narrating the Organization: Dramas of Institutional Identity*. Chicago: University of Chicago Press.

Danilov, V. (1992) *A Planning Guide For Corporate Museums, Galleries And Visitor Centres*. Westport, Conn.: Greenwood Press.

De Chernatony, L. (2001) *From Brand Vision to Brand Evaluation. Strategically Building and Sustaining Brands*. Oxford: Butterworth Heinemann.

Deal, T. E. and Kennedy, A. A. (1982) *Corporate Cultures: The Rites and Rituals of Corporate Life*. Harmondsworth: Penguin Books.

Deaux, K. (1996) "Social identification." In E. T. Higgins and A. W. Kruglanski (eds), *Social Psychology: Handbook of Basic Principles*. New York: Guilford.

Deephouse, D. L. (1999) "To be different, or to be the same? It's a question (and theory) of strategic balance." *Strategic Management Journal*, 20: 147–166.

Dierickx, I. and Cool, K. (1989) "Asset stock accumulation and sustainability of competitive advantage." *Management Science*, 35(12): 1504–1511.

DiMaggio, P. J. and Powell, W. W. (1983) "The iron cage revisited: institutional isomorphism and collective rationality in organizational fields." *American Sociological Review*, 48: 147–160.

Dowling, G. R. (1986) "Managing your corporate images." *Industrial Marketing Management*, 15: 109–115.

Dowling, G. R. (2001) *Creating Corporate Reputations. Identity, Image and Performance*. Oxford: Oxford University Press.

Dube, L., Chattopadhyay, A., and Letarte, A. (1996) "Should advertising appeals match the basis of consumers' attitudes?" *Journal of Advertising Research*, 36(6): 82–89.

Dukerich, J. E., Golden, B., and Shortell, S. M. (2002) "Beauty is in the eye of the beholder: the impact of organizational identification, identity, and image on the cooperative behaviors of physicians." *Administrative Science Quarterly*, 47: 507–533.

Dutton, J. E. (1993) "Interpretations on the automatic: a different view of strategic issue diagnosis." *Journal of Management Studies*, 30: 339–357.

Dutton, J. E. and Dukerich, J. (1991) "Keeping an eye on the mirror: image and identity in organizational adaptation." *Academy of Management Journal*, 34: 517–554.

Dutton, J. E., Dukerich, J. M., and Harquail, C. (1994) "Organizational images and member identification." *Administrative Science Quarterly*, 39: 239–263.

Einar, B.-M. (1995) "Kontorsnätet förblir intact trots ny konkurrensbild." *Veckans Affärer*, April 11.

Ellemers, N., Haslam, S. A., Platow, M. J., and van Knippenberg, D. (2003) "Social identity at work, developments, debates, directions." In S. A. Haslam, D. van Knippenberg, M. J. Platow, and N. Ellemers (eds), *Social Identity at Work: Developing Theory for Organizational Practice*. New York: Psychology Press, 3–26.

Elsbach, K. D. (1994) "Managing organizational legitimacy in the California cattle industry – the construction and effectiveness of verbal accounts." *Administrative Science Quarterly*, 39(1): 57–88.

Elsbach, K. D. (2003) "Relating physical environment to self-categorizations: identity threat and affirmation in a non-territorial office space." *Administrative Science Quarterly*, 48(4): 622–654.

Elsbach, K. D. and Sutton, R. (1992) "Acquiring organizational legitimacy through illegitimate actions: a marriage of institutional and impression management theories." *Academy of Management Journal*, 35(4): 699–738.

Elsbach, K. D. and Kramer, R. M. (1996) "Member's responses to organizational identity threats: encountering and countering the Business Week rankings." *Administrative Science Quarterly*, 41: 442–476.

Elsbach, K. D. and Bhattacharya, C. B. (2001) "Defining what you are by what you're not: organizational disidentification and the national rifle association." *Organization Science*, 12: 393–413.

Fiol, C. M. (1991) "Managing culture as a competitive resource: an identity-based view of sustainable competitive advantage." *Journal of Management*, 17: 191–211.

Fiol, C. M. (2002) "Capitalizing on paradox: the role of language in transforming organizational identities." *Organization Science*, 13: 653–666.

Fiol, C. M. and Huff, A. S. (1992) "Maps for managers: Where are we? Where do we go from here?" *Journal of Management Studies*, 29: 267–285.

Fiske, S. and Taylor, S. (1991) *Social Cognition*. New York: McGraw-Hill.

Fombrun, C. J. (1996) *Reputation: Realizing Value from the Corporate Image*. Boston, Mass.: Harvard Business School Press.

Fombrun, C. J. and van Riel, C. B. M. (2004) *Fame and Fortune. How Successful Companies Build Winning Reputations*. New York: Financial Times/Prentice-Hall.

Foreman, P. and Whetten, D. A. (2002) "Members identification with multiple-identity organizations." *Organization Science*, 13: 618–635.

Fox-Wolfgramm, S. J., Boal, K. B., and Hunt, J. G. (1998) "Organizational adaptation to institutional change: a comparative study of first-order change in prospector and defender banks." *Administrative Science Quarterly*, 43: 87–126.

Gatewood, R. D., Gowan, M. A., and Lautenschlager, G. J. (1993) "Corporate image, recruitment image, and initial job decisions." *Academy of Management Journal*, 32: 414–427.

Geertz, C. (1973) *The Interpretation of Culture*. New York: Basic Books.

Gellner, A. (1988) *Nations and Nationalism*. Oxford: Blackwell.

Ginzel, L., Kramer, R., and Sutton, B. (1993) "Organizational impression management as a reciprocal influence process: the neglected role of the organizational audience." In L. L. Cummings and M. M. Staw (eds), *Research in Organizational Behavior*, 15: 227–266.

Gioia, D. A. (2000) "Organizational identity, image and adaptive instability." *Academy of Management Review*, 25: 63–81.

Gioia, D. A. (1998) "From individual to organizational identity." In D. A. Whetten and P. C. Godfrey (eds), *Identity in Organizations: Building Theory Through Conversations*. London: Sage Publications.

Gioia, D. A. and Thomas, J. B. (1996) "Identity, image and issue interpretation: sense-making during strategic change in academia." *Administrative Science Quarterly*, 41: 370–403.

Gioia, D. A., Schultz, M., and Corley, K. G. (2000) "Organizational identity, image, and adaptive instability." *Academy of Management Review*, 25(1): 63–81.

Glaser, J. and Strauss, A. (1967) *The Discovery of Grounded Theory*. Chicago: Aldine Publishing Co.

Glynn, M. A. (2000) "When cymbals become symbols: conflict over organizational identity within a symphony orchestra." *Organization Science*, 11: 285–298.

Gobe, M. (2001) *Emotional Branding: The New Paradigm for Connecting Brands to People*. New York: Allworth Press.

Goffman, E. (1959) *The Presentation of Self in Everyday Life*. London: Penguin.

Golden-Biddle, K. and Rao, H. (1997) "Breaches in the boardroom: organizational identity and conflicts of commitment in a nonprofit organization." *Organization Science*, 8: 593–611.

Greenwood, R. and Hinings, C. R. (1996) "Understanding radical organizational change: bringing together the old and the new institutionalism." *Academy of Management Review*, 21(4): 1022–1054.

Handelsbanken (2004) *Our Way 2004*. Stockholm: Handelsbanken.

Harquail, C. V. (2005) "Employees as animate artefacts: employee branding by 'wearing the brand.'" In A. Rafaeli and M. Pratt (eds), *Artefacts and Organizations: Beyond Mere Symbolism*. Mahwah, N.J.: Lawrence Erlbaum Associates, 161–181.

Hatch, M. J. and Schultz, M. (1997) "Relations between organizational culture, identity and image." *European Journal of Marketing*, 31(5/6): 356–365.

Hatch, M. J. and Schultz, M. (2000) "Scaling the Tower of Babel: relational differences between identity, image and culture in organizations." In M. Schultz, M. J. Hatch, and M. H. Larsen (eds), *The Expressive Organization*. Oxford: Oxford University Press, 11–36.

Hatch, M. J. and Schultz, M. (2001) "Are the strategic stars aligned for your corporate brand?" *Harvard Business Review*, 79(2): 128:135.

Hatch, M. J. and Schultz, M. (2002) "The dynamics of organizational identity." *Human Relations*, 55: 989–1018.

Heil, O. and Robertson, T. S. (1991) "Toward a theory of competitive market signaling – a research agenda." *Strategic Management Journal*, 12(6): 403–418.

Hobsbawm, E. (1990) *Nations and Nationalism Since 1780*. Cambridge: Cambridge University Press.

Hogg, M. A. and Terry, D. J. (2000) "Social identity and self-categorization processes in organizational contexts." *Academy of Management Review*, 25: 121–140.

Holbrook, M. B. and Hirschman, E. C. (1982) "The experiential aspects of consumption – consumer fantasies, feelings, and fun." *Journal of Consumer Research*, 9(2): 132–140.

Hollander, B. S. and Ellman, N. S. (1988) "Family-owned businesses: an emerging field of inquiry." *Family Business Review*, 1(2): 145–164.

Hoorn, J. S. and Konijn, E. A. (2003) "Proceeding and experiencing fictional characters: an integrative account." *Japanese Psychological Research*, 45(4): 250–268.

Humphreys, M. and Brown, A. D. (2002) "Narratives of organizational identity and identification: a case study of hegemony and resistance." *Organization Studies*, 23(3): 421–447.

Ibarra, H. (1999) "Provisional selves: experimenting with image and identity in professional adaptation." *Administrative Science Quarterly*, 44: 764–791.

Ind, N. (2001) *Living the Brand: How to Transform Every Member of Your Organization into a Brand Champion*. London: Kogan Page.

Jones, T. M. (1995) "Instrumental Stakeholder Theory – a synthesis of ethics and economics." *Academy of Management Review*, 20(2): 404–437.

Kapferer, J. N. (2004) *The New Strategic Brand Management – Creating and Sustaining Brand Equity Long Term*, 3rd edn. London: Kogan Page.

Keller, K. L. (2000) "Building and managing corporate brand equity." In M. Schultz, M. J. Hatch, and M. H. Larsen (eds), *The Expressive Organization – Linking Identity, Reputation, and the Corporate Brand*. Oxford: Oxford University Press.

Keller, K. L. (2003) *Strategic Brand Management. Building, Measuring and Managing Brand Equity*, 2nd edn. Upper Saddle River, N.J.: Pearson Education.

Kling, K. and Goteman, I. (2003) "IKEA CEO Anders Dahlvig on international growth and IKEA's unique corporate culture and brand identity." *Academy of Management Executive*, 17: 31–37.

Kotler, P. (1991) *Marketing Management*. Englewood Cliffs, N.J.: Prentice-Hall.

Kulik, C. T. and Ambrose, M. L. (1992) "Personal and situational determinants of referent choice." *Academy of Management Review*, 17: 212–237.

Labianca, G., Fairbank, J. F., Thomas, J. B., Gioia, D. A., and Umphress, E. E. (2001) "Emulation in academia: balancing structure and identity." *Organization Science*, 12: 312–330.

Larçon, J.-P. and Reitter, R. (1979) *Structure de pouvoir et identité d'entreprise*. Paris: Fernand Nathan.

Lave, J. and Wenger, E. (1991) *Situated Learning: Legitimate Peripheral Participation*. New York: Cambridge University Press.

Lounsbury, M. and Glynn, M. A. (2001) "Cultural entrepreneurship: stories, legitimacy, and the acquisition of resources." *Strategic Management Journal*, 22: 545–564.

McAlexander, J. H., Schouten, J. W., and Koenig, H. F. (2002) "Building brand community." *Journal of Marketing*, 66: 38–54.

McGee, J. and Thomas, H. (1986) "Strategic groups: a useful linkage between industry structure and strategic management." *Strategic Management Journal*, 7: 141–160.

McGuire, W. J. and McGuire, C. V. (1981) "The spontaneous self-concept as affected by personal distinctiveness." In M. D. Lynch, A. A. Norem-Herbeisen, and K. J. Gergen (eds), *Self-concept, Advances in Theory and Research*, Cambridge, Mass.: Ballinger Publishing Company, 147–171.

McKinsey & Co. (1989) *Developing a Successful International E&P Business, Statoil A/S*. Oslo: McKinsey/ Statoil.

Marcus, H. and Nurius, P. (1986) "Possible selves." *American Psychologist*, 41: 954–969.

Martin, J. (1993) *Cultures in Organizations. Three Perspectives*. Oxford: Oxford University Press.

Martin, J. (2002) *Organizational Culture: Mapping the Terrain*. Thousand Oaks, Calif.: Sage Publications.

Melewar, T. C. (2003) "Determinants of the corporate identity construct: a review of the literature." *Journal of Marketing Communication*, 9, 195–220.

Miller, D. T., Turnbull, W., and McFarland, C. (1988) "Particularistic and universalistic evaluation in the social comparison process." *Journal of Personality and Social Psychology*, 55: 908–917.

Mintzberg, H., Raisinghani, D., and Theoret, A. (1976) "The structure of unstructured decision processes." *Administrative Science Quarterly*, 21: 246–275.

Mintzberg, H., Ahlstrand, B., and Lampel, J. (1998) *Strategy Safari: A Guided Tour Through the Wilds of Strategic Management*. New York: Free Press.

Moran, P. and Goshal, S. (1996) "Value creation by firms." *Academy of Management Best Papers Proceedings*. Cincinnati, OH.

Moran, P. and Goshal, S. (1999) "Markets, firms, and the process of economic development." *Academy of Management Review*, 24: 390–412.

Muniz, A. R. and O'Guinn, T. C. (2001) "Brand community." *Journal of Consumer Research*, 27: 412–432.

Nahapiet, J. and Goshal, S. (1998) "Social capital, intellectual capital, and the organizational advantage." *Academy of Management Review*, 23(2): 242–266.

Nardon, L. and Aten, K. J. (2004) "Identity, scanning, and organizational action." Paper presented at the Egos Colloquium, Ljubljana, July 2–4.

Nissley, N. and Casey, A. (2002) "The politics of the exhibition: viewing corporate museums through the paradigmatic lens of organizational memory." *British Journal of Management*, 13: S35–S45.

O'Reilly III, C. A. and Pfeffer, J. (2000) *Hidden Value. How Great Companies Achieve Extraordinary Results with Ordinary People*. Boston, Mass.: Harvard Business School Press.

Ocasio, W. (1997) "Towards an attention based-view of the firm." *Strategic Management Journal*, 18 (Summer Special Issue): 187–207.

Olins, W. (1989) *Corporate Identity: Making Business Strategy Visible through Design*. Boston, Mass.: Harvard Business School Press.

Ouchi, W. G. (1979) "A conceptual framework for the design of organizational control mechanisms." *Management Science*, 25: 833–848.

Palmer, T. B. and Short, J. C. (2001) "Why do Goliaths fail? Performance referents in successful organizations." *Corporate Reputation Review*, 4: 209–222.

Peteraf, M. and Shanley, M. (1997) "Getting to know you: a theory of strategic group identity." *Strategic Management Journal*, 18: 165–187.

Pettersson, R. (1993) *Visual Information*. Englewood Cliffs, N.J.: Education Technology Publications.

Plutchik, R. (1980) *Emotion: A Psychoevolutionary Analysis*. New York: Harper & Row.

Porac, J. F., Thomas, H., and Baden-Fuller, C. (1989) "Competitive groups as cognitive communities: the case of Scottish knitwear manufacturers." *Journal of Management Studies*, 26(4): 397–416.

Porter, M. (1985) *Competitive Advantage*. New York: Free Press.

Porter, M. E. (1980) *Competitive Strategy: Techniques for Analyzing Industries and Competitors*. New York: Free Press.

Pratt, M.G. and Rafaeli, A. (1997) "Organizational dress as a symbol of multilayered social identities." *Academy of Management Journal*, 40: 862–899.

Pratt, M. G. and Dutton, J. E. (2000) "Owning up or opting out: the role of emotions and identities in issue ownership." In N. M. Ashkanasy, C. E. Hartel, and W. J. Zerbe (eds), *Emotions in the Workplace*. London: Quorum, 103–129.

Pratt, M. G. and Foreman, P. O. (2000) "Classifying managerial responses to multiple organizational identities." *Academy of Management Review*, 25: 18–42.

Pratt, M. G. and Rafaeli, A. (2001) "Symbols as the language of organizational relationships." *Research in Organizational Behavior*, 23: 93–133.

Preston, A. M., Wright, C., and Young, J. J. (1996) "Imag[in]ing annual reports." *Accounting Organizations and Society*, 21(1): 113–137.

Rafaeli, A. and Pratt, M. G. (1993) "Tailored meanings: on the meaning and impact of organizational dress." *Academy of Management Review*, 18(1): 32–55.

Rafaeli, N. and Vilnai-Yavetz, I. (2004) "Emotion as a connection of physical artefacts and organizations." *Organization Science*, 15: 671–686.

Rao, H. (1994) "The social construction of reputation: certification contests, legitimacy, and the survival of organizations in the American automobile industry: 1895–1912." *Strategic Management Journal*, 15: 29–44

Rao, H., Davis, G. F., and Ward, A. (2000) "Embeddedness, social identity and mobility: why firms leave the NASDAQ and join the New York Stock Exchange." *Administrative Science Quarterly*, 45: 268–292.

Ravasi D. and van Rekom, J. (2003) "Key issues in organizational identity and identification theory." *Corporate Reputation Review*, 6: 118–132.

Ravasi, D. and Schultz, M. (2006) "Responding to organizational identity threats: exploring the role of organizational culture." *Academy of Management Journal*, 49(3): 433–458.

Reeve, J. (1992) *Understanding Motivation and Emotion*. Philadelphia, Pa.: Harcourt Brace Jovanovich.

Reger, R. K. and Huff, A. S. (1993) "Strategic groups: a cognitive perspective." *Strategic Management Journal*, 14: 103–124.

Reger, R. K. and Palmer, T. B. (1996) "Managerial categorization of competitors: using old maps to navigate new environments." *Organization Science*, 7: 22–39.

Reger, R. K., Gustafson, L. T., DeMarie, S. M., and Mullane, J. V. (1994) "Reframing the organization: why implementing total quality is easier said than done." *Academy of Management Review*, 19: 565–584.

Rindova, V. P. and Schultz, M. (1998) "Identity within and identity without: lessons from corporate and organizational identity." In D. A. Whetten and P. C. Godfrey (eds), *Identity in Organizations. Building Theory through Conversations*. Thousand Oaks, Calif.: Sage, 46–51.

Rindova, V. P. and Fombrun, C. J. (1999) "Constructing competitive advantage: the role of firm–constituent interactions." *Strategic Management Journal*, 20(8): 691–710.

Rindova, V. P., Becerra, M., and Contardo, I. (2004) "Enacting competitive wars: competitive activity, language games, and market consequences." *Academy of Management Review*, 29(4): 670–686.

Ritchie, B. (1995) *Portrait in Oil: An Illustrated History of BP*. London: British Petroleum Company.

Ryggvik, H. (2000) "Norsk oljevirksomhet mellom det nasjonale og det internasjonale: en studie av selvskapstrukturer og internasjonalisering." Ph.D. thesis, University of Oslo.

Sarason, Y. (1997) "Identity and the Baby Bells: Applying structuration theory to strategic management." Unpublished dissertation, University of Colorado at Boulder.

Sarason, Y. (1998a) "U.S. West Inc." In D. A. Whetten and P. C. Godfrey (eds), *Identity in Organizations: Building Theory through Conversations*. Thousand Oaks, Calif.: Sage, 128–132.

Sarason, Y. (1998b) "Deregulation – telecommunications: the case of the Baby Bells." In R. Dorf (ed.), *The Technology Management Handbook*. Boca Raton, Fla.: CRC Press, 2–20 to 2–26.

SBC (2005) "SBC communications to adopt AT&T name." Press release, October 27, 2005. Available: http://www.sbc.com/gen/press-room?pid=4800&cdvn=news&newsarticleid=21850 (accessed November 11, 2005).

Scania (2000) *Scania Product Identity. Guiding Principles*. Södertälje: Scania.

Scania (2002) "Industrial designers peer into the future: tomorrow's rugged T-trucks." *Scania World*, 3: 25–30.

Schein, E. H. (1992) *Organizational Culture and Leadership*. San Francisco: Jossey-Bass.

Schmitt, B. and Simonson, A. (1997) *Marketing Aesthetics*. New York: Free Press.

Schmitt, B., Simonson, A., and Marcus, J. (1995) "Managing corporate image and identity." *Long Range Planning*, 28(5): 82–92.

Schneider, G. (2002) "Ford invents the Model Two: the firm that got America rolling was desperate for customers. So it designed a pair." *Washington Post*, October 27, H1 and H8.

Schouten, J. W. and McAlexander, J. H. (1995) "Subcultures of consumption: an ethnography of the New Bikers." *Journal of Consumer Research*, 22: 43–61.

Schultz, M. (2005) "A cross-disciplinary perspective on corporate branding." In M. Schultz, Y. M. Antorini, and F. F. Csaba (eds), *Corporate Branding. Purpose, People and Process*. Copenhagen: Business School Press, 23–55.

Schultz, M., Hatch, M. J., and Larsen, M. H. (2000) *The Expressive Organization: Linking Identity, Reputation and the Corporate Brand*. Oxford: Oxford University Press.

Schultz, M., Antorini, Y. M., and Csaba, F. F. (2005) *Corporate Branding: Purpose, People and Process*. Copenhagen: Copenhagen Business School Press.

Scott, S. G. and Lane, V. R. (2000) "A stakeholder approach to organizational identity." *Academy of Management Review*, 25(1): 43–62.

SEB (2000) *Årsredovisning 1999*. Stockholm: SEB.

Shapiro, C. (1983) "Premiums for high-quality products as returns to reputations." *Quarterly Journal of Economics*, 98: 659–679.

Short, J. C. and Palmer, T. B. (2003) "Organizational performance referents: an empirical examination of their content and influences." *Organizational Behavior and Human Decision Processes*, 90: 209–244.

Smidts, A., Pruyn, A. T. H., and van Riel, C. B. M. (2001) "The impact of employee communication and perceived external prestige on organizational identification." *Academy of Management Journal*, 49: 1051–1062.

Smircich, L. and Stubbart, C. (1985) "Strategic management in an enacted world." *Academy of Management Review*, 10: 724–736.

Søderberg, A.-M. and Björkman, I. (2003) "From words to action? Socio-cultural integration initiatives in a cross-border merger." In A.-M. Søderberg and E. Vaara (eds), *Merging Across Borders: People, Cultures and Politics*. Copenhagen: Copenhagen Business School Press.

Søderberg, A.-M. and Vaara, E. (eds) (2003) *Merging Across Borders: People, Cultures and Politics*. Copenhagen: Copenhagen Business School Press.

Soenen, G. and Moingeon, B. (2002) "The five facets of collective identities: integrating corporate and organizational identity." In B. Moingeon and G. Soenen (eds), *Corporate and Organizational Identities: Integrating Strategy, Marketing, Communication, and Organizational Perspectives*. London: Routledge, 13–34.

Spender, J.-C. (1989) *Industry Recipes*. Oxford: Basil Blackwell.

Stern, S. (1988) "Symbolic representation of organizational identity." In M. O. Jones, M. D. Moore, and R. C. Snyder (eds), *Inside Organizations*. Beverly Hills, Calif.: Sage, 281–295.

Stiglitz, J. E. and Weiss, A. (1981) "Credit rationing in markets with imperfect information." *American Economic Review*, 71: 393–410.

Strauss, A. and Corbin, J. (1990) *Basics of Qualitative Research*. Newbury Park, Calif.: Sage.

Sutton, R. I. and Callahan, A. (1987) "The stigma of bankruptcy: spoiled organizational image and its management." *Academy of Management Journal*, 30: 405–436.

Sveningsson, S. and Alvesson, M. (2003) "Managing managerial identities: organizational fragmentation, discourse, and identity struggle." *Human Relations*, 56(10): 1163–1193.

Tajfel, H. and Turner, J. C. (1979) "An integrative theory of intergroup conflict." In W. G. Austin and S. Worchel (eds), *The Social Psychology of Intergroup Relations*. Monterey, Calif.: Brooks/Cole, 7–24.

Tapper, G. (2001) "SHB har stått modell för SEBs nya strategi. Thunell tar intryck av missnöjda kunder." *Dagens Industri*, October 24.

Tenkasi, R. and Boland, R. (1993) "Locating meaning making in organizational learning: the narrative basis of cognition." *Research in Organizational Change and Development*, 7: 77–103.

Thibault, P.-M. (2005) *Inflight Mythologies*. Paris: Galimard.

Thoits, P. A. (1983) "Multiple identities and psychological well-being – a reformulation and test of the Social-Isolation Hypothesis." *American Sociological Review*, 48(2): 174–187.

Thomson, J. D. (1967) *Organizations in Action*. New York: McGraw-Hill.

Tienari, J., Vaara, E., and Björkman, I. (2003) "Global capitalism meets national spirit. Discourses in media texts on a cross-border acquisition." *Journal of Management Inquiry*, 12: 377–393.

Trice, H. and Beyer, J. (1984) "Studying organizational cultures through rites and ceremonies." *Academy of Management Review*, 9: 653–669.

Tyler, T. (2001) "Cooperation in organizations." In M. A. Hogg and D. J. Terry (eds), *Social Identity Processes in Organizational Contexts*. Ann Arbor, Mich.: Sheridan Books.

US West (2000) "Letter to shareholders." *US West Annual Report*, March 3. Denver, Colo.: US West.

Vaara, E., Tienari, J., and Björkman, I. (2003) "Knowledge transfer around 'best practices': a sensemaking perspective." *Nordic Organization Studies/Nordiske Organisasjonsstudier*, Special issue, 5: 37–57.

Van Rekom, J. (1997) "Deriving an operational measure of corporate identity." *European Journal of Marketing*, 31(5/6): 412–424.

Van Riel, C. B. M. (1995) *Principles of Corporate Communication*. London: Prentice-Hall.

Van Riel, C. B. M. and Balmer, J. (1997) "Corporate identity: the concept, its measurement and management." *European Journal of Marketing*, 31(5/6): 340–355.

Van Riel, C. B. M. and Fombrun, C. J. (2004). *Essentials of Corporate Communication*. London: Routledge.

Vilnai-Yavetz, I. and Rafaeli, A. (2006) "Managing artefacts to avoid artefact myopia." In A. Rafaeli and M. G. Pratt (eds), *Artefacts and Organizations*. London: Lawrence Erlbaum Associates, 9–22.

Von Feilitzen, C. and Linne, O. (1975) "Identifying with television characters." *Journal of Communication*, 25: 51–55.

Weick, K. E. (1995) *Sense-making in Organizations*. Thousand Oaks, Calif.: Sage.

Wenger, E. (1998) *Communities of Practice. Learning, Meaning and Identity*. Cambridge: Cambridge University Press.

Wert, S. R. and Salovey, P. (2004) "A social comparison account of gossip." *Review of General Psychology*, 8: 122–137.

Whetten, D. A. (1998) "Preface: Why organizational identity and why conversations?" In D. A. Whetten and P. C. Godfrey (eds), *Identity in Organizations: Developing Theory through Conversations*. Thousand Oaks, Calif.: Sage, vii–xi.

Whetten, D. A. (2006) "Albert and Whetten revisited: strengthening the concept of organizational identity." *Journal of Management Inquiry*, 15(3): 219–234.

Whetten, D. A. and Godfrey, P. C. (1998) *Identity in Organizations. Building Theory through Conversations*. Thousand Oaks, Calif.: Sage.

Whetten, D. A. and Mackey, A. (2002) "A social actor conception of organizational identity and its implications for the study of organizational reputation." *Business and Society*, 41(4): 393–414.

Wilkins, A. L. (1983) "Organizational stories as symbols." In L. R. Pondy, P. J. Frost, G. Morgan, and T. C. Dandridge (eds), *Organizational Symbolism*. Greenwich, Conn.: JAI Press, 81–92.

Wodak, R., de Cillia, R., Reisigl, M., and Liebhart, K. (1999) *The Discursive Construction of National Identity*. Edinburgh: Edinburgh University Press.

Yergin, D. (1991) *The Prize: The Epic Quest for Oil, Money and Power*. New York: Touchstone.

Yin, R. K. (1994) *Case Study Research: Design and Methods*. Thousand Oaks, Calif.: Sage.

Index